THE HEALTHY GARDEN
HANDBOOK

AN ILLUSTRATED GUIDE TO COMBATING
INSECTS, GARDEN PESTS, AND PLANT DISEASES
BY THE EDITORS OF ✧ MOTHER EARTH NEWS
FOREWORD BY HUGH JOHNSON

F
FIRESIDE

A FIRESIDE BOOK
PUBLISHED BY SIMON & SCHUSTER INC.

NEW YORK   LONDON   TORONTO   SYDNEY   TOKYO

Fireside
Simon & Schuster Building
Rockefeller Center
1230 Avenue of the Americas
New York, New York 10020

Grateful acknowledgment is made for
permission to reprint: Map and table on
pages 70–71 from *Prescription for Your
Vegetable Garden*. Copyright © 1982,
Duane Newcomb. Reprinted through special arrangement with J.P. Tarcher, Inc.,
Los Angeles. Excerpt on pages 54–56
from *Organic Plant Protection*. Copyright
© 1976 by Rodale Press, Inc. Permission
granted by Rodale Press, Inc., Emmaus,
PA 18049.

Designed by Will Hopkins Group
Manufactured in the United States of
America

10 9 8 7 6 5 4 3 2 1

Library of Congress Cataloging in Publication Data

ISBN 0-671-65788-7

Acknowledgments

Although gardening is quintessentially an individual enterprise, creating a garden book is definitely a group effort. *The Healthy Garden Handbook* could not have been brought to full fruition without the generous assistance of many people.

For scientific advice, we thank John Gowan, New York State Department of Environmental Conservation; Kenneth Sorensen, North Carolina State Entomology Department; and Louis N. Sorkin, American Museum of Natural History. For their professional gardening contributions, we are indebted to David Duhon, Kate and Fairman Jayne, Greg and Pat Williams, Kerry and Barbara Sullivan, and Walker and Olivia Able. Art direction came from Will Hopkins, Ira Friedlander and John Baxter, for which we are deeply grateful; they were ably assisted by Nazan Akyavas, Linda Patterson Eger,

Thomas Egly, Bill Lessner, Rita Pocock, Sandra McKee, Kathleen Seabe, Sergio Girgenti, Genia Gould, Robert Graf, Don Osby and Kay Holmes Stafford. Editorial assistance was conscientiously supplied by Assistant Managing Editor Christie Lyon and Liz Brennan, Klara Blair, Julie Brown, Wilma Dingley, Judy Gold, Judy Janes, Lorna K. Loveless, Betty N. Mack, Karen Murray, Rita Norton and Carol Taylor. Finally, Susan Sides, Head Gardener, *Mother Earth News* research gardens, and Kate Stuart, Managing Editor, *Mother Earth News*, deserve special praise. They made it all happen.

Alfred Meyer
Editor at Large, Mother Earth News
Pat Stone
Garden Editor, Mother Earth News

Contents

Acknowledgments 3
Foreword 7
Introduction 9

PART I
Creating the Healthy Garden .11

A guide to building good soil and keeping plants nourished

Preventive Gardening 12
Preparing the Soil 14
Compost 19
Deep Mulch 24
Green Manure 27
Garden Teas 30
Seed Starting Secrets 32
Seedlings: Handle With Care 38
Watering 42
Weeding 46
Weatherproofing 48
Companion Planting 53
Resistant Plants 56
Crop Rotation 59

PART II
Coping With Garden Pests . . .61

How to control everything from aphids, loopers and borers, to rabbits, woodchucks and crows

Never Cry Bug 63
Intervention 64
Peak Infestation Times 70
What Makes an Insect 72
Shape Guide 74
Key Players 76
Harmful Insects 78
Helpful Insects 102

Plant Allies 118
Harmful Animals 126
Helpful Animals 132
New Natural Controls 135
Shopping for Insects 136

PART III
Overcoming Plant Diseases . .139

Diagnosis and treatment for the main afflictions that can strike the garden

Rots, Smuts & Blights 140

PART IV
Remedies for Common Garden Problems 145

A vegetable-by-vegetable guide for identifying and reversing crop failure

Curatives 146

PART V
References 177

Useful information from other people and places to help your garden flourish

Major Seed Companies 178
Specialty Seed Companies 179
Plant Yields 182
Soil Nutrients 183
Planting Times 184
Spring & Fall Frost 186
Plant Hardiness 187
Index .188
Credits 192

Foreword

I have a friend who runs what she calls a "plant hospital," to which her friends and neighbors and acquaintances regularly bring plants that are off-color, under the weather, infested with nameless diseases or even apparently dead.

A few days in her healing hands and all except the last category are on their way to being show specimens. Even the apparently dead often have a fat little bud to prove that life was not extinguished after all. My friend's thumbs are green up to the elbows. I sometimes wonder if she is not the sort of woman our superstitious ancestors would have called a witch.

It is true she has special powers. There is nothing sinister or occult about them, though: They are powers we could all have, but most of us are too idle or distracted to acquire them.

My friend simply uses her faculties to observe and her experience to deduce what the plant's problems are. There is a parallel with a veterinarian, who can only commune with his patient to a limited extent, if at all.

Diagnosing what is wrong with a plant needs not only keen observation, but the blend of imagination, knowledge and experience that few of us possess—and none of us can obtain without a significant amount of study.

The problem, up to now, has been to know what to study. There has been no medical dictionary, as it were, of the plant kingdom. I have a terrifying volume called *Pathology of Trees and Shrubs* in which I seek to recognize, among the Latin names of fungi, what it is that ails my lilac. But even if I thought I had found out, I would not know what to do about it. "Cut out and burn infected wood" is as far as this scholarly volume goes in the direction of solid homely advice.

The editors of *Mother Earth News* are a different breed. One has the feeling that they are seldom indoors, that Mother Earth is literally under the fingernails bashing the typewriter.

This book is the very antithesis of a scientist's lofty pronouncements from his desk in a laboratory. The laboratory here is the vegetable garden itself, constantly involved as we learn to create healthy conditions for *all* our plants and then to react with precise unpanicked measures when something does go wrong.

It is important (and comforting) to be able to look up the insect that is devouring our vegetables, to learn its behavior pattern and how best to defeat it. It is even more important to appreciate, as *Mother Earth News'* editors do, the interdependence of all the creatures that make a garden a living ecosystem. Few creatures are all bad, however they may seem to gardeners. To understand their place in the system is to know how best to thwart them without throwing the switch on the system itself.

There is not a gardener who has not puzzled and grieved over the fate of plants he has nurtured. Too often in the past we have all felt the helplessness of ignorance.

This book is going to live no further from this gardener's hands than his trowel and his twine. Reading it has made me full of resolution. Referring to it will make me a physician to my plants and a terrible foe to their adversaries.

Hugh Johnson, one of the world's foremost wine authorities, is also a passionate gardener.

Introduction

"How can I keep flea beetles off my eggplants?"

"What causes those black spots on my green beans?"

"Why won't my spinach sprout?"

"Why doesn't my broccoli head?"

In spite of all our experience, hopes and efforts, every garden is, in part, a lesson in humility. Oh, the tomatoes may bulge like balloons, and the lettuce grow so fast it needs to be mowed. But tucked away in a back corner of the plot is always something (or a few somethings) that just isn't making it. Such garden disappointments are reminders that we don't know—and can't always grow—everything.

Most vegetable-raising texts start from scratch and teach you to grow each individual crop. *The Healthy Garden Handbook* takes a different tack. It assumes you already garden and now want answers to specific problems you may be encountering.

If you go to a physician and describe the symptoms of some ailment, the doctor may consult the *PDR*, the *Physician's Desk Reference*, to find which prescription would most likely serve you as a remedy. This guide is your own *GDR*, a *Gardener's Desk Reference*.

The Healthy Garden Handbook is divided into five sections:

Part One: "Creating the Healthy Garden" is based on the premise that most times it's easier to prevent a problem than to fix it. Healthy plants have far fewer pest, disease and growth problems than do unhealthy ones. So the sound soil-building and crop-tending practices in this section will keep you from ever having to deal with the vast majority of gardening problems.

Part Two: "Coping With Garden Pests" is a complete practical field guide to the common harmful and beneficial insects—and other residents—of the garden. As far as we know, this is the *first* time good pest identification photos and solid advice for organic controls have been brought together in the same book.

Part Three: "Overcoming Plant Diseases" describes common plant maladies and offers the best organic treatments for them. In truth, many diseases are quite difficult to treat. Here, more than anywhere else, the preventive advice of Part One can come into play. Horticultural hygiene, crop rotation and resistant varieties fend off plant diseases far better than most remedies cure them.

Part Four: "Remedies for Common Garden Problems" is the nitty-gritty section. It gets right out there in the dirt, taking each commonly raised vegetable, citing the likely problems you may have growing it and describing the best treatments for each problem. If you've ever wished some wise gardening grandmother lived next door who could answer all the questions you have about puzzling crop failures, you'll be only too glad to find the straightforward counsel of this section.

Part Five: "References" contains the basic statistics of vegetable raising—everything from where to get your seeds to how many quarts of produce you can expect them to yield. Consult it for planting times and sequences, crop rotation guidelines and more.

The advice in these pages has been carefully collected, edited and checked for accuracy, but it's more than just information being passed from one book to another. It actually comes from *several* voices of experience—the master gardeners who, through the years, have worked at the *Mother Earth News* research gardens. Kerry and Barbara Sullivan, Walker and Olivia Abel, and Franklin and Susan Sides have all tended our demonstration and experimental plots. The showcase gardens they created have been home to hundreds of bountiful crops and the solving grounds for many a horticultural headache. There, dozens of apprentices, under the tutelage of our head gardeners, have learned how to correct their own mistakes. The lovely plots have also been seen by thousands of visitors—visitors who, thinking of their home gardens, asked many of those hard-to-tackle questions we've tried to answer here. So the base of experience in this guidebook is deep, as deep as taproots in a well-tilled bed.

The single person most responsible for the dirt-under-the-fingernail truth of *The Healthy Garden Handbook* is Susan Sides, current head gardener. She's been raising vegetables, flowers and herbs organically for over 13 years, from the sands of Florida to the clay loam of the western North Carolina mountains. She's experimented with everything from seed-starting kits to homemade compost bins. One summer she even grew 64 exotic crops—from chocolate peppers to Chinese chives—as hands-on research for an unusual-vegetable guide we published. And not only have her hands turned the soil of many a spring bed, but they've also pounded a lot of typewriter keys. Sides wrote almost all of both Part Two and Part Four, and several other chapters, as well. Between words and vegetables, she has had an incredibly busy year, but her compassion for plants and the people who grow them pulled her through, as did all the help and encouragement she got from her husband, Franklin.

As useful as *The Healthy Garden Handbook* will become to you, remember that it takes a problem-solving approach to gardening. As a result, it could lead a beginning gardener to see vegetable raising as an enterprise fraught with trouble. Indeed, learning about all the damaging insects, gruesome diseases and surprising mishaps that can afflict home-raised vegetables might make such a person feel like never even trying to nurse a crop from the ground to begin with.

Clearly, however, gardening offers far more pleasures than pitfalls, which is why it ranks as the most popular leisure activity in the country. To make our guide as thorough as possible, we've had to cover as many problems as possible. But only a small fraction of these are ever likely to afflict your garden (we simply didn't know *which* ones *you'd* get). If you follow good gardening practices, the vast majority of your vegetable offspring will practically rear themselves.

One last thought: Every garden and every gardening season is unique—one of the joys of the activity is its variability—so while our advice is the absolute best we could come up with, there are no guarantees it will always work. Gardens are not mechanical devices that submit to simple repairs. They are small, living communities filled with plants, animals, insects, humans, bacteria.

So please consider each of our suggestions as a possible solution, not the final word; then experiment with open eyes and a caring heart. Let your plants be your real guides—they are true teachers and never lie. Through it all, enjoy the growth both failures and successes bring to you as a gardener. Cherish the opportunities your garden offers to touch these children of the earth, to listen and learn directly from the natural world.

—*Pat Stone*
Garden Editor
Mother Earth News

Creating the Healthy Garden

Building good soil
and nourishing the crops
can keep most
garden problems from
ever occurring.

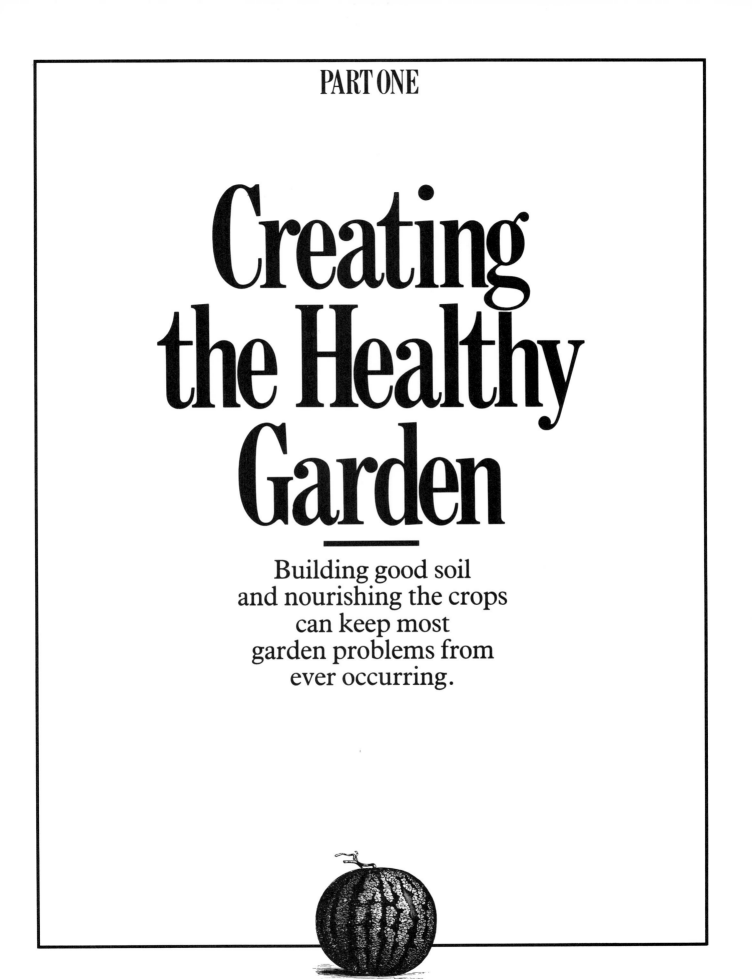

Preventive Gardening

Healthy plants form the best defense.

"I suspect that the insects which have harassed you have been encouraged by the feebleness of your plants; and that has been produced by the lean state of your soil."
—*Thomas Jefferson*

Much of the information in this guide is therapeutic—it's meant to help fix a problem *after* it has occurred. Many times, however, you can prevent a garden calamity in advance by observing good soil and crop husbandry. This section is devoted to promoting garden health. Hence it covers the basic practices and principles of good gardening. Here, in a nutshell, are its 10 major points:

1. Compost

Organic gardeners have claimed for years that using compost and other organic matter as fertilizers, rather than feeding the soil an all-chemical diet (such as a standard nitrogen-phosphorus-potassium, or NPK, fertilizer), helps plants resist pests. Researchers at Cornell University have recently found that this credo has a basis in fact. Their results show that "significantly smaller pest-insect populations are associated with use of organic fertilizers relative to controls fertilized with highly soluble NPK materials or left unfertilized, at least for the particular experiment situation studied."

Such results are hardly surprising. It is common knowledge that a good, well-balanced diet makes humans less prone to disease and other health problems. The same holds true for plants, as Jefferson knew.

2. Stress

Poor diet reduces health in humans; so does stress. Again, the same holds true for plants. Plants subject to such conditions as cold weather, lack of water or air pollution produce glutathione, an amino acid that helps shield them from environmental stress. The trouble is that some insects find glutathione-rich plants all the more attractive.

To increase their vigor, plants should be kept well watered (the equivalent of at least an inch of rain a week) but not soggy. They should be shielded from extreme cold and wind by such means as cold frames, plastic covering devices, spunbond row covers such as Reemay or windbreaks. All in all, it is best to attempt to keep environmental extremes at a minimum.

3. Resistant Varieties

Certain plant varieties are less vulnerable to insect damage than others. Globemaster radishes, for example, are prone to attack by flea beetles each spring. The Champion radish, on the other hand, is a flea-resistant variety that grows equally well. (For a listing of other cultivars that can help fend off chronic infestations, see "Resistant Plants" on page 56.)

4. Timed Plantings

In most areas, each problem pest reaches its peak population about the same time every year. Knowing when that time is likely to occur means that the alert gardener can often plan to harvest before that date or plant after it. Timed plantings cost nothing and require little more than common sense, yet they can be one of the most effective ways to avoid insect problems. (To find emergence times, see "Peak Infestation Times" on page 70 or consult a local agricultural extension agent.)

5. Companion Planting

Herbs and vegetables that beneficially affect each other can be companion-planted—that is, interplanted or grown in close proximity. Experience has shown that some crops help deter the pests of others. For example, green beans deter the chief pest of potatoes—the Colorado potato beetle—while potatoes repel the Mexican bean beetle, nemesis of the bean. Companion planting works on the principle that insects tend not to seek out a plant they like if it's surrounded by ones that repel them.

The concept of companion planting can be taken one step further. The more diversified the plantings in a garden, the less likely that insect problems will arise. The jumble of sight and scent signals simply makes it harder for specific pests to locate their preferred foods. Conversely, large plantings of a single crop—a practice known as monoculture—fairly scream "Come and get it!"

6. Mulch

Mulching a garden—that is, covering the soil with a layer of organic (or sometimes inorganic) material—can often reduce plant stress caused by weather and water extremes. It helps to moderate soil temperature and to keep the ground from drying out. Mulches such as cedar and oak bark can also serve as physical deterrents to pests.

But mulches have drawbacks, too. Mulching too early in a cool climate can keep the soil from warming up quickly, or it may encourage rot during overly wet periods. A simple straw or grass mulch will provide extra shelter to slugs and snails in plots where they are a problem. So gardeners must weigh the factors of soil type, climate and pests to decide when mulch will help a plot's health and when it will hinder it.

7. Crop Rotation

Rotating crops means not planting the same crop in one place twice in succession. Typically, a heavy nutrient feeder such as tomatoes, corn, cabbage or squash is followed by a leguminous crop such as beans or peas that add nitrogen to the soil. This, in turn, is followed by a light-feeding root crop such as carrots or beets.

Rotating crops helps keep soil and produce healthy, which helps ward off pests. Moreover, as biointensive gardener John Jeavons puts it, "crop rotation is a way of companion planting over time." Many insects overwinter or lay their eggs in the soil near favored feeding sites. But if in the next growing season they emerge only to find different and distasteful foliage, they will be well on their way to being thwarted.

8. Sanitation

Many pests find good places to hide, sleep, mate, lay eggs or overwinter in decaying, uncollected garden litter. Consequently, old leaves, vines, stalks, fruit and other debris should be raked onto the compost pile as soon as possible.

9. Cultivation

Digging or tilling up the soil can interrupt the life cycles of insects. Exposing underground grubs, eggs and pupae to hungry birds and cold temperatures is an excellent way to be rid of pests likely to cause *next* year's infestation. Late fall and/or early spring is generally the best time for such preventive cultivations.

10. The Gardener's Shadow

According to an oft-quoted Chinese proverb, "the best fertilizer is the gardener's own shadow." Spending time just *being* in the garden—watching the birds at work, observing plants, insects and animals and noting the day-to-day changes and interactions—can teach one more about a garden than days of studied work. Casting your shadow in the garden will open up worlds of knowledge not found in books, know-how that can't but help improve the health and productivity of your plot.

The best
fertilizer is the
gardener's
own shadow.

Preparing the Soil

Good texture and fertility in the earth lead to good crops from it.

It wasn't that long ago that farmers were called sodbusters—a term derogatory to people who worked with the soil. Today, more and more men and women seem to be eager to get out and bust some very special bits of sod—their home gardens.

At *Mother Earth News'* research garden, we look forward to that moment in spring when the soil has warmed and dried. From then on until early summer, our backs will bend and our sweat will flow as the earth beneath us is lifted, tilthed and reawakened to its full life.

This year, though, before beginning to break ground, let's pause and review the basic reasons and techniques for preparing the soil. This section will be of special interest to people with new gardens, but it should prove useful for experienced growers tending years-old plots, as well.

Cultivation

Usually, we think of garden cultivation in terms of plowing, tilling, digging or hoeing—that is, simply turning and loosening the soil. This is accurate as far as it goes, but there's much more implied by the word *cultivation*, and no doubt the farmers of old intended for these additional meanings to be understood when they chose this term to describe their practices.

If a teacher stands before a class and says, "In this school, we cultivate the characters of young men and women," that person is stating an intent to nurture, refine and improve the students' basic natures. These meanings are equally applicable in the garden. The full intention of soil cultivation is to nurture and improve the ground so that crops will grow better. And just as the teacher must know what attributes the students are intended to gain, so must the gardener have a clear image of what is to be achieved by working the soil.

For the *organic* grower, that image has two central aspects: The soil should be loose, friable and evenly textured, and the life it contains should be fully encouraged and nurtured.

Part I: Soil Texture

It's said that the early Greeks began their transition to agriculture when they observed

Turning soil: a rite of spring.

that plants grew particularly well in the loosened soil of a landslide. That was the example in nature that they tried to imitate with their digging and planting. (Nature also texturizes soil through the action of glaciers, frost, wind, earthworms, gophers, moles, the probing of deep-rooted plants and so on.) Whatever model you follow with your own ground-disturbing activities, you'll be striving to loosen the soil to a good depth and create an even texture in its upper inches. Such cultivation—in the narrow sense of the word—performs several important functions:

It provides *aeration*. Roots need oxygen in order to carry on cell respiration and thus grow. Indeed, well-aerated soil may be almost half air space.

It provides *drainage*. Most garden plants don't like soggy soil. And the deeper the soil is dug, the better the drainage.

It provides *easy root movement*. In compacted soil, the roots must slowly pry their way down. This slows overall growth. In loosened soil, the roots can move freely to get the water and nutrients they need.

And it provides *a good seedbed.* The fine, even texture of the upper inches allows the soil to snugly cradle each seed and assures reliable germination.

Of course, you aren't likely to achieve such ideally textured soil in your first gardening season, but you can take a giant step toward that goal. Then again, you could also take a giant step *backward,* if you're not careful.

Many enthusiastic beginning gardeners rush outdoors and work their soil before it's ready. It takes some experience to know when the right time has come. The critical factor is soil *moisture:* If your plot is either too wet or too dry when you start to dig or till, you can cause serious damage that may take years to heal. (This is particularly true of clay soil; sandy soil is more forgiving.) Too wet ground may turn into large, hard clumps that are difficult to break, while overly dry soil may pulverize into such fine dust that it loses all its texture.

To tell if all or part of your soil is ready to work, pick up a clump in your hand and lightly roll it into a ball. Then either drop it or prod it with a finger. If the ball breaks easily into smaller sections, your soil is ready. If it's still rubbery or puttylike, wait for drier weather. On the other hand, if the clod is *too* dry (if it feels hard or crumbles easily into small, brittle fragments), water the ground thoroughly and check it again in another day or two.

You might also want to dig deeply into your garden to get a general sense of its current quality. Dark red or brown coloration is a sign of good drainage, while gray mixed with yellow or red means your plot's drainage is probably poor. Pale ground is subsoil: If that's all you've got, your soil-building work is cut out for you. Mottled soil may indicate that the water table sometimes rises near your plot's surface. And black soil is rich in organic matter.

If your ground's ready to work, first clear and remove the dead weeds and crop residue, and scythe or mow down any tall, live vegetation. You can then either rake this growth off and compost it or—while it's still green—turn it under. Note, however, that cellulose-rich plant matter requires nitrogen to

One way to break up soil clods is tilthing—hitting the soil with glancing blows from a garden fork. This can produce fine soil texture.

break down, so if you till in the plant material, you'll also be temporarily reducing your soil's supply of that important nutrient. Wait a month after turning in green matter before you plant.

You can, of course, choose one of several ways to break the ground. If you have a small plot and a strong back, you can dig the whole area by hand. As another option, you can rent or buy a rotary tiller to work the plot. It may take a large number of passes with the machine's tines set at increasing depths, but eventually you should be able to finely break up the top 4″ to 8″ of soil.

Then again, you may live in an area where you can pay a tractor owner to plow and disk

your plot. Although the machine probably won't work the ground any deeper than a tiller would, it will do the job more quickly and easily. In fact, if you're preparing a large first-year garden on a plot with a thick layer of sod, you'll definitely be better off if you let a tractor do that initial ground breaking.

Still another method, called double-digging, uses hand tools and involves loosening the soil with a spade and garden fork to a depth of as much as 24″ to better work in organic matter and to promote texture deep in the soil. The process demands a lot of hard work, but the results usually justify the effort. In fact, yields from double-dug beds can be four times as great as those from conventionally dug areas.

While a lot of factors can influence your choice of ground-breaking technique, one element crucial to good soil texture is *depth.* A rotary tiller or tractor will do a fine job of texturizing the top 4″ to 8″ of your plot, but those machines won't touch anything beneath that. In fact, with repeated use they can actually compact that subsoil into hardpan.

Double-digging, obviously, loosens soil to the greatest depth, but it also takes the greatest amount of labor. For a "middle ground" alternative, divide your tilled garden into pathways and raised beds, and rake the loosened pathway earth onto the beds; that'll help increase the depth of texturized soil for your crops, no matter how you initially break the ground.

Part II: Soil Life

Mechanical and manual methods of soil conditioning can be likened to an inhalation: The soil has fluffed and expanded as a chest does when the lungs are filled. But just as our lungs are not simply inert balloons but are alive with blood that moves and uses this air, so the life in the soil responds to the increased air flow, leading to fertility.

And the organisms that make up a living soil must be carefully nurtured. They form an intricate system that is by no means completely understood. According to one estimate, a single teaspoonful of fertile soil contains 4 billion bacteria, 40 to 100 meters of mold filament, 144,000,000 actinomycetes and large quantities of algae and other microorganisms. All of these, along with the organic matter that sustains them, transform inert, mineral dirt into healthy, living soil.

Such life-forms are important for a number of reasons. Like some intestinal bacteria in animals, they digest nutrients and change them into a form that higher organisms (in this case, plants) are able to use. Also, by tying up nutrients in their bodies as they grow and then dying and releasing them, these organisms regulate the flow of food to the plants and create a sustained fertility. In addition, their excretions, sometimes called soil glue, bind earthen particles into small aggregates, helping to build a loose, friable soil.

These beneficial microorganisms will *not* live in a soil that is fertilized only with chemicals. They rely, instead, upon a *steady* supply of actively decomposing organic matter for their food and energy. Note the word *steady:* Organic matter needs to be supplied on an ongoing basis.

And important as its role of supporting microorganisms is, organic matter does even more. It helps aerate the soil, retains water through dry periods, holds nutrients that would otherwise be leached out by rains and—unlike chemical fertilizers—releases these nutrients slowly as its decomposition proceeds.

At our garden, we spread 1″ of fresh compost over the surface of every just-dug bed and then work this material in with a fork so that it's dispersed through the upper 4″ to 6″ of the soil. That is our fundamental fertilization program. The compost will nurture the crop throughout the season and leave some residue for long-term soil improvement. We do occasionally work in some bone meal to provide extra phosphorus and hardwood ashes for potash.

When our compost production is high, we're able to add as much as 2″ or 3″ of the homemade amendment per bed to help build up the organic matter in the soil. Ideally, a garden will eventually have a standing ratio of at least 5% organic matter. This can be difficult to achieve in sandy soils or in regions with very hot summers.

There are, of course, other sources of organic matter for your soil. In many areas, you can gather leaf mold from municipal leaf dumps. This is an excellent, long-lasting source of organic "fiber"; use only well-decomposed mold, not fresh leaves. Well-aged manure is also effective; if you can only

Double-Digging Steps

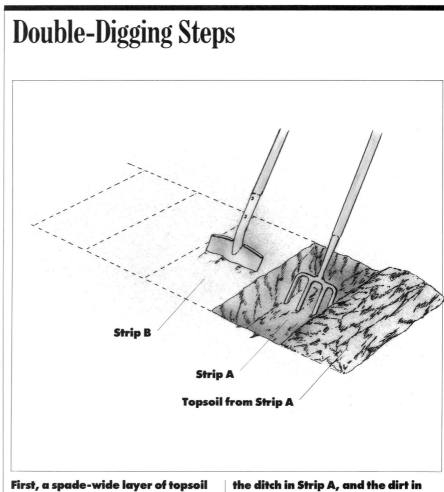

Strip B

Strip A

Topsoil from Strip A

First, a spade-wide layer of topsoil is removed from Strip A. Next, after the lower layer of soil in that trench is loosened with a garden fork, topsoil from Strip B is shoveled into the ditch in Strip A, and the dirt in the lower level of Strip B is also loosened. Finally, the topsoil from Strip A is used to fill in the remaining ditch.

get hold of fresh, "hot" manure, compost it a few months so it won't burn your plants. And you can raise your own organic matter by growing cover crops like rye, hairy vetch or buckwheat and then composting or turning them under. Remember to wait a month before planting after turning under green matter.

Building up the life and organic matter in your soil is an ongoing, never-ending garden task. You'll want to work each year at "growing" good soil, just as you'll work at growing good crops. Eventually, you should be able to maintain your soil's health and fertility by doing little more than proper com-

posting, crop rotation and cover cropping.

However, because most soils have been mistreated in the past—through poor agricultural practices or by natural erosion—they need some initial "medicinal" help to reach a sustainable level of fertility.

Experienced farmers of old could look at the relative quantities of various weeds or the way crops were growing and diagnose their soils. Such "living soil analyses" can be extremely accurate, since they reveal how the soil is actually functioning in relation to plant growth.

Of course, very few people today have such observational skills. Most of us must rely on chemical soil tests to gain some sense of our plots' strengths and weaknesses. You can buy a kit at a garden supply store or get a test done through your county extension service. But don't rely completely on any test results—the accuracy of soil testing is a subject of much controversy; instead, use them to identify glaring deficiencies you should address.

Potential Hydrogen

The first thing you should test for is pH, that indicator of acidity or alkalinity. Balancing your garden's pH is important, because a soil that's too acidic (a pH of 6.0 or lower) or too alkaline (a pH of 8.0 or higher) will tie up essential minerals in the earth, making them unavailable to your vegetables.

If your soil is too acidic, you'll need to add limestone or hardwood ashes to your garden—on the day you break ground—to increase the pH. Be sure, though, to use only agricultural-grade (not hydrated, or slaked) lime, and if you have a choice, opt for dolomitic limestone rather than calcic limestone, because of the former's more favorable magnesium content. To raise your soil's pH one full point, you'll need at least three pounds of finely ground limestone per 100 square feet, and the denser your soil is, the more limestone you'll have to add. Very heavy clays sometimes need as much as eight pounds per 100 square feet. Alternatively, hardwood ashes—which are faster-acting—can be applied at roughly the same rate as lime. Actually, you might be wise to use a *combination* of ashes and limestone, to give your garden both an immediate and a sustained boost.

On the other hand, your garden may be alkaline—particularly if you live in the Southwest—in which case you'll need to *reduce* the pH. A 1″ layer of peat moss, worked into the earth when you till or dig your plot, should lower the rating a point. You can also use agricultural gypsum, at a rate of two pounds per 100 square feet, for the same purpose.

Inorganic Elements

After checking your soil's pH, you'll next be interested in its nutritional balance. Of the 216 elements that most affect plant growth, all but three must come from the soil. The exceptions are carbon, hydrogen and oxygen, which are derived mainly from water and air. And among the most important of those remaining, nitrogen, phosphorus and potassium—the famous N, P and K of commercial fertilizer formulas—are generally classified as major nutrients, while 10 others are labeled minor, or trace, elements.

Nitrogen

As most gardeners know, nitrogen is essential to plant growth and vigor. It's often considered the nutrient that most promotes leaf development. (How're your spinach crops?) An ongoing supply of good compost and other organic matter should take care of the nitrogen needs of a healthy garden. To supplement the nitrogen of a soil that already tests out very high in that element, Jeavons—in his eminently useful book *How to Grow More Vegetables*—recommends either .75 pound of blood meal (14% N), one pound of fish meal (10% N), two pounds of cottonseed meal (8% N) or .75 pound of hoof and horn meal (14% N) per 100 square feet of garden. For a garden rated medium in nitrogen, he triples this dosage. And he roughly quintuples the proportions for a plot ranked very low in the element. In case you'd like to try working out some substitutions of your own, feather meal contains 10% to 13% nitrogen; processed municipal sludge, 4% to 5%; poultry manure, 4% to 6%; and most animal manures, 2% to 4%.

Phosphorus

Phosphorus promotes cell division, root development and—most notably—fruit growth. If your soil tests show a very low phosphorus content, or if last year your green crops exhibited a reddish purple coloration in their stems and leaf veins or if your fruiting crops were leafy but unproductive, you may need to add this element to your soil. For soils already rated very high in phosphorus, Jeavons recommends either one pound of bonemeal (24% to 28% P) or two pounds finely ground phosphate rock (30% P, but slow-releasing). Double the dose for ground rated medium and triple it for plots rated very low. Colloidal phosphate (20% P) and single superphosphate (20% P) are other good—and relatively fast-acting—sources.

Potassium

Also known as potash, potassium is indispensable for cell division and growth, helps plants form strong stems and fight off disease and promotes root growth. (Have a problem with your root crops last year? Notice a lot of yellow-streaked leaves and spindly plants?)

For plots with a very high potassium rating, use one pound of kelp meal (3% K), two pounds of greensand (7% K) or three pounds of crushed granite (4% K). For soil rated medium in potash, use one pound of kelp plus 1.33 pounds of greensand (or two pounds of crushed granite), 3.33 pounds of greensand or five pounds of crushed granite. And for soil with a very low potassium rating, double all of the "medium" numbers except the kelp. Because kelp meal contains some growth hormones, you should be careful to never add more than one pound of it per 100 square feet per year. Some additional organic sources of potash are feldspar dust (5% to 15%), wood ashes (8%) and sulphate of potash-magnesia—or Sul-po-mag—(22%).

Trace Elements

These micronutrients—boron, calcium, chlorine, copper, iron, magnesium, manganese, molybdenum, sulfur and zinc—are necessary in smaller amounts than nitrogen, phosphorus or potassium, but, like the spices in a good recipe, are no less important to the end result.

Not only are trace elements valuable as direct nutrients, they also work as catalysts to prompt chemical reactions that dissolve other soil-borne minerals, making them available to plants. Many of the 10 micronutrients, in fact, work best only when present in proper proportion with others.

Good composting and other soil-building practices should provide a balanced meal of trace elements in the long run. If you want to give your plot a trace-element boost now—or periodically—seaweed (kelp) is an excellent source. Apply one pound of seaweed meal (or three pounds of raw seaweed) per 100 square feet of soil area. Another good, commercially available source is FTE (fritted trace elements).

Complete Organic Fertilizers

You can buy or make balanced organic fertilizers to help boost your garden's soil quality. At our garden we've often used Erth-Rite fertilizer on poor soils. (It's available in different blends from Zook & Ranck, Rt. 1, Gap, PA 17527.)

John Jeavons has a general fertilizer program for first- and second-year gardens, assuming that the soil is poor and the owner hasn't—for one reason or another—done a soil test. His recipe is meant to be applied per 100 square feet at each planting.

For *nitrogen:*
10 pounds cottonseed meal, or 5 pounds fish meal, or 5 pounds blood meal or 4 pounds hoof and horn meal

For *phosphorus:*
4–5 pounds bonemeal, or 10 pounds phosphate rock or 10 pounds soft phosphate

For *potash* and *trace minerals:*
1 pound kelp meal and 2 pounds wood ashes, or 10 pounds crushed granite or 10 pounds greensand

As a *texturizer:*
2 cubic feet of manure

For *microbiotic life* and *humus:*
up to 1 cubic yard of compost

For *calcium:*
2 pounds eggshells

For *humic acid* (to release tied-up nutrients):
1 pound Clodbuster (a commercial product)

Lee Fryer also provides some good homemade fertilizer recipes in his book *The Bio-Gardener's Bible*. Each of his three formulas makes about 100 pounds of fertilizer and provides at least 3% nitrogen, 6% phosphorus and 6% potash. Lee recommends applying a total of four pounds of these mixtures per 100 square feet of garden per season (applied both throughout the garden and under seed rows prior to planting) if—in his words—

Tilthing takes time but produces finely textured soil that's just right for sprouting seeds and young seedlings.

"you want to grow a garden that'll impress the neighbors."

Recipe I
Feather meal	20 pounds
Superphosphate	30 pounds
Sulfate of potash	10 pounds
Compost	40 pounds
FTE	2 pounds

Recipe II
Feather meal	10 pounds
Dehydrated manure	10 pounds
Rock phosphate (or colloidal phosphate)	25 pounds
Bonemeal	5 pounds
Greensand (or granite dust)	20 pounds
Compost	30 pounds
FTE	2 pounds

Recipe III
Any good organic-based garden fertilizer	40 pounds
Blood meal (or ureaform)	5 pounds
Bonemeal (or superphosphate)	10 pounds
Epsom salts (or Sul-po-mag)	3 pounds
Seaweed meal (or compost)	10 pounds
FTE	2 pounds
Compost (or dry manure)	30 pounds

A good mail-order source for most of these supplements, in case you want to purchase some to remedy specific deficiencies or make your own fertilizer, is Necessary Trading Company, 328 Main St., New Castle, VA 24127.

Compost

Making and using humus are two of the most important things you can do to improve your garden.

Rural author Wendell Berry once wrote of the farmer, "He has seen the light lie down in the dung heap and rise again in the corn." These words deftly sum up the agricultural life cycle—or, even better, *light cycle.* Plants convert solar energy into food for animals (ourselves included). Then the wastes from those animals, along with dead plant and animal bodies, "lie down in the dung heap," are composted and "rise again in the corn."

This cycle of light is the central reason that composting is such an important link in organic food production: It returns solar energy to the soil. In this context, such common compost ingredients as onion skins, hair trimmings, eggshells, vegetable parings and even burnt toast are no longer seen as garbage, but rather as sunlight on the move from one form to another.

By making use of such substances, composting enables us to have large amounts of "dung" for our gardens without necessarily passing most of the ingredients through an animal first. It also greatly speeds up the earth's own soil-building processes so we can get the results in months instead of centuries.

The benefits of using compost are so legion that it's no exaggeration to say that it is *the* key to soil fertility. The end product of composting is *humus*, the broken-down organic matter that is the basis of soil life. And the billions of microorganisms that are in a single teaspoon of fertile soil perform numerous functions. They change nutrients into a form that your plants can use; provide a sustained, ongoing flow of that food; and bind earthen particles into small aggregates, helping to build a friable soil.

There are other benefits of composting:

Control of pH. Acid or alkaline soil can lock up many nutrients so that they're unavailable to plants. The regular addition of compost rounds off such sharp edges, helping to bring soil to the crop-favoring pH range of between 6.5 and 7.5.

Heat absorption. Finished compost will help darken most soils, helping them to better absorb heat from sunlight. This can actually extend your spring and fall growing seasons.

Drainage, water retention and aeration. Imagine the life of a root for a moment, ever tunneling in search of water and food. If the soil is clayey, the roots will have trouble making headway. They become shallow, never reaching the food and water reserves deeper down. And their oxygen supply is easily cut off in the tightly packed soil.

Sandy soil creates a different problem; it's like a long stretch of good road with nowhere to get food and water. Nutrients and moisture simply percolate down out of reach.

So we want it all—good drainage, good water retention (even though the two sound almost contradictory) *and* openness for the incorporation of air. Again, humus is the cure-all. It opens up packed soils and binds together loose ones. Acting like a sponge, humus helps hold moisture, food and air so plants can have access to them at will.

Nutrient retention. Chemical fertilizers provide quick-fix doses of three major nutrients: nitrogen (N), phosphorus (P) and potassium (K). Since such garden additives are highly water-soluble, plants can take them up quickly, but they can also be easily washed away by rain or irrigation. In fact, it's estimated that from 25% to 85% of the chemical nitrogen applied to soil and 15% to 20% of the phosphorus and potassium are lost to leaching.

Humus holds those water-soluble nutrients inside itself, keeping them safe from run-off and releasing them slowly to plants. (Even better, the soil microorganisms in humus release nutrients more slowly during cool weather—when crops are growing more slowly—and most quickly during warm weather—when plants are growing most actively.)

Free choice feeding. The way in which roots and humus directly interact is probably the most fascinating argument for the use of compost. It's a miraculous process whereby plants choose their own diet.

You may have seen the words *cation exchange* on a soil test. Cations are positively charged molecules of different minerals like ammonium, iron, potassium, magnesium and calcium. Since opposites attract, the negatively charged molecules of humus (and, to a lesser extent, clay as well) attract and hold the positive cations.

When a searching root comes along, surrounded by an aura of positive hydrogen ions, it strikes up a friendly exchange with the humus (or clay) molecules: The root trades its hydrogen ions for the nutrient ions of its choice. Thus humus allows plants to choose what nutrients they need.

And more. Compost also helps control nematodes and soil diseases, attracts soil-building earthworms, helps plants produce their own growth stimulators, helps fix heavy metals and other toxins in the soil (instead of letting them be absorbed by the crops), adds trace minerals to the soil, and makes plants hardier and more resistant to insects and diseases. It can even be used as a healing poultice on tree wounds.

Last, compost can be made virtually free at home, by mimicking the earth's recycling system. Chemical fertilizers, on the other hand, cost money and use nonrenewable fossil fuels both as ingredients and in their manufacture.

Where

If you are ready to start your own pile of black soil magic, the first concern is where you'll build it. When choosing a spot, take into account these suggestions:
1. Try to locate your pile near your garden—a wheelbarrow loaded with compost is heavy.
2. If you're going to be importing some compost-building ingredients by vehicle, try to build your pile in a spot you can drive to.
3. Wetting the pile will be a lot easier if you locate near a water source.
4. A good deciduous shade tree near the pile can provide some shelter from heavy thunderstorms and excessively hot summer sun, while it lets warmth-boosting fall and winter light through. It'll even provide leaf material. However, evergreens (which have acidic needles), walnuts (which exude a toxin through their roots) and eucalyptuses (which have resinous leaves) are not good choices.

In What

Now you need something to put your ingredients in. Actually, a straight-sided pile can be constructed with no bin or supports. That's a perfectly acceptable way to compost.

But it takes time to shape a freestanding pile; being able to toss the makings into a container can really speed the process along. In addition, if your neighbors live nearby, they may voice aesthetic objections to a freestanding pile of decomposing materials. In that case, you can compost incognito by using an attractive homemade or commercial

Top to bottom: Fresh green matter— like this comfrey—helps add nitrogen and mass to a compost pile. Turning the mound in a compost bin is a simple task if you can open one of the container's sides. Work the finished humus into your soil before planting.

bin. Privacy fencing (plant or wire) might also help shut out the critical eyes.

The creative scrounger will find that numerous materials make good bin build-ings. Boards, poles, screen, wire, old pallets, concrete blocks, snow fencing and hay bales will all serve well. At the other end of the spectrum are the $70 to $200 commercial composters you can buy through garden supply catalogues.

In the middle, between total scrounging and total spending, are the two composters designed by gardeners at *Mother Earth News*. The "quickie" version is a mobile pen made out of hog wire panels. This low-cost model allows you to use it to make a pile and then easily move the pen when you want to start a new pile or turn the old one. The "uptown" model is meant to be more aesthetically acceptable, yet still entirely practical. Although you could build it with just one bin (the design is basically modular), you'll do better if you build more than one enclosure so you can turn compost from one bin to the other. Better still, build a three-bin version so you can turn two half-decomposed "side" piles into the middle bin to finish cooking.

Any pile, freestanding or contained, should be at least 3' X 3' X 3' to insure that there's sufficient mass for the composting process to take place. The bottom of the pile should be exposed to the earth, and the top should be covered with black plastic or a waterproof tarp to protect it from extreme rain or drying sun. Contained piles should also have enough open spaces in their sides to allow for good air circulation.

Kosher and Nonkosher Materials

So many types of organic matter can be composted that it's almost easier to list what shouldn't be put in a compost pile. Here's a partial list of what not to use:
Cat feces. While almost every other kind of animal manure makes an excellent compost ingredient, cat feces can contain a parasite (*Toxoplasma gondii*) or roundworm (*Toxocara cati*). Either of these organisms can spread serious disease to pregnant women, unborn babies and children.
Grease and fat. OK in small amounts, but too much will clog up the composting process.
Coal, coal ashes and barbecue briquettes. These have overly high amounts of iron and sulfur (and who knows what else in the briquettes).

Diseased plant matter. Actually, you can place diseased plants in the center of a compost pile that will be prepared in the hot method—where temperatures reach a pathogen-killing 140°F. Otherwise, burn them before composting.

Polyester, plastics and other synthetics. They just don't rot.

Urban floor sweepings. In high-traffic areas, these can contain as much as 500 parts per million of lead.

Food preserved with BHT. Recent research has shown that even very small amounts of this antioxidant can alter plant growth profoundly.

Overly bulky or hard material. Cornstalks, sunflower stalks, nutshells, sticks thicker than a pencil, large bones, and oyster and clam shells should be shredded or pulverized before composting. If you can't do that, put them in a long-range pile of their own or burn what you can and add the ashes.

Sludge. Commercially reprocessed sludge is an increasingly popular soil amendment and is almost certainly pathogen-free, but there is concern about the heavy metals and insecticides it may contain.

And what are *good* compost makings? Well, for starters, how about these:

Plant residues (nonsprayed). Candidates include kitchen and garden wastes, weeds, grass clippings, leaves (go light on those from eucalyptuses, walnuts and evergreens), straw, hay, hedge clippings, seaweed, aquatic plants and green manure crops.

Commercial wastes. These include buckwheat hulls, rice hulls, molasses-making residue, spent hops, fruit-processing wastes, commercial fishing scraps, lake dredgings, sawdust, feathers, wood ashes (in moderation), utility-company tree trimmings and vegetable or dairy wastes from grocery stores.

Home wastes. Eggshells, hair, wool scraps, etc., all apply.

Manures. Horses, fowl, cows, pigs, sheep, etc., will fill the bill. Manure is even better if it's mixed with straw (i.e., used stall bedding).

The Six Essentials

Once you've assembled lots of appropriate organic matter from the "compost pile shopping list" above, you're just about ready to start cooking. The funny thing, though, is

Top to bottom: This quickie model composter is a snap to use and little bother to make. You can open the door all the way to start building the pile. Close the bottom half of the doorway as your mound grows. Then secure a polyethylene tarp for a rain cover when you're done. (And when the time comes to turn the heap, just take the pen off the pile, move it a couple of feet, and start the process over.)

there is no *one* way to make compost—indeed, there are almost as many methods as there are experts to advocate them.

It's like baking bread: There are thousands of different recipes, but all of them have in common some basic practices and vital main ingredients. So before you build that long-awaited heap, let's quickly review the six essentials of successful composting:

Nitrogen. For a compost to cook properly and to have maximum value for plants, it needs nitrogen, the leaf-growth-promoting element. Good sources of N are pig, chicken, sheep, horse and cow manures (ranked in descending amounts of nitrogen); fresh *green* plant waste (especially legumes); kitchen wastes; blood, bone, cottonseed, hoof, horn and alfalfa meals (readily available from garden supply centers, but somewhat costly); and urine. This last nitrogen source may be animal or—if you're not made squeamish by the thought—human. Indeed, "household liquid activator," as human urine has been dubbed, is practically sterile, available to everyone and a perfect nitrogenous compost catalyst. (You can collect it in a lidded bucket—a chamber pot, our forebears called it—and dilute it with water, then add it once the pile is *hot*. A week's urine should provide plenty of N for a good-size pile.)

Carbon. The vast bulk of any compost pile should be carbonaceous material: dried leaves, hay, straw, partially dried garden gleanings, shredded stalks—almost any dried organic matter. This is the key humus-building material and the substance that binds nitrogen (an otherwise ephemeral element) into the compost.

Air. Although organic matter can decay anaerobically (without oxygen), it will do so much quicker, retain more nutrient value and—for that matter—cook with much less stink if it composts aerobically (with oxygen). To provide good airflow to a pile, you should, if possible, place thick, hollow material like cornstalks and sunflower stalks at the bottom of a pile. Also, be sure that any compost bins or pens have perforated sides.

Once the pile is built, you can try poking holes in numerous places with poles or branches to increase aeration. You can try using a "compost aerator," a pole with a flap like a toggle bolt that opens up when you pull it up out of your pile (available from garden supply companies). Or you can just break down and use the age-old method of adding oxygen to a pile: turning it. Periodically, take a garden fork and turn the pile—upside down and inside out—over on an adjacent spot.

Water. A compost pile needs moisture to cure. However, too much water will drown out the air and stop the process. The ideal heap, then, is damp but not soggy.

Mass. As pointed out earlier, a compost pile needs to have at least a cubic yard of bulk to heat up properly. And the bigger the better—up to a point. A pile can hardly be too long or wide, but one that is too tall (say over 5' high) may mash down and squeeze out air. **Beneficial microorganisms.** These are the guys who actually do all the work. You can buy beneficial bacteria packets to inoculate your compost, but these little fellows are pretty much everywhere and will thrive if you give them an environment they like. One simple way to inoculate your piles for free is to occasionally sprinkle some good garden soil—or compost from a previous pile—on the one you're constructing.

Putting It All Together

Now that you know the six essential ingredients of a good compost pile, you need to know how to combine them. The basic tech-

Any Way You Stack It

The great thing about organic decomposition is that it's always ready to start without you. However, if you want to be assured of consistently composted material on a regular basis, you'll need to take the matter into your own hands and provide a setting in which the breakdown process can occur under the best conditions and with your supervision.

Fortunately, compost doesn't ask much in the way of accommodations. So, depending on how much you're willing to spend, your bin can be as unassuming as a simple wire enclosure, or as fancy as the covered "post-and-beam" model featured in the photograph on page 20.

If you're short on time and not ready to spend much money on a composter, the "quickie" version is right up your alley. It'll take about $40 and less than two hours to put together, and it's made of a 16'-long, 1/4"-wire stock panel hacksawed into 48" X 52" sections and clipped together at the corners with quick-connecting chain links. To ease the chore of filling it up, one of the wire sections can be cut in two, halfway up its 4' height, and similarly linked at the horizontal split to make a hinged flap which you can secure at the top with a couple of snap hooks.

Since the panels' wire openings are 2" X 8" at the bottom and increase to 6" X 8" toward the top, it's necessary to line the walls with cage fencing (or some other product with openings no larger than 2" X 4"); this inner grid can be secured to the outer with baling wire or leftover strands from the trimmed-down panels. To put the lid on the

DELUXE COMPOSTER

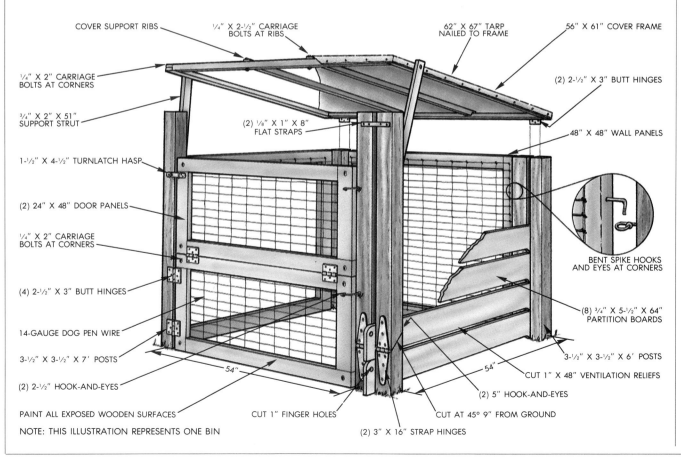

COVER SUPPORT RIBS

1/4" X 2-1/2" CARRIAGE BOLTS AT RIBS

62" X 67" TARP NAILED TO FRAME

56" X 61" COVER FRAME

1/4" X 2" CARRIAGE BOLTS AT CORNERS

(2) 2-1/2" X 3" BUTT HINGES

3/4" X 2" X 51" SUPPORT STRUT

(2) 1/8" X 1" X 8" FLAT STRAPS

48" X 48" WALL PANELS

1-1/2" X 4-1/2" TURNLATCH HASP

(2) 24" X 48" DOOR PANELS

1/4" X 2" CARRIAGE BOLTS AT CORNERS

BENT SPIKE HOOKS AND EYES AT CORNERS

(4) 2-1/2" X 3" BUTT HINGES

(8) 3/4" X 5-1/2" X 64" PARTITION BOARDS

14-GAUGE DOG PEN WIRE

3-1/2" X 3-1/2" X 6' POSTS

3-1/2" X 3-1/2" X 7' POSTS

54"

54"

CUT 1" X 48" VENTILATION RELIEFS

(2) 2-1/2" HOOK-AND-EYES

(2) 5" HOOK-AND-EYES

PAINT ALL EXPOSED WOODEN SURFACES

CUT 1" FINGER HOLES

CUT AT 45° 9" FROM GROUND

NOTE: THIS ILLUSTRATION REPRESENTS ONE BIN

(2) 3" X 16" STRAP HINGES

nique is simply to alternate layers of nitrogenous and carbonaceous materials. If your pile is all carbon or all nitrogen, your bacteria's diet will be too far out of whack for them to do their job.

The ideal carbon-to-nitrogen ratio is about

kettle, just invest a couple of bucks in a 5' X 7' polyethylene tarp and some S-hooks or rope to keep the heavy rain off your working pile. Then when it comes time to start a new heap, simply open one corner of the enclosure, remove it, and set it up at a different location.

The "uptown" model shown in the illustration costs considerably more—perhaps as much as $200, depending on where you get your materials—and is nothing less than a weekend project. In return for this investment, though, you'll get a sturdy and attractive compost crib that's been specifically designed for ease of use. This version has two bins, though it could be built as a single or a triple, depending upon your compost rotation schedule. Its front doors hinge both down and outward, the ventilated partition between the bins can be lowered in stages, and the front center-posts fold down against the ground; fully opened, with the framed covers flipped back on their supports, each stall is surprisingly accessible for routine turning.

The illustration indicates the number and placement of hinges, fasteners, hooks and other hardware. The 4 X 4 posts should be sunk 2' into the ground if possible, leaving 5' exposed at the front and 4' at the rear. All posts are centered about 54" apart. The wall panels are 2 X 4s notched at the ends to make bolted-together half-lap joints; they're secured to the posts with 40d spikes driven into the wood and bent to form slipout hook-and-eye fasteners. Cut sections of dog pen wire are stapled to the frames.

The tarp covers are framed in 2 X 2s, which are half-lap jointed like the wall panels. Each lid has two support ribs that are lapped and bolted in place. Wooden struts fastened to the cover frames hold them up or support them when they're flipped back, but normally they're just tied to looped spikes fastened to the center posts.

If you take the time to build either version now, you should soon have a ready supply of valuable organic material for your garden.

25 to one, but you'd need all sorts of time and charts to figure out how to achieve that precise ratio out of the materials you may have on hand. It's easier—and perfectly effective—to just take some ingredients from the carbon list and some from the nitrogen list and layer them, experimenting with proportions until you find what works for you.

In a nutshell, then: 1) Lay down some stalky material, preferably on bare soil you have forked up some to allow easier passage for bacteria and earthworms. 2) Fork on a layer of carbonaceous material. 3) Fork on a layer of nitrogenous matter. Each layer—N or C—should be about 2" to 8" thick. And fluff it up as you add it to promote airflow. 4) Repeat steps two and three until you've finished building your pile. Sprinkle on a spadeful or two of soil or cured compost occasionally, and if your materials seem dry, spray on some water periodically as you work. 5) Cover the pile with a waterproof tarp to protect it.

You'll have to experiment to find the best ratio of materials for you, but one "old reliable" combination is alternating in a 5:5:2 pattern: a 5" layer of green matter, a 5" layer of dry matter and a 2" layer of manure. But—contrary to some opinions—good compost piles can be made with vegetative matter and *no* manure. Just make sure you have enough nitrogen (here's where something like blood meal or human urine is invaluable).

If It Didn't Work

If all goes well, in about four or five days the interior of your compost pile should have heated up. Indeed, before long a hand poked inside the heap will get uncomfortably hot.

If that happens, congratulations. Your compost is cooking. If your pile doesn't heat up, something's wrong. First check to see if the pile is too wet or too dry. If it's too soggy, turn it, adding more dry material as you do. If it's too dry, wet it.

Assuming the pile is properly moistened and isn't too compressed for good air circulation, your problem is that the compost mixture needs *more nitrogen*. Turn the pile, incorporating more nitrogenous material as you do so.

You may have a different problem—namely, the cooking mound will smell like

ammonia. In that case, you've got *too much nitrogen*. So turn the pile, adding more carbonaceous matter.

Fast, Medium or Slow

There's one last step to making compost: turning the pile. And there you have some choices. If you want to get your compost quickly, you'll turn the pile every time its most intense heat (104° to 170°F) starts to drop—about every three to five days. That will add more oxygen and kick up the process. Keep that up and you should have finished compost in two months or less. If all the ingredients have been finely shredded, thinly layered and turned every three days, it's even possible to make usable compost in two weeks.

If you want your compost in a medium amount of time, turn the pile approximately six weeks after you make it and again six weeks later. Your humus should be ready four to six months after you started it.

And if you're long on patience and short on turning time, just leave the mound alone. Such a slow pile should be ready to use after a year (or even a little longer).

Time is not the only consideration here—there are raging debates about whether "quick" or "slow" compost is better. Since quick-cured piles get well above the pathogen-killing temperature of 140°F, they're the way to go if you want to compost diseased materials (or kill weed seeds).

On the other hand, slow-pile advocates claim that cold-cured compost (which cooks at around 100°F) retains more nutrients.

So relax, dig in, and don't be afraid to experiment. Whichever way you compost, you'll be making the best soil builder your garden could have. You'll also be participating in the light cycle that connects all life on this planet—plant, animal and even human. As Leandre Poisson has pointed out, we ourselves are "light's ultimate art."

Deep Mulch

A year-round blanket of organic material makes for an almost labor-free garden.

Paul G. Dennis, Jr., senior master gardener with the University of Illinois Extension Service, began an "affair" with mulch more than 15 years ago when he encountered the now-classic gardening guide called The Ruth Stout No-Work Garden Book. *Here's his report.*

Talk about love at first sight. Ever since I was a boy, I'd enjoyed gardening—but I'd hated hoeing and weeding. So when I opened the book to the first chapter and read the title, "Throw Away Your Spade and Hoe," I knew I'd found something worth trying.

For the next several years, I followed my new mentor's advice, covering the garden with a deep blanket of organic material to smother weeds, help the soil retain moisture, and virtually eliminate the need to till, plow or hoe. Vegetables thrived amidst the nurturing mulch, protected from temperature extremes and fertilized by the decomposing straw or leaves.

But, of course, no good gardener stops searching for ways to improve. I became interested in biodynamic/French intensive (BFI) gardening, which involves growing plants in permanent raised beds that have been double-dug to a depth of 2' or more. Because of the deeply loosened, compost-enriched soil, plants can be spaced closer together, resulting in dramatically increased yields. I liked being able to raise more food in less space, but there was a lot of labor involved in double-digging. Furthermore, I found making and hauling compost—which BFI practitioners apply to their beds liberally and often—to be hard work. Finally, BFI gardeners tend to shun mulch, preferring instead the "living mulch" created by the overlapping foliage of closely spaced plants.

Experiment, Adopt, Adapt

If I'd learned anything from experience and from Ruth Stout's books, it was to *experiment*—to try different methods, to be open to the ideas of others, but always to temper those ideas with common sense. What works for another gardener may not suit your particular gardening conditions; sometimes it's necessary to adapt deep-mulch methods to your own situation.

"Gardening is like cooking: Read the recipe and then use your head," Stout wrote in her landmark book about low-labor growing, *How to Have a Green Thumb Without an Aching Back*. "A dash of skepticism can do no harm. Go lightly on caution, heavily on adventure, and see what comes out. If you make a mistake, what of it? That is one way to learn, and tomorrow is another day."

Applying that principle, over the years I've blended components of BFI, mulch and conventional gardening techniques into a system that works for me, and that (here in USDA Zone 5, at least) seems to allow its various elements to complement one another. The result is a hybrid: a no-till, permanent-raised-bed, deep-mulch garden system that provides several key benefits over other methods I've tried:

● Raised beds provide superior drainage in wet weather, allowing a garden to be deeply mulched without keeping the soil too wet for too long. Raised beds also help you produce noticeably larger yields in less space, and (because you walk only between beds, never on them) they prevent soil compaction from foot traffic.

● Deep mulch virtually eliminates weeding and hoeing, fertilizes plants, prevents soil compaction (and muddy gardening conditions) due to rain, creates a fertilizing humus, improves tilth and encourages a thriving population of worms, beneficial bacteria and fungi.

● The combination of dense planting and deep mulch provides a double layer of mulch—both living foliage and dead organic material—that protects the soil far better than either of the two methods would alone.

● Because it requires so much less labor, a mulched garden makes gardening possible and fun even for small children (kids love to spread mulch) and for senior citizens and handicapped people. For the same reason, you can leave a mulched garden for two or three weeks—to go on vacation, for example—and not come back to a jungle of weeds. During the busy harvest season, you can concentrate on picking, preparing and preserving your vegetables rather than on hoeing and weeding.

Bed Preparation

You don't *have* to double-dig to make a raised bed; you can single-dig, plow or rototill the ground. (Keep in mind, though,

© MICHELLE WHITE

Hot plants hate hot feet. Gardeners hate weeds. Deep mulch satisfies both.

---

that every time you till you destroy worms.) The important thing is to produce a mound of loosened soil 3″ to 5″ deep and 3′ to 4′ wide; the length and shape of the bed are entirely up to you. You also have a choice of many methods for holding the soil in the beds. Some gardeners build borders from planks staked or nailed into place, while others use landscape ties, fieldstones, bricks or cement blocks. Most of my beds are simply heaped earth with the sides sloped at 45°

angles. Mulch prevents the beds from eroding away. This method works fine in clay or loam soils but probably wouldn't be effective in sandy soils.

When I start beds from scratch in sod, I rototill the area several times over a two- or three-month period to kill the grasses. (Quack grass, however, is so persistent that I dig it out by hand; rototilling a single clump chops it into hundreds of pieces that become hundreds of plants.) Then I simply heap topsoil from around the bed—in other words, from the aisles—to form the bed itself. I make most paths between the beds 15″ wide, and main aisles wheelbarrow width.

Once I've dug and formed a bed, I'll never dig or till it again, so at this point I work compost or other amendments into the area. This is an especially good idea in heavy clay or sandy soils.

Planting

You plant a raised-bed mulch garden just as you would *any* raised-bed garden: Place the seeds close enough so that, when the plants are mature, their leaves will overlap to form a continuous canopy. If it's a new, unmulched bed, sow the seeds as you normally would. Make a furrow (or hole, or whatever is appropriate) in the ground, plant the seeds, and cover them with soil. Then sprinkle a little well-rotted mulch or compost on top of the earth to prevent soil crusting, and place mulch on either side of the planted area to limit weed growth and compaction from rain. As the plants grow, tuck mulch around them.

If the garden is already mulched, it's an easy task to move the thin (1″ to 2″) layer remaining in spring and plant. For example, to plant peas I rake the mulch back to form a 1′-wide strip of bare earth. Then I plant just as I do in unmulched beds. With finer seeds such as lettuce or carrots, I'll rake off an area about 4′ square, sprinkle the seeds directly on the ground and cover them with a bit of compost or rotted mulch. This is as close to planting the way Mother Nature does as any method I know.

What Mulch?

You can use newspapers or plastic sheeting as mulch, but they add little (in the case of newspaper, which decomposes slowly) or nothing (in the case of plastic) to the soil, and they leave a lot to be desired aesthetically. Newspapers do work well for mulching aisles, though. I take care not to use newspapers printed in color, however (harmful chemicals can leach into the soil), and I cover the papers with hay to hide them and to keep them from blowing away.

I prefer organic mulches, which not only fertilize the soil but feed my plow jockeys (worms). Hay and straw are excellent and long-lasting. Grass clippings are good but decay more quickly. Be careful not to use clippings from lawns that have been treated with weed killers; traces of herbicides can be deadly to tomatoes, although, in my experience, they don't seem to harm fruit trees and some other garden plants. Bark chips make an attractive mulch. Leaves are fine, too, but only if they've been shredded or composted for a year. Freshly raked tree leaves cake together and smother the soil, retarding plant growth; raspberries, however, thrive in such material. Finely chipped tree limbs make a good, enduring mulch, but let the chips age and soften a year before you try to walk in your garden barefoot.

I've heard people say that sawdust and some other organic mulches pull the nitro-

gen out of the soil; as far as I can tell, this is true only at the surface and doesn't extend into the earth. I've never noticed such a problem in all my years of mulching.

There are many kinds of other materials you can use for mulch: corncobs, cocoa shells, rice hulls, etc. Availability is probably the most important consideration; the best choice is usually whatever is easiest to find and least expensive. A good bale of hay can cost $3 or more, although some farmers will give spoiled hay away. Wood chips from a nursery can be pricey, but tree trimmers will sometimes *deliver* chips to your garden for free. Just keep an eye out for prospects; you'll be surprised at how much material is out there.

When to Mulch

Anytime is the right time to start mulching. Here in Illinois, I keep a comparatively thin (2″) layer of mulch on my garden most of the year, because in this climate a thicker mulch during cool seasons would chill heat-loving plants. Sometimes I rake the mulch off a vacant bed in order to plant, or to let the soil warm up for a few weeks before planting (though my thin mulch seldom retards soil warm-up significantly). I don't mulch my garden deeply until the weather gets hot and dry. Then I really pile it on: up to 8″ deep if I can. Obviously, with short plants such as lettuce this is difficult, but with potatoes, broccoli and other tall cultivars it's easy to do, and the plants love it.

I also adjust my mulching to suit the particular plant. For example, broccoli prefers cool soil, so I pile mulch on my broccoli beds early in the season. Tomatoes like it hot, so I don't mulch them heavily until summer starts to hit hard—usually June but sometimes as late as July. Of course, I also throw mulch on any spots where the layer is thinning out, or where weeds start popping up.

As the season progresses into fall and the weather cools, I no longer need to add mulch —which is convenient, since I need the time for harvesting and preserving my garden's bounty. If I notice a patch of bare soil, I'll put a little mulch on it, and if a bed seems particularly wet, I might pull a little of the material off.

By the following spring the mulch, having settled and decomposed, is no more than a

couple of inches thick, but that's enough to prevent soil crusting and to discourage early weeds. There's no need to till or plow mulch-conditioned soil, so I don't have to wait several weeks—as most gardeners do— for the garden to dry enough to tolerate tines or a plow blade. I plant peas, lettuce and other cool-loving crops as soon as the ground thaws in the weak sunlight of early spring.

The Great Moderator

There is no single right depth for mulch, no more than there is a single best material to use or a perfect time to use it. You can add mulch or take it away, apply a thin layer or heap it on thick. More than just a way for lazy gardeners to avoid tilling and weeding, mulch is a great moderator—you can use it to adjust soil moisture and temperature, to protect against frost and drought, to create just the right conditions for a particular type of vegetable or flower.

If you try some of my mulching techniques (or Ruth Stout's, or anyone's) and they don't quite work, don't dismiss the method altogether. Instead, see if you can find out how to change the way you use mulch to suit your own situation. For example, if mulch seems to keep your soil too moist for too long, perhaps you're applying too much too early. If you garden in sandy soil, a conventional flat row garden may be a better idea than raised beds. If insects become a problem in your mulched garden, the kind of mulch you're using could be to blame—or (even more likely) perhaps the cause is entirely unrelated to mulch. *[Editor's Note: Some types of mulch are used to fight pests. A deep mulch of leaves, straw or hay discourages potato and cucumber beetles; sharp sand repels slugs.]*

I think the advantages of using mulch— not the least of which are less labor, a longer season, more control over soil conditions and a garden that improves year after year—are well worth a little trial and error.

Green Manure

Each year, grow some crops that feed your soil.

John Jeavons and Bill Bruneau, co-founders of Ecology Action of the Midpeninsula in Willits, California, have had dramatic success improving poor soils through a process called green manuring. Here's their report.

When we first started Ecology Action of the Midpeninsula in 1974, we were minifarming a site in the Stanford Industrial Park that had no topsoil or subsoil: It had all been scraped off in anticipation of future construction. Eight years later, we had improved the soil to a depth of over 2'.

Then in 1982, we moved to our current steep hillside location in northern California. Its thin rocky topsoil had few available nutrients. Indeed, some feel the site approximated marginal Third World growing conditions. But now, it is becoming a beautiful and productive garden/minifarm.

In both cases, we were able to dramatically improve the soil by deep cultivation, intensive plant spacing, the addition of composts and aged manures and a continuous program of growing green manure crops.

Green manuring will help your soil in many ways. Perhaps most important, it boosts your plot's organic matter (O.M.) level. And a high O.M. level (2.5% to 4%) keeps nutrients from leaching down beyond reach of crops, provides food for microbial soil life, helps legumes fix nitrogen in their root nodules, and helps the soil produce good structure and maintain the air-pore spaces essential to good crop health.

In addition, your green manure crops will till the soil for you. Alfalfa, for instance, can send down roots as deep as 60', pulling up nutrients for next year's crops. A single rye plant grown in good soil can produce an average of three miles of roots per day—387 miles of roots and 6,603 miles of root hairs in a season. Such root and root-hair growth will fiberize the soil, helping loose soils bind together and clay ones open up.

Green manures also provide a living mulch that will protect soil from erosion and other weathering effects. Indeed, during the late summer and early fall is an excellent time to put in a green manure crop. The plants will protect your garden from winter damage and will produce organic matter during the off-season, when much of your plot would otherwise lie fallow. Then next spring, you'll find that your soil will have good tilth instead of being hard and compacted.

Many fall-planted green manure crops will also pump excess water out of the soil, allowing you to prepare the soil and plant crops much earlier than usual. Fava beans, for instance, can pump soil dry in as little as five days of warm weather. (If, on the other hand, you are trying to conserve soil moisture in early spring, you can harvest your green manure crop on the first warm day.)

Compost It

To get the maximum benefit from a green manure crop, you should compost it. If, instead, you spade or till it directly into the soil, you'll have to wait 30 days for it to decompose before you can plant again.

You'll do far better if you compost the current green manure crop, while using compost made from the previous growing season's green manure to fertilize the current planting. You can harvest the crop by pulling it out by hand or skimming it off with a sharpened spade. In our experience, a 1" layer of cured compost—about eight cubic feet per 100 square feet—appears to maintain fertile soil in good health. Other organic fertilizers may be needed to initially build up a soil's nutrient reserve, or even to maintain that level if not all waste nutrients are returned to the soil.

We feel the secret to composting green manures successfully is to combine lots of fresh green matter—from a legume crop, when possible—with lots of dry carbonaceous matter and one-third topsoil by weight. The green matter—from your freshly cut manure crop—provides nitrogen to the pile. The dry matter—from a previously cut manure crop, or other dry material such as leaves and straw—provides the carbon that holds the water-soluble nitrogen in the compost and, later, in the soil. And the topsoil slows and cools the composting process. There are indications that slow-cooked compost will produce 12% to 40% more compost—excluding the soil itself from these percentages—than hot-cooked piles. Hotter piles, in effect, burn off part of their mass.

Four Old Standbys

Below are some good green manure crops you might think about growing. When choosing one green manure over another, consider how much O.M. it will add to the soil, how much nitrogen it will return to the soil (many soils need up to .5 pound of nitrogen per 100 square feet per year), if it can pull up nutrients from the substrate below, if the crop fits your particular soil and weather conditions, and if you want the harvest to also provide food for your family.

Remember that two or more green manure crops can often be grown together to their mutual benefit, and that you can frequently save seed from your current crops so you can reseed for free next year.

The first four crops we'll list are old standbys: ones that have served often and well.

Cereal rye produces lots of organic matter (the rye straw grows up to 7' high) and lots of roots (which makes it very good for fiberizing compacted soil). It's also drought-tolerant and very winter-hardy and, of course, can give you food: rye grain.

Sow this rye in cool weather—in many areas, you can plant it in fall and expect it to overwinter and produce abundantly the next spring. It matures in as little as 16 to 18 weeks of growing season. If you want to harvest the grain, time your planting so the rye will have only about one month of hot weather before it matures. Yields are up to 60 pounds of rye straw per 100 square feet plus four to 26 pounds of grain.

Agricultural mustard is a very fast way to get lots of green matter: It can mature in as little as six weeks and yield 180 to 270 pounds of green matter per 100 square feet.

Other benefits are that agricultural mustard will grow in cold or hot weather and that it apparently has the ability to bring health back to rundown soil. It's often used in orchards to reclaim and "invigorate" land. It also attracts honeybees.

You can harvest this O.M. crop at any growing stage, but just after flowering is best.

Alfalfa can be grown for just one growing season, but this perennial is better used for long-term soil build-up—say, in an area you plan to start cultivating in a year or two. A deep-rooting crop, it boosts fertility by pulling nutrients up from subsoil. And since it's a legume, its roots fix nitrogen in the soil: from .36 to .57 pounds per 100 square feet per year.

Drought-tolerant alfalfa thrives in all growing seasons, maturing in about 17 weeks

Sowing Green Manure Crops

Almost all of the green manure crops mentioned here can be directly sown into prepared soil by hand-broadcasting. When doing so, *under*broadcast at first, so you'll have some seed left to fill in any gaps. Then gently chop the seed into the soil by poking holes in the area with a rake. You may also want to tamp the soil down with a wide board to eliminate excess air spaces. Finally, water the area thoroughly.

Some of the crops will produce more, and more quickly, if you first sprout them in soil on 1" centers in growing flats. After five to 10 days, when the seedlings are about 1½" to 2" tall, transplant them into the garden. This works well with cereal rye, alfalfa, hard red spring wheat, barley and oats—all of which set out on 5" centers.

Banner fava bean seed should be directly planted on 7" centers, and foul muddammas fava beans should be directly planted on 6" centers.

(although it can take a while to get a stand established). You can harvest it—use it for green matter, not dry—repeatedly through the season. Traditionally, farmers cut their alfalfa at nine-week intervals, but the best times are when about 10% of the plants are in bloom; those can be anytime from three to 12 weeks apart depending on climate and season. Alfalfa can provide from three to six cuttings a year and from 80 to 360 pounds and more of green matter.

When you want to clear the land for other crops, you'll have to dig the roots out—a job hard enough to keep you in shape without jogging. If you clear the crop out when it's just three months old, you won't have to dig the roots out, but can let them decompose in the ground.

Banner fava beans are quite hardy legumes that are very good for spring growing. If your winters don't drop below 10°F, a fall planting will keep growing throughout the cold months. The plant grows from 4' to 6' high, produces lots of green O.M. and, as noted earlier, can bring up excess moisture from damp spring ground. It also tolerates acidic soil conditions. When we minifarmed in mild-climate Stanford, fava beans made our garden productive year-round and were our favorite green manure crop.

Banner favas mature in 11 to 26 weeks. They fix .16 pounds or more of nitrogen per 100 square feet per season, and can yield 90 to 360 pounds of green matter. They also can yield five to 18 pounds of dry beans. Many people enjoy eating fava beans—they are a staple in Egypt—but a few people are fatally allergic to them.

The next four crops we'll discuss are some unusual, specialty, ones you might consider growing.

Specialty Crops

Alsike clover is the "poor soil workhorse." It grows in any temperature except severe cold, tolerates depleted, acidic and poorly drained ground and stands up well to drought. The legume produces an adequate (not large) amount of green matter and nitrogen (about .27 pounds of nitrogen per 100 square feet). Sow it in spring or autumn for best results.

Fodder radish has a deep taproot for bringing up nutrients from the subsoil and produces more organic matter per day than almost any other green manure crop. Although you can use it for green matter, it will also produce a great deal of carbonaceous dry matter if you let it grow for several months until the plants are "woody."

Fodder radish grows well in hot or cool weather, but it's best sown in late summer, early autumn or early spring. It will mature in as little as 17 weeks and can yield 100 to 500 pounds of green matter per 100 square feet.

Woollypod vetch, like alsike clover, is good at growing in poor soil and under conditions such as heat or drought. In addition, it's very hardy—it can handle cold down to 0°F. (It's more cold-tolerant, but less productive, than its cousins purple and hairy vetch.) It can also help knock out weeds in a garden by outcompeting them.

A medium-fast-growing legume, woolly-

After only two years of green manure cropping, Ecology Action's gardens were transformed from barren ground to the verdancy shown here.

pod vetch produces only an adequate amount of green matter (about 50 to 200 pounds per 100 square feet) and nitrogen (up to .25 pounds). It matures in 12 weeks and can be harvested more than once at approximately nine-week intervals.

Foul muddammas beans grow well in heat, so they're suitable for late spring and summer sowing. They also have a good root system which can fix up to .16 or more pounds of nitrogen per 100 square feet.

Foul muddammas mature in 11 to 26 weeks, depending on season, and yield 45 to 180 pounds of green matter per 100 square feet and five to 30 pounds of beans.

The last green manure crops we'll mention have an extra "by-product": They can be harvested for food as well as for dry carbonaceous organic matter.

Double-duty Crops

Drought-tolerant *hard red spring wheat* should be planted early so it will mature after only about one month of hot weather. (Its growing season is from 16 to 18 weeks.) It produces a lot of straw for dry O.M.: 20 to 60 pounds per 100 square feet.

The grain yield is four to 26 pounds per 100 square feet (the average American consumes about 110 pounds of wheat per year).

Like spring wheat, *barley* should be planted to mature after only one month of hot weather. But barley has a much shorter growing season—from nine to 10 weeks—so you can sneak it in a spot you can spare for only two to three months. It actually contains somewhat less protein and calcium per pound than wheat or oats, but—due to its shorter growing season—produces more of these nutrients per day of growing time.

Barley is a good straw producer (up to 60 pounds per 100 square feet) and yields five to 24 pounds of grain (the average American consumes only about 1.2 pounds of barley each year).

Grow your own oatmeal. Cold-hardy *oats* mature in 13 to 17 weeks and, like barley and spring wheat, need about one month of hot weather near harvest.

One hundred square feet will yield up to 60 pounds of oat straw and four to 17 pounds of oats (the average American consumes about 3.2 pounds of oats each year).

There are many other good green manure crops. Two commonly used ones are winter rye mixed with hairy vetch for fall-to-spring plantings and buckwheat for short-term, warm-season growing. Any of them will help you build a living soil from which you can harvest increased crop yields.

Building your own soil is important for broader reasons, as well. When we use fertilizers and organic matter from somewhere else for our gardens, we may actually be depleting the soil resource base of another growing area. By improving our own soil base with "homegrown" materials, we're taking a small step toward improving our whole planet's soil and life resources.

In fact, in a world of diminishing agricultural petrochemical resources, green manure is as precious as gold. From 1975 to the year 2000, it is expected that the percentage of desert on the earth's land surface will increase from 49% to 63% or more—and one-third of this process is expected to occur in the United States. Each back-yard garden or homestead can contribute to our planet's much-needed increase in soil fertility.

Garden Teas

Homemade fertilizing teas make wonderful pick-me-ups for stressed garden crops.

Even if your vegetables get enough major nutrients from the surrounding air and soil, fertilizing teas can fill in their dietary blanks. These nutrient-laden solutions—made by aging compost, manure or plant matter in water—supply enzymes, hormones, micronutrients and minerals to crops. They can be just the shot in the arm needed to help plants through such stress periods as seedling growth, transplanting, blossoming and fruiting. Some mixes can help protect against mold, mildew and fungus, and others can even make crops more healthful to eat.

What's more, these magic potions are easy to brew. Just steep the main ingredient in a large, water-filled trash can or a 55-gallon drum. Cover the brew, but stir the tea once a day to help supply oxygen. This will promote aerobic, rather than foul-smelling anaerobic, decomposition. You might also add a little compost, stinging nettle or mail-order compost starter to help kick off the fermentation process.

In two or three weeks, your tea should be ready. You can then strain the solids and siphon the liquid onto your waiting garden. If you keep the steeping materials in a porous bag, you don't even have to strain the brew: Just empty the bag onto a compost pile.

You can use your garden refresher full strength or diluted to a light color. And you can scale the job down—by using, say, a bucket for your container—if you want to make small batches of liquid fertilizer.

While many substances work for fertilizer teas, gardeners usually brew with one of six ingredients: compost, manure, comfrey, stinging nettle, chamomile or horsetail.

Compost

Compost tea is a fine garden tonic. It's most often used to help plants during transplanting, flowering and fruiting stages. Three or four shovelfuls of compost per 30 gallons of water makes a good batch. Some gardeners use an all-vegetative compost tea on older seedlings. But never apply a tea made from composted *manure* to seedlings, because it may encourage damping off.

Manure

For raw manure teas, use the same recipe as for compost tea and also apply as an all-purpose garden tonic. (Again, don't use manure solutions on seedlings.) Some gardeners claim specific manures can do specific jobs. Nitrogen-rich chicken manure may be especially good for heavy feeders like cauliflower, corn, tomatoes, squash and okra. Sheep and goat manures are supposed to help increase the aroma of fruits and the oil content of herbs. Rabbit manure tea benefits foliage, stems and shrubbery. Horse manure tea boosts leaf development. Potash-rich pig manure is best for potatoes, leeks, celeriac and root crops in general. Cow manure also promotes root development.

Comfrey

Comfrey (*Symphytum officinale*) is another general tonic for transplanted, flowering or fruiting vegetables. Rich in potash, calcium, phosphorus, magnesium and many vitamins, this herb also has a nitrogen-phosphorus-potash balance that gives tomatoes a special lift.

To make comfrey tea, fill your container half to three-quarters full with leaves, add water all the way to the top, and ferment as previously described.

This large-leaved perennial is easy to grow, but watch out: It's invasive. Keep your comfrey patch separate from other crops.

Stinging Nettle

Stinging nettle (*Urtica dioica*) is a useful general tonic to strengthen plants and help them resist rot. Rich in iron (which is used in the production of chlorophyll), it helps increase the essential oils in herbs. Nettle tea and leaves added to compost piles also help activate microbiotic life in soil. Nettle may even stimulate bacteria in cool spring soil and thus give crops a head start.

The perennial thrives once established. But be careful when gathering its "stinging" leaves: Use clippers and wear gloves, long pants and a long-sleeved shirt.

Chamomile

Chamomile tea is widely known for its ability to discourage damping-off disease. Use it on seedlings (even before they emerge), on plants in cloches, on greenhouse crops and anyplace else you find where moist, humid, enclosed conditions prevail.

This herb also concentrates calcium, sulfur and potash, and can help make soil more alkaline.

Chamomile tea brews easily in small batches. Just steep fresh or dry flowers in hot, boiled water until the mixture cools. Strain and apply.

Horsetail

Horsetail (*Equisetum arvense*) tea may protect squashes, seedlings and greenhouse or cloched plants from mildew, fungus and rust. Biodynamic growers believe the silicon-rich plant helps a crop resist these waterborne diseases by enhancing its light-absorbing ability.

To make horsetail tea, boil the plant—fresh or dry—for about 20 minutes. Then cool, strain, and dilute until you have a weak solution. Spray or mist the mixture onto the leaves of the plants you're treating. Since equisetum has been known to be difficult to grow, you may want to buy dried plants.

Other Brews

Many other plants can be brewed to make garden teas. For example, cabbage leaf tea adds sulfur to crops, oak bark tea adds calcium and helps plants resist disease, and yarrow tea enhances growth and wards off pests. Even many weeds, natural mineral concentrators, may make good teas.

The whole subject is open to study, so test your own hunches. But do start using fertilizer teas—you'll be pleased with the results.

Seed Starting Secrets

First days are crucial days.

The seed is awakened in the darkness of the
Earth,
The leaves are quickened in the power of the
Air,
And all fruit is ripened in the might of the
Sun.
So awakens the Soul in the shrine of the
Heart.
So quickens the Spirit in the Light of the
World.
So ripens man's power in the glory of God.
—*Rudolf Steiner*,
Verses and Meditations

Between the gleaming fantasies in seed catalogues and the mishmashed cornucopia that
is a full-blown summer garden stand the tiny
kernels known as seeds. Seed starting is the
first—and therefore most important—task of
the gardener's year. Unless you go to the expense of buying all your garden plants
(which will severely restrict your varietal
choices) or simply wait for the weather to
warm up enough to sow everything directly
in the ground (which will severely curtail the
length of your growing season), you'll want
to start many of your future foods and flowers indoors, in containers, under close personal supervision.

The little home births you'll be attending
demand a lot of knowledgeable care. While
there are plenty of other good seed-starting

systems (you may have a different approach
that works fine for you), the following techniques used by *Mother Earth News'* gardeners have proved to be very successful.

Materials

The first thing you'll need to do is to make
wooden seed trays. Sturdy and inexpensive
ones are made from cedar or redwood; both
species resist rotting and are less likely than
other woods to harbor diseases.

All you have to do is nail together sides of
3″-wide wood and then nail on some bottom
slats, leaving ⅛″ gaps between the lower
boards so excess water can drain out. A good
size for flats is 12″ X 24″. Don't make yours
much bigger—a tray full of plants and wet
soil can get pretty heavy.

Next, make your own soil mix to go in the
flats. Not only will this save you money, but
it will also let you provide the optimum living soil for your plants. A good flat mix consists of the following (by volume, not
weight): five parts leaf mold (or compost),
four parts good topsoil, two parts sharp sand.

You can gather leaf mold (decomposed
leaves) on a visit to a forested area—but don't
take it all from one place. Leave some for the
plants growing there. The soil should be the
best topsoil you can gather. And sharp sand
is the coarse builders' sand that's sold at
hardware or lumber stores. Smooth creekside or ocean sand packs too densely
when wet.

If you use any compost, it should be from
the best, most thoroughly processed batch
you have. Note that flowers definitely don't
start as well in manure-based composts as
they do in compost made entirely from
vegetable materials. Feel free to adjust the
formula to suit your own particular experiences or growing conditions. For example, you could add more sand if your topsoil
is very clayey.

Contrary to the popular opinion that one
should bake potting soil, you won't need to
sterilize this mixture. (Baking your mix kills
all the *beneficial* bacteria, as well as any harmful ones.) You shouldn't have to add any
store-bought "supplements" to fortify the
growing medium, either. Your mix will supply all the nutrients that your seeds will need.

Before you start stirring up your first batch
of flat mix, you should sift the compost, leaf

mold and topsoil through ¼″ mesh hardware cloth. The fine particles thus produced
will give the starts' roots room to grow. For
this task, build a simple sifting screen by
tacking a piece of ¼″-mesh hardware cloth
onto a simple frame of laid-flat 2 X 4s. (A
hand-protecting rim of 2 X 2s will cover the
cloth's sharp edges.) You can make this aid
any size you want, perhaps one designed to
fit conveniently over a wheelbarrow.

Sift each coarse ingredient through your
screen (this'll be easier if the materials are
dry), mix the correct spadefuls of each one
and the sand on a hard surface, and you'll be
ready to plant.

Oversow and Undercover

First, line the bottom of your seed flat with
partly decomposed leaves broken into
small—say, quarter-size—pieces. This will
cover the cracks in your tray bottoms so that
soil won't fall through, yet will still provide
necessary drainage.

Next, fill the tray with your sowing mix,
dropping a corner of the flat from a short
height once or twice to help the mixture settle and fill the box evenly. Run a board that's
wider than the tray along the top of the soil
to level and smooth it. And then tamp
the mix some with a smaller board to pack
it a bit.

Done? Then get your seed packet, hold it
over the tray (so if you spill any precious
plant starters, they'll land in your soil), and
tear open—but wait. Did you make labels?
Always label each flat (or flat section) before
you sow. Use a Popsicle stick, or something
similar, on which you've written the name
of the plant—including the variety—the date
sown and your sources, all in indelible ink.
Fail to do this step beforehand, and you'll
pay in confusion later.

Now you can sow your seeds. You may just
want to sprinkle them from the packet, dribble them off the edge of your hand or run
them through your thumb and forefinger.
However you work, be sure you distribute
the seeds evenly—you might start at the corners and edges to make sure you don't miss
those hard-to-get spaces before you sow in
the middle of the tray. And don't be afraid
to plant more seeds than you think you'll
need; you can always thin the weakest seedlings later.

Seeds sprout underground, hidden from view. The gardener must nurture these miracles of birth.

Then lightly sift some additional soil mix over the flat to a depth of three to five times the smallest diameter of the seeds (use a kitchen sieve or the like, and stir the mix as you sift, or mostly sand will fall out). Don't overdo it. Go light, rather than heavy, on this topping for now.

How close should you set your seeds? That depends on whether you plan to transplant the young seedlings to another flat for a time before you set them out in the garden. This two-step plant-starting approach allows seeds to be sown densely. Seeds seem to germinate and grow better in clusters that form little microclimates than when spaced farther apart. It also gives you an opportunity to provide the soil nutrition that's most appropriate for each stage of growth, and to start more seeds (so you can cull the least healthy ones while transplanting). Repeated transplanting is even said to stimulate root growth in much the same way that pruning does.

If you're going to *prick out* (as it's called) your starts to a second flat, broadcast your seeds about ½" apart. If, however, you intend to keep your seedlings in the same tray until set-out time, try to sow the kernels about 1" to 2" apart.

Oftentimes, you'll have room to plant more than one type of seed in a single flat. When that happens, lay a stick border or two on top to divide the tray surface into sections, cover areas with cardboard (or whatever) when they're not being sown, to prevent misplaced seeding, and make sure you label each section. The best "flatmates" are plants that have pretty much the same germination and growth rates. Then you can transplant the whole trayful at once and cause less root disturbance.

Moist and Warm

If you just pour some water on your flat, the soil mix will splash all around while your little seeds will get washed every which way. Instead, water carefully. An excellent help is a Haws watering can (available from Smith & Hawken, 25 Corte Madera, Mill Valley, CA 94941, or Walter F. Nicke, Box 667, Hudson, NY 12534), because —thanks to its finely perforated, upward-pointing rose—it sprinkles water very gently on the seeds. Start and end the watering off the flat to avoid any hard splashing. If you're watering from a bucket or can, trickle the liquid over one hand and use your fingers to break up and place the droplets.

Water the seed flats well initially, and then lightly whenever the surface of the soil begins to dry out. Use tepid—not cold—water, and if your household supply is chlorinated, let the liquid stand overnight before using it, so the chemicals in it will volatilize.

Start Warm, Grow Cool

So far, you've maintained a warm, moist haven—a womb, in a way—for your incubating seeds. (Some growers even construct little plastic tents over their newly planted trays.) But once they start to sprout, everything changes. If you kept your seedlings in that type of environment, they'd be quite likely to succumb to *damping off*, a fungal disease that rots the stems of young plants at the groundline, causing the seedlings to topple over and die. Even just-planted seeds can succumb to damping off and will rot unsprouted if they're kept too wet.

To prevent this calamity, you need to make sure your starts are well ventilated and not overly warm. The ideal temperature range for seedling growth is about 55° to 70°F. It's better to overdo ventilation and let the crops stay a little cool than risk creating the "tropical jungle" that is prime territory for damping off.

At this point, you should also change your watering habits. Instead of keeping the flats constantly moist, water the plants less often, but give the trays more water when you do add the liquid. Eventually, you should be letting the top ½" to 1" of soil start to dry out before you rewater. The bottom of the tray, though, should still be moist. (Just poke your finger in somewhere to find out.) And water your flats early in the day so that the surface of the potting mix can start to dry by nightfall. If damping off is really a problem, you can even "bottom water" by submerging flats halfway in a tub of water.

Give your growing starts plenty of light. If you're stuck with using a windowsill, you'd better supplement what sunshine you get with artificial light. Plain old fluorescent tubes (not incandescent bulbs) will do fine. Work out some way to get those tubes as close to the plants as possible—no more than a few inches away—and to raise the lights (or lower the plants) as the seedlings grow to keep that distance the same.

Many growers strive to give their starts as much as 16 hours of sunlight a day, because if the plants don't get adequate light, they'll become spindly, leggy and weak. They may even fall over. Interestingly enough, one partial antidote for low-light troubles is to grow your plants in a cooler environment. Since their growth rate will thereby be slightly reduced, they'll be less likely to be starved for illumination.

Breakfast—Lunch—Dinner

If you're going to keep the plants in the same tray until set-out time, you should occasionally provide some form of supplemental fertilization for the seedlings to help them prosper during their long weeks in the planting trays. Diluted fish emulsion is a common commercial amendment. You can also use homegrown nutrient-rich teas made from stinging nettle, comfrey or very well aged compost. Each of these is made by simply steeping its name ingredient in water for several days (chop and bruise either kind of soaking plant with a spade). Don't overfertilize: A diluted supplement every five days or so should be plenty. It's best to not use manure tea, as that solution may promote disproportionate growth (because of its high nitrogen content) or encourage damping off.

In addition, thin your plants as necessary to keep them from getting too crowded (leaves barely touching is the ideal density).

As noted before, you can prick out your seedlings to another flat to grow for a period before setting them out in the garden. Do this as soon as the seedlings set their first *true* leaves (the very first bits of greenery to appear on a new sprout are the temporary *seed* leaves).

Try using 4"- to 6"-deep flats—instead of 3" ones—for prick-outs, in order to give the growing roots plenty of room. You see, if the roots strike bottom, they're likely to think it's time to flower and go to seed. Well-known biointensive pioneer John Jeavons recalls that he once reared some shallow-trayed broccoli seedlings that produced heads, each the size of a little fingernail. To avoid any such problems, you can even clip off the ends of exceptionally long roots to keep them from getting squished in the bottoms of their new trays.

You might also use a richer soil mix for your transplants than the plain 5:4:2 mix advised for seed trays. Seeds carry a good deal of the nutrients needed to start off and are encouraged to grow longer roots when grown in a lean mix, but seedlings need more to eat.

Top: Layering the bottom of a seed tray with crumbled leaf mold will add nutrients while reducing leaks. Fill the tray with a good soil mix, and level the mix with a tamping block. Middle: Be sure to put a label tag in each tray. Bottom: When you water in the seeds, begin and end the sprinkling off the tray to avoid splashing the soil and seeds.

A good mix can be made up of five spadefuls of leaf mold, four spadefuls of good garden soil, two spadefuls of sharp sand and two spadefuls of compost, with an additional two handfuls of bone meal. In addition, seed trays that will hold tomatoes, blue flowers or brassicas—such as broccoli, cauliflower, cabbage, kale, collards and Brussels sprouts—get a layer of dried eggshell chips sprinkled on the leaf mold in the bottom of the flat, to provide those particular seedlings with the extra calcium they thrive on.

The idea is to give the plants better and better nutrition during each stage of growth, so that transplanting won't be a temporary setback but, rather, an immediate improvement. This concept is sometimes called "Breakfast—Lunch—Dinner": Give plants a lean breakfast in their first flat, a nutritious lunch in their next one and a robust dinner in their compost-filled final garden bed.

Pricking Out

When the seed leaves have flopped all the way open, two or three true leaves have appeared on each seedling and your transplanting trays are all filled and ready, it's time to prick out. Transplanting's going to come as a shock to your plants, so you'll want to do everything you can to soften the blow. Choose a fairly shady spot in which to carry out the operation, and work smoothly and quickly. The job will go faster if you let the seedling trays get a little dry before you transplant. The soil in the prick-out flats, though, should be moistened just a bit.

With a hand garden fork or other tool, dig out a clump of seedlings, roots and all, and drop them gently onto a wet cloth. Dropping them helps to separate the roots, while using a damp cloth keeps the roots from drying out. Indeed, you should cover the root ball with the cloth whenever you're not working with it. Don't leave the roots exposed to air for long: If they dry out, the plants will be damaged and may not survive.

Gently work the roots apart, dig a little hole in the soil in your transplant tray (a regular butter knife works fine for this), and pick up a plant by its seed leaves to move it to its new home. Don't carry the transplant by the roots, true leaves or stem; if any one of those breaks, you'll hurt the plant. The seed leaves, though, are going to fall off soon anyway, so they make safe carrying handles.

Set the plant in so the soil reaches just below the true leaves—even if that means burying the seed leaves—and tamp the soil down around it to hold it in place. (Perennial flowers, however, should be set at their previous depth.)

Space your plants evenly along a row, 2" to 3" apart, depending on how big they will grow and how long you intend to keep them in the tray. Then set your second row of transplants so that each one of them forms an equilateral triangle with its two closest neighbors in the first row. This staggered planting makes better use of tray space and lets the foliage fill the tray more without crowding.

And by all means, cull, cull, cull. Get rid of the tiny specimens, the ones with crown scars and the spindly ones. Transplant only the best.

Once you have your crops pricked out and in place, water the tray well at the base with an ordinary spouted watering can (from now on, try not to wet the leaves when you water; it fools the plants into actually *losing* needed moisture). After watering, set the trays in a shaded, moderately warm place until they're completely over the shock of moving. They may wilt for a day or so, but should then recover. Once they perk up, give them all the sun or other light you can.

More About Damping Off

What if damping off does strike, and some of your nurslings begin to keel over from this seed-starter's plague? First off, dig out any afflicted plants and dispose of them in a place where they can't infect other crops. (Then clean your hands and tools before you touch healthy specimens.) Increase the ventilation around your remaining starts, and if the area is fairly warm, cool their environment some, too. You can also lightly dust the trays with flowers of sulfur (available at drugstores) to help "treat" the seedlings.

If a whole flat has been infected, you'll have to dump out all the plants and soil mix, and start over. But first try to determine what caused the problem, and do what you can to prevent recurrence. Maybe you're using "green" (non-broken-down) manure in your mix or tea. Do you need to add more sand to your flat mix to provide better drainage?

Are you reusing the same soil mix? (Don't.) Are you thoroughly brushing out all flats with a wire brush and then sun-airing and -drying them before reusing them? (Do.) With a little care and thoughtfulness, you should be able to bring this common problem under control.

Of course, the best cure for this malady is prevention: Always provide adequate ventilation and drainage. Some growers highly recommend a foliar feed of kelp (add ²/₃ cup of the seaweed powder to a gallon of warm water) or of chamomile tea (made from soaking dried blossoms in water for a day or two) as good fungal preventives. The chamomile tea can also be used—to the same end—as a seed soak before planting.

Garden Time

Taking care of pricked-out seedlings is very similar to managing just-started ones: Give them lots of light, thorough waterings as needed and occasional fertilizing with a homemade plant tea or similar nutrient. When the time to put them out in their real garden home is only a week or so away, you can begin hardening off your plants (adjusting them to the outdoors) by setting the trays outside for a few hours a day or moving them into a cold frame.

Then late one afternoon or on a cloudy day—don't set plants out at the start of a sunny day—you can grab a trowel and, just as you moved the starts before, set them out in your prepared garden soil—hale, hardy and ready to grow. You'll have successfully nurtured dozens or hundreds of young plants from mere seeds to healthy garden stock. And that's a feat that any gardener could be mighty proud of.

Some Specific Seeds

To understand seeds' needs, break them into two groups: monocots and dicots.

Monocots

Lily family—alliums: Alliums include onions, leeks, chives and garlic. Onions ger-

minate in seven to 21 days and can be grown indoors from seed, directly sown or grown into sets that can be used the following year. Cool temperatures (55° to 65°F) and firm, light-textured soil are ideal for good germination. Do not "help" the emerging seedling by straightening it or removing the seed coat from the first stalk, and keep house-bound starts trimmed back to about 3" high. For direct sowing in spring, tilth up the bed, then

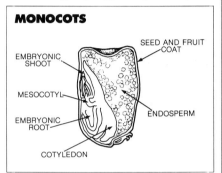

firm it down a bit and plant in shallow furrows. The seedlings will be thinned later.

The little onion sets that you purchase at the feed and seed or the nursery can also be produced successfully at home. To experiment, prepare a small section of bed, say 3' to 4' long, and broadcast seed in early spring. Chop it in with a leaf rake, tamp the soil to firm it, sprinkle on straw or some other light mulch, and just weed and wait.

Don't be concerned about thinning, because come late July, you'll harvest these baby bulbs. Dry them outdoors for a week or two, trim the tops off, and store them, as you would mature onions, in a cool dry place till next spring. Then simply set them out about 6" apart for an early-season jump.

Leeks, which germinate in seven to 21 days, are similar to onions but should be planted in trenches that you slowly fill in, in order to blanch the stems.

Though many folks plant garlic cloves in spring, others get the best results from bedding them down in the lull of fall. Planted about 1" under the surface, pointed end facing upward, they get a bit of growth on them before winter, then really take off come spring. If you place them in a diamond pattern and mulch with leaves under a layer of straw, you'll keep weeds at bay and you'll know where to feel for bulbs when the tops have died back. Mulch heavily in areas with severe winter temperatures.

Dicots

Pea or pulse family: These dicots are directly sown and include all of the peas and beans (broad beans, lima beans, bush and snap beans, soybeans, etc.). An initial soaking in warm water for an hour or two can be used to start things happening, but don't soak the seeds longer or you'll risk their splitting open. Once soaked, they can be wrapped in a damp paper towel and—until germination begins—kept at a temperature above 65°F (preferably 80° to 90°). *Rhizobium* bacteria, usually found in powdered form at garden supply stores, can be dusted on damp seeds before sowing to increase yields as well as soil nitrogen. Sprinkle water from your fingertips onto the seeds, stir them around gently, and then shake them in a paper bag containing this nitrogen-fixing bacteria.

Beans are planted outdoors when all danger of frost is past, about 6" apart for most varieties. Peas like it cool, so they're grown in spring and fall in most climates or over the winter in such very southern locales

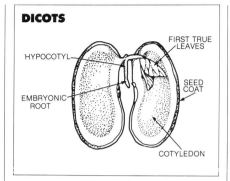

DICOTS

HYPOCOTYL
FIRST TRUE LEAVES
EMBRYONIC ROOT
SEED COAT
COTYLEDON

as parts of Florida, Texas and California. Typically planted around St. Patrick's Day in the North, or as soon as the ground can be worked in central states, peas are often the first seeds to be sown in spring. They can be planted fairly close together, with only 2" to 3" required between seeds.

Parsley family: This group includes carrots, parsnips, parsley and celery.

Direct-sown and slow to germinate (requiring up to 30 days), the seeds of parsley and carrots can be hurried along by soaking them overnight in warm water and then "towel drying" them for easier sowing. Some people swear by mixing fine carrot seed with

dried, already-used coffee grounds, claiming this provides better distribution of seeds as well as a nutritional boost for the young plants. Others suggest that using fresh grounds helps prevent visits from the carrot fly by confusing its ability to home in on the carrot scent. You may also want to try a technique that's good for most root crops: Mix some of your accumulation of winter's wood ashes into the soil or use them as a side-dressing. The ash will add potassium, sweeten acidic earth and deter wireworms.

Parsnips are a good choice for gardeners young in age or in experience, because they're difficult to oversow. It's not that they love overcrowding, but that the germination rate is usually low enough to allow everything to come out just right. (For this reason, careful planters should be sure to use only the freshest of seed.) In clay soils, radishes can be interplanted with parsnips to break up the surface and thus ease the slower seedlings' passage. Since parsnip germination takes three to four weeks and the vegetable requires a long growing season, get those seeds in as soon as the ground can be worked in spring.

Another lover of cool temperatures, celery

A SEED-STARTING TIMETABLE	–10 WEEKS	–8 WEEKS	–6 WEEKS	–4 WEEKS	–2 WEEKS	LAST EXPECTED FROST	+2 WEEKS	+4 WEEKS
This chart shows average dates for sowing, germination, pricking out and final garden transplanting relative to average date of last spring frost. Germination times, in days, are in parentheses; prickout dates are marked with an X. Actual times vary according to local conditions.								
					PEPPERS (10-28) X			
					TOMATOES (7-14) X			
	BROCCOLI (5-14)		X					
	CABBAGE (5-14)		X					
	CAULIFLOWER (5-14)		X					
		CELERY (14-21)			X			
	COLLARDS (5-14)		X					
			EGGPLANT (7-14)		X			
	KALE (5-14)		X					
			KOHLRABI (5-14)					
	LEEKS (7-21)							
		LETTUCE (2-3)						
	ONIONS (7-21)							
	PARSLEY (10-30)		X					
				COSMOS (3-5)		X		
				ZINNIAS (3-5)		X		
				MARIGOLDS (3-5)		X		
		CALENDULAS (7-10)	X					
		SNAPDRAGONS (7-10)	X					
			STRAWFLOWERS (3-5)		X			

may not even sprout if its environment is too warm. To encourage germination, you can try exposing the seeds to light for a day before planting. Celery can take up to three weeks to sprout, so you may try speeding things up with, again, the old warm water bath. The key to growing celery is in knowing that it has a very shallow root system, and for this reason, requires its food and water to be served up within easy reach.

Mustard family: These dicots make up a large family that includes kale, cabbage, Brussels sprouts, cauliflower, broccoli, mustards, kohlrabi, rutabagas, turnips and some of the Chinese greens.

Cabbage, cauliflower and broccoli thrive during the crisp, cool days of spring. They're generally started indoors, about eight to 10 weeks before the last frost date, in order to give the plants time to mature before the mercury climbs too high. When the midsummer heat is on, you can either start seed outdoors for a fall crop, or indoors (especially in extreme southern climates) where the temperatures will (it's hoped) be a bit cooler. There are even midseason cabbage varieties available to fill the dog-days gap. Brussels sprouts benefit from frost and are usually started in early summer and grown as very hardy fall and winter vegetables.

All of the members of this gang prefer firm soil and good contact around both seeds and seedlings. When sprouts show their first two true leaves, it's time to transfer them to another container. Bury the roots and stem to just below the bottom leaves whenever you transplant, and your cole crops will always have a strong and sturdy base from which to head up. Stocky aboveground stems and leaves are developed by giving seedlings plenty of elbow room and sunlight, yet keeping the air temperature a bit on the chilly side (60° to 65°F). Germination times will run about five to 14 days, unless mice eat them for a midnight snack.

Goosefoot family: This group of dicots includes beets, spinach and Swiss chard.

Beet seeds germinate in about 10 to 14 days. Each "seed" is actually a fruit with two to six seeds inside. (You'll want to keep this in mind when spacing.) The germination will be quicker, and sometimes more reliable, when seed is soaked in warm water for 24 hours. Most gardeners simply direct-sow the seeds and cover them with a layer of sifted leaf mold, sand and soil mixture. Beet seeds need good contact with the soil, so it's a good idea to pat the covering earth down with your hands, or with the back of a shovel or spade. You may want to check your pH and adjust accordingly, too; these crimson roots don't like acid soil, nor will they tolerate fresh manures (as with most root crops).

Spinach, which germinates in about eight to 10 days, is direct-sown for spring and fall because hot weather will send it bolting. Even the seeds need cool weather if they're to break free from their dormancy. So, if you're coaxing Popeye's favorite food in late summer, you might mummy-wrap the seeds and put them in the fridge for five to seven days. Spinach is usually broadcast, but can be hand-placed if the plot is small.

Swiss chard germinates in about one to two weeks, and all gardeners should have a bit of it tucked into a partially shaded spot. It's like the best of spinach and oriental cabbage in one plant. And it seems to have nine lives; just when you think it's frozen or fried, it'll come back to surprise you. Swiss chard enjoys the same planting preparations as its relative, the beet.

Nightshade family: This group includes tomatoes, bell peppers, eggplants and potatoes.

Tomatoes take up more pages in seed catalogues, and are grown in more American gardens, than probably any other vegetable. Six to eight weeks before the last frost date, you'll want to start your seeds indoors, making sure they're in good contact with the soil. Tomatoes germinate best at around 80° to 85°F, but should be cooled down to around 60° to 65° as seedlings. Keep in mind, too, that tobacco can carry tobacco mosaic virus to your seedlings; smokers are well advised to wash their hands thoroughly before working with nightshade family seeds or plants.

You may notice that your young plants develop a purplish tinge to their leaves—a sign of phosphorus deficiency. If so, don't despair; just add a little bone meal or rock phosphate to your mix to correct the problem. And if you're using a live organic soil mix, don't use leaf mold from around walnut trees; tomatoes are affected by a toxin given off by this tree's roots.

Nightshades love heat, and the eggplant is no exception. It germinates in seven to 14 days at around 70°F, and more quickly than that if it's presprouted between moist paper towels or cloth and placed inside a plastic bag. Start seeds eight to 10 weeks before the last expected frost date, and don't set out seedlings till all danger of frost is past and the soil has warmed.

Each year quite a few flats or pots of pepper seeds get thrown out, either because the soil was too cold (below 60°F) and they rotted, or because most people simply find it hard to believe something can take as long as peppers do (up to four weeks) to germinate. The optimum temperature you should shoot for is 85°F, and presoaking seeds in warm water may help a little.

The gourd family: These plants include winter and summer squashes, pumpkins, watermelon, cantaloupe and cucumbers.

Most all of the members of this group can wait until the soil is warmed up after the last frost before being planted directly; set three or four seeds to a hill that has a core made up of a few shovelfuls of good compost or well-aged manure.

Gourds are prolific crawlers and climbers and don't enjoy having their roots jostled, so if you want to get a head start, grow them in flats with plenty of space between the seeds, or in individual containers. They germinate best at temperatures above 75°F.

Compositae family: Leaf and head lettuce, endive, chicory, and globe and Jerusalem artichokes are among the more popular members of this group.

Next to tomatoes, lettuce is quite the most popular salad-garden vegetable. You can raise iceberg lettuce, which is bland in appearance as well as in nutritional value; the easy-to-grow cos, or romaine, which is dark green and upright; the butterhead, with its delicate flavor; or any of the many varieties of leaf lettuce, which are probably the favorites of most home gardeners.

Lettuce seed germinates best at between 70° to 75°F and thereafter prefers to be kept at 60° to 65°. This is easy enough to accomplish in spring, but at the end of July—as you are starting your fall salad crop—a day in the refrigerator may help to remind the seed of cool weather to come and cause it to germinate a bit more reliably. Exposure to light for a day can also help. Shade and continuous moisture are the two conditions that your growing salad greens would ask for if only they could.

Seedlings: Handle With Care

Setting out spring seedlings demands careful preparation and a delicate touch.

Hardening off seedlings is a gardener's way of getting young plants adjusted to seasonal temperature changes. You can't just take young sprouts that have grown vigorously in a warm indoor environment, plunk them outside into the cool spring ground and expect them to thrive. Instead, you must toughen them up for the transition by gradually adjusting their *temperature*, *water*, *food* and exposure to *wind* and *sunlight*. In this way, you'll produce stocky, thick growth that's less vulnerable to cold, wind and disease.

Begin this process one to two weeks before transplanting by setting your starts outdoors for a few hours in the afternoon. Choose a sunny location that's protected from strong winds. Cold frames are wonderful tools for this, but there are plenty of other suitable methods, such as placing the plants on a protected patio or by the sunny side of a building. After two or three days of this initiation, your plants will be ready to stay out from morning to late afternoon for the remainder of the week. Then, if the weather promises to be mild, let them "camp out" for a few nights in final preparation.

Early evening is the best time of day for transplanting. A damp cloth will keep exposed roots moist while you're forking open a plant's new home.

Temperature

Some gardeners like to further ease their seedlings' transition by surrounding them with cool temperatures right from the start. It may surprise you to know that, although most plants prefer a warm atmosphere for germination, their optimum *growing* temperatures are on the cool side (see the chart on the following page). For instance, while broccoli, Brussels sprouts, cabbage, cauliflower, Swiss chard, collards, Chinese cabbage, kale, lettuce and parsley prefer germination temperatures from the mid-70s to the 80s, they actually grow best between 60° and 65°F.

Water

To help a plant harden off, you should also restrict its water supply. So give your seedlings' soil a chance to dry out some during those transition days. You might even let leaves droop just a little before you water. (And try to water only on sunny days—doing so reduces overchilling.)

Food

Alan Chadwick, founder of the biodynamic/French intensive method, used to speak of the "breakfast, lunch and dinner" concept of nurturing young plants: Give them a good "breakfast" in their first seed tray, a nutritious "lunch" in their second flat and—when they're hungry and ready—a hearty "supper" in the fertile soil of their garden home. By the time you're ready to plant out, the breakfast and lunch you've provided for your plants indoors should be almost used up. Then the plants will respond all the more eagerly to the rich dinner you've prepared for them in the garden.

Wind

So far, to "hardy up" your plants, you've been decreasing warmth, water and—in a way—food. But wind and light are two factors you'll want to increase. Vegetables that get doses of mild wind make more xylem (tough) cells and shorter internodes (the stem distances between leaves). This means stockier, sturdier plants.

Never pick up a seedling by its stem. Instead, support it by its root ball (and leaves, too, if necessary).

Be sure to press down the dirt around the stem to eliminate air pockets and ensure good contact between the root ball and the surrounding soil.

Light

Although you need to increase your plants' exposure to sunlight, you don't want to overdo it: Moving plants directly from partial light into full sun can "burn" leaves. By gradually increasing light exposure during the hardening-off process, you'll allow the plant time to form carotenoids—pigments that act sort of like temporary sunglasses for the leaves until their chlorophyll levels have time to adjust.

Transplanting

The best time to plant out is late afternoon, early evening or on a day that is decidedly overcast. (A light misting rain is an added bonus.) Water the flats or containers well a few hours before transplanting. This helps the roots slip free without tearing. You'll need a tool for making holes in the ground, a damp cloth to wrap the roots in, a source of water *and* a sense of not being pressed for time.

To begin, carefully get the seedlings out of their containers. (Peat pots and the like can be planted directly in the soil.) If a plant has its own individual pot, you can tap the sides gently until the roots slide out easily. Loosen any tightly balled roots before you put the plant in the soil.

If you raised your starts in flats, use a hand garden fork to lift out a small block of soil. You don't want to let any roots dry out, so wrap that bunch in a moist cloth. Then gently separate and transplant one start at a time.

Never pick a seedling up by its stem. While it may look like a naturally tough "handle," the stem is truly a seedling's most vulnerable spot. A young plant can survive some root damage or even losing a leaf or two. (Indeed, some growers recommend deliberately pinching off a few lower leaves of lettuce, parsley, celery and brassica transplants to reduce wilt and stimulate root growth.) But if you squeeze a stem too tightly, you'll injure the seedling's food and water transport system and make the plant more vulnerable to disease. The correct way to handle a transplant is to support its root ball in your palm while holding the tips of either cotyledon or true leaves between two fingers.

Once you've got a seedling ready, open a small pocket in the earth with a trowel, dibble or large spoon, and put the plant in. (Actually, if the soil is light enough, you may prefer to dig down with your fingers. Doing so allows you to feel a more direct bond between the darkness of past lives and the coming of new ones.) Don't dig too large a hole, or an air space that could harm the roots may form when you're filling in around the plant.

Bury most stems up to their first set of true leaves to provide a firm anchor for the surge of new growth to come. This is especially important for top-heavy crops like cabbage, broccoli, cauliflower and Brussels sprouts. With tomatoes, you can produce a long, lush root system by pinching off all but the top set of leaves and burying the bare stem.

The most critical factor in successful transplanting is creating a cohesive bond between the root ball and the surrounding soil so there'll be an uninterrupted uptake of nutrients and water. To ensure this, lightly press the soil around the stem with your hands. This firm footing is particularly important for brassicas.

Some experts recommend watering the transplants after each bed or row is complete, and others swear that you should do it plant by plant. If the soil is moist and the humidity high, go with the first method. If opposite conditions prevail, water as you go. Be sure to do one or the other: Watering in helps establish good root contact and provides the medium for nutrient uptake.

Try hard *not* to wet your transplants' leaves as you water the soil. The cold could shock the plant. What's more, the moisture could make the leaves "think" it's raining, open their stomata and "perspire" to balance the perceived moisture. The end effect? The plant could actually *lose* water.

You may also want to give your new transplants a dose of fertilizing tea—manure, comfrey or stinging nettle—to help ease their transition and boost their strength.

A Pact Renewed

There's something enchanting about this ancient, early-evening ritual of planting out seedlings. It's a special time of day and year, when skin seems to glow a deeper color, bees slow down and return to the hive, newly green surroundings take on a richer intensity, and gardeners renew their promise of stewardship of the earth.

Optimum Germination Temperature (& Range) °F

Crop	Temperature	Range
Cucumber	95	(60-95)
Squash		(70-95)
Watermelon		(70-95)
Cantaloupe	90	(75-95)
Broccoli		(45-95)
Cabbage	85	(45-95)
Chard		(50-85)
Eggplant		(75-90)
Pepper	80	(65-95)
Tomato		(60-85)
Cauliflower		(45-85)
Lettuce	75	(40-80)
Parsley		(50-85)
Celery	70	(60-70)
	65	

Optimum Growing Temperature (& Range) °F

Crop	Temperature	Range
	85	
Eggplant	70-85	(65-95)
Pepper		(65-95)
Watermelon	80	(65-95)
Tomato	70-75	(65-95)
Cantaloupe	75	65-75 / (60-90)
Cucumber		(60-90)
Squash		(50-90)
Broccoli	70	60-65 / (40-75)
Cabbage		(40-75)
Cauliflower		(45-75)
Celery	65	(45-75)
Chard		(40-75)
Lettuce		(45-75)
Parsley	60	(45-75)
	55	

STEVEN J. CHARNY

Watering

How to get the job done as efficiently and effectively as possible

Most of us—with the twist of a spigot—can turn a garden hose into an umbilical cord linking us to vast (yet *not* inexhaustible) underground rivers. And since many of us don't need to worry about the availability of water, being blessed with adequate supplies, we can often afford to fret about *when* to water, *how much* moisture to put down, what *implements* and *techniques* are most appropriate to use and how to *conserve* as much water as possible while still nurturing the crops.

Water provides more than just liquid to a plant; it's also the medium that enables nutrients and minerals to enter the roots. (Roots don't digest dirt—they're not "woody earthworms"—but instead obtain their nutrients only in solution.) What's more, through the process of photosynthesis, some of water's hydrogen is split off to become a constituent of the carbohydrate compounds that make up most of the body tissue of growing plants.

Interestingly, water also enables plant roots to obtain nutrients that are beyond their physical reach. At varying depths below our feet lies the water table. Above that is soil containing minute, air-filled vestibules. When enough moisture surrounds each soil particle to create a continuous film from roots to water table, plants can, by capillary action, draw water and thus food from places far beneath their roots. (When this happens, the soil is said to have reached field capacity.)

If, on hot summer days, the crops use more water than is replaced, dry air spaces are created within the soil, and the bridge to the water table is broken. Conversely, if a real downpour hits and the air spaces become flooded to the point of excluding oxygen altogether, plants can literally drown—because roots must have air as well as water.

Whether or not your garden soil will retain water well without becoming oversaturated is determined, for the most part, by its structure. But don't feel that you must live with the type of soil that's currently in your plot. The great equalizer, compost, can help improve any ground that has trouble properly absorbing or retaining water.

Take sandy soils, for instance. They often have large spaces between their particles that allow for excellent drainage—*if* there is existing moisture in the soil. If, however, as might be the case in an extremely sandy soil, those spaces are completely filled with air,

they can actually become a barrier to water penetration. Rain will be able to penetrate only the first few inches, so even though the garden has gotten a good soaking, deeper levels will remain bone-dry. When that happens, plant roots tend to seek out only the upper few inches of soil and will thus be quite susceptible to heat and moisture loss.

Compost added to such a sandy soil will act as a moisture-retaining wick. It should be incorporated deeply—say, 6" to 8"—so it will also help attract roots downward.

Silty soil acts in much the same way. Its powdery, flourlike texture can let water slip right through, just as the soil itself would sift through your open fingers. In the process, that water will quickly leach nutrients from your plants. Here again, compost will give your plot a better water-retaining capacity.

Clay soils have another problem: They have so few air spaces that they're too easily flooded by water. A sticky, slimy, wet clay soil can easily drown roots. The addition of as much organic matter as possible is a definite must in order to lighten the soil to allow plant roots more room to breathe.

Turning under green manure (or cover) crops is often another good way to add more humus to the soil. If you have a clay pot, however, it won't have sufficient belowground air to stimulate the needed decomposition of turned-under crops, so cut down most of the green matter and compost it before working it in. On the other hand, adding *sand* to clayey soil is *not* supposed to help its texture—the clay allegedly "swallows" it up. As an old gardening maxim puts it: Put clay in sand, money in the hand; put sand in clay, throw money away.

When to Water

Early mornings and evenings are almost magical times in a garden. The low rays of the sun impart a certain aura to leaves and fruit that's lacking in the harsh light and heat of midday. And, as chance would have it, those are also the best times of day to water.

The soil, heated throughout the day, will warm the water as it percolates downward, making the liquid less chilling (and stressful)

Watering the base of tomato plants keeps leaves dry, reducing the risks of foliage disease.

to the plants. Furthermore, watering in the early evening allows time for the foliage to dry before nightfall—preventing the sustained dampness that favors the spread of fungi and mildews. In addition, plants do much of their actual growing at night (employing the stored products of photosynthesis), so they can well use a late-day boost to their aqueous reserves. And evening is generally a time of reduced wind and cooler temperatures—so water added then will be less likely to evaporate (an important conservation consideration).

Of course, if you find that you spend most of your time in the garden during morning hours, you can water then instead. While doing so may not provide quite as many advantages as does early-evening watering, at least it avoids the hazards of adding water in the heat of the day (which can seriously stress plants) or at nightfall (which encourages disease). It also provides the earth with a deep, long drink early on that can help bring your plants through the coming hot afternoon.

Do remember one thing, though: It's never a good idea to work in your garden when the plants are wet (whether from rainfall or overhead watering). You can easily damage crops at such a time or—worse—spread disease. (Carrots, tomatoes, beans and squash are especially vulnerable to hand-spread disease.)

How Often and How Much

Just as you may choose between two generally preferred times to water, there are also two schools of thought on how often to water. *Daily light* watering regularly replenishes the water that growth and evaporation use up. This way, the soil's water "arteries" remain intact and reach deep into the ground. And *occasional deep* watering accomplishes the same goal by periodically drenching the soil thoroughly.

Choose whichever technique you prefer—just *don't* go with *occasional light* watering. Such halfhearted efforts will keep only the top inch or two of soil moist, coaxing roots to grow only near the surface, where they can readily dry out.

To make sure you're watering enough—whether you go for the daily-light or the occasional-deep method—get a trowel, a soil tube or an auger, and after you've watered, dig down about 1' to see just how deep your added moisture is penetrating. This is a very important learning step. With time, you'll develop a feel for how to keep the soil at its optimum saturation level.

The first time or two you check, you may well discover that you've been watering too shallowly. Many people make that mistake, failing to realize that it can take three-quarters of an hour to fully water one 10′ X 10′ plot. Indeed, the average garden needs about 1″ of rain or irrigation per week, which figures out to about 62 gallons per 100 square feet. If you provide that much in one weekly watering, it should soak the ground to a depth of about 1′.

Of course, most times, natural rainfall will provide some of that moisture, and you'll only have to make up the difference. You can estimate the amount of natural precipitation you've received by following your local weather reports, by putting a large can in the garden and measuring how deep the water in it is after each rain or—if you like precision—by making your own rain gauge from a funnel and cylindrical tube. For the last method, use a funnel with steep sides, and set it where it's not exposed to ground splashings or heavy winds (about 1′ off the ground is good). You can also add a thin film of oil to the cylinder to reduce evaporation losses. To determine the number of inches of rainwater in the cylinder that will equal 1″ of rainfall, divide the squared radius of the funnel by the squared radius of the cylinder. Thus, if your funnel has a 3″ radius and your collecting tube a 1″ radius, every nine ($3^2 \div 1^2$) inches of water collected in the cylinder will equal 1″ of rainfall.

What about droopy leaves? Won't they tell you that you need to water? Well, not necessarily. Plants often wilt some on a hot summer day as a way of shutting down their systems to conserve moisture. If you water at that time, you can shock the flowers and vegetables and cause more harm than good. (In fact, if you overhead-water on such occasions, the plants may actually lose moisture; the leaves will give up internal liquid to try to balance the perceived atmospheric humidity and end up worse off.)

Instead, look for signs of wilting during morning and evening hours. If the leaves are drooping then, it's almost a sure sign that your plants need water—and fast. (One exception: Plants can also wilt if their roots are so wet that they're flooded. A quick trowel-in-the-dirt will determine the true cause if you have any doubts.) Remember, though, that some waxy-leaved plants, such as cabbage, onions and garlic, don't show water stress as clearly as others. On the other hand, peas, celery, spinach and lettuce are very susceptible to drought conditions and will let you know in no uncertain terms.

Tools

A quality garden hose is the heart of any watering system. A hose that will resist its inborn urge to kink and cut off flow is all but priceless. So don't skimp on this purchase—you'll never regret it. Standard diameters are $^1/_2$″, $^5/_8$″ and $^3/_4$″. The larger the diameter, of course, the greater the flow. (By the way, if you garden with raised beds, you can set rebar posts—with bamboo or PVC collars—at the corners of your growing areas, and the posts will conveniently steer your hose *around* the beds.)

A watering wand is a hose attachment that consists of a long tube with a rose nozzle at the end. It's kind to your back, allowing you to stand upright while gently but thoroughly soaking the soil at ground level. The wand is just the thing for ground-watering melons, squashes, tomatoes and other plants susceptible to leaf molds and fungi. It's also an efficient water user, since it places the liquid right where you want it, rather than spraying it all through the air and garden.

There are other common hose attachments for hand-held watering, including the fireman-type nozzle, the spray gun and fan sprayers. All of these can be useful, but you do have to stand there and hold them, which takes time and increases the likelihood that you may skimp on watering. To make your operation a bit more automated, use a rotary or oscillating sprinkler. (The latter is generally easier to use, since most of us lay out our gardens in rectangular—not circular—patterns.) Sprinklers won't apply water entirely evenly, however, and they need to be moved periodically to prevent spot-flooding and run-off problems. (You can buy automatic timers to shut them off after specified periods.) A good source for sprinklers and other hose attachments is Smith & Hawken, 25 Corte Madera, Mill Valley, CA 94941.

Sprinklers have other drawbacks. They waste a lot of water, both by evaporative loss and by wetting pathways—and weeds—as much as crops. They can increase salt build-up in your soil or on your plants (do your crops' leaves have a powdery residue on them or a burned-edge look?). And they wet the leaves of your disease-susceptible crops.

The most water-efficient, automated system around is drip irrigation—invented when an Israeli engineer, Symcha Blass, spotted the beneficial effects of a leaky spigot on the growth of a nearby tree. Drip irrigation systems today come in two types: plastic hoses with small valves—called emitters—spaced every couple of feet, and microporous plastic pipes that weep liquid along their entire length. Both systems use from one-third to one-half less water than do overhead watering methods, put the liquid right at your crops' roots and help increase yields by reducing the stress of extreme fluctuations in moisture levels. Indeed, tests at Ohio State University have shown that peppers and cantaloupes grown with drip irrigation and black plastic mulch produced more than twice the yield of those grown without those two aids.

Drip systems do have some possible drawbacks. Their openings can clog (to avoid that, put an appropriate filter in your waterline). They can start to break down after prolonged exposure to sunlight (that won't happen if you keep the line just underground). And they must be moved whenever you're going to do any serious cultivation.

Their biggest disadvantage, at least for people with larger gardens, is cost: around $15 to $30 per hundred feet of tubing. Perhaps the best way to deal with that consideration is to buy a small "starter" drip system and try it out for a season so you can evaluate its effectiveness.

Water Conservation

Many times, conserving water will be as important as getting some to your crops. Particularly during July or August dry spells, you'll want to make sure your garden *uses* and *loses* as little water as possible.

In a row garden, one of the easiest ways to cut water demand is to plant three to five rows close together and thereby reduce wasted (and watered) pathway space. Of course, gardening in raised beds will save even more

For prolonged watering, punch tiny holes in the bottoms or tops of large cans or plastic milk jugs, and set them next to thirsty plants.

space. Since such beds incorporate a greater depth of loosened soil, they also absorb water better than row plantings do. In addition, raised-bed gardening frequently incorporates the art of spacing plants so that their mature leaves just touch—thus creating a "living mulch" that further blocks evaporation and conserves moisture.

Combine raised beds, living mulch *and* double-digging (to loosen the soil as deep as possible), and you'll have a highly efficient water-conserving garden. John Jeavons' Ecology Action group in Willitts, California, has obtained excellent yields of vegetables using these biodynamic/French intensive techniques and *one-eighth* the water of conventional gardening.

While you obviously want to establish your garden away from the drip line of trees (their roots practically inhale water), those large plants do have their place as windbreaks. Much more water is lost to evaporation from wind than most of us realize. So you'd do well to utilize any available trees, houses, hedges or fences to slow down the drying effects of hot summer breezes.

Mulching with dry materials such as hay, straw, wood chips or even black-and-white newspaper pages most definitely helps protect bare soil from evaporative water loss. Keep in mind, though, that you shouldn't mulch too early in the growing year, or the covering will retard the warming of your soil. Also, carbon-laden mulches do tie up nitrogen while they're decomposing, so you should be sure that heavily mulched soil has ample nitrogen. (Fish emulsion, blood meal, cottonseed meal and well-aged manure are some good nitrogen supplements.)

The Fundamental Point

Finally, always remember that while expensive irrigation systems or conservation strategies will help you save water, the most significant way to conserve moisture is to make soil improvement your top priority. A humus-rich soil—created by using lots of compost and cover crops—will hold the water it gets while still allowing for aeration. Indeed, the soil should be our first concern in all aspects of farming and gardening, because nurturing the diverse life it sustains is the strongest step we can take toward growing healthy plants.

Weeding

You don't have to kill yourself killing weeds.

"A weed," someone once said, "is anything growing in an inappropriate place and making a nuisance of itself." Keeping weeds at bay is a perpetual task that's vital to the good health—and good appearance—of your garden.

They can grow so rapidly and densely that the shade they create may stunt the growth of the crop they've infiltrated. What's more, these invaders rob your crops of needed moisture and nutrients.

Unless you're gardening in containers or raised beds, the most obvious solution to eliminating already-sprouted weeds would seem to be hoeing or hand weeding on your knees. Mulching is a great preventive measure, but it's nearly impossible to mulch thickly in a close row of plants. (After the final thinning of some crops, a mulch can sometimes be effectively applied between plants that are far enough apart to develop fully.)

Vegetables usually have shallow root systems. Because their roots are near the surface, vegetables are easily damaged by deep hoeing. Ideally, the soil should be disturbed no deeper than 1″. Even if hoeing takes place some distance from the furrows, the gardener must exercise caution: Vegetables, especially those in less than fertile soil, send out shallow but far-ranging root systems. A scuffle hoe is particularly effective for chopping off weeds at ground level, because its blade will lie flat on the surface of the soil and will behead weeds when pushed forward or pulled backward (other types work only when dragged toward the hoer). Leveling weeds may not always kill them, but neither does it damage the roots of surrounding crops. Besides, if you lop the weeds regularly, even resprouting ones are kept under control, as they never grow large enough to be a problem.

Unfortunately for the gardener, weeding is best done in the heat of the day, when the hot sun can help kill exposed roots. Weeds pulled in the late afternoon or in the evening may recover unless they're completely removed from the garden.

Don't attempt to weed the vegetable garden right after a rain. Bumping against wet foliage can increase the likelihood of plant injury and disease, and walking on wet

Good care means weeding.

soil packs it down and drives out the air.

Some weeds are annuals, and some are perennials. Annuals grow only one season, but they create thousands of seeds. Examples are chickweed, lamb's-quarters, spurge, purslane and green amaranth. Perennials send up new growth every year, not only from seeds but also from underground stems and roots, so simply hoeing or tilling doesn't usually get rid of them; as long as bits of stems and roots remain in the soil and can get sun and water, these pieces will send up new shoots. Examples are Bermuda grass, quack grass, crabgrass, nut grass and bindweed.

The first purging of annual weeds should take place before they're even visible. The seeds are small and therefore germinate only in the top $1/4''$ of soil; those below that depth haven't the strength to push their way up. Annual weeds can be successfully controlled in several ways. First, work the soil *just before* planting. This last-minute disturbance of the soil exposes the tender weed seeds in the top $1/4''$ and kills them before they can germinate. Vegetable and flower seedlings then have a head start. Second, as soon as vegetable seedlings are $1/4''$ to $1/2''$ tall, thin them with a rake, as this will also loosen and kill sprouting weed seedlings. Third, when the surface of the ground has had a chance to dry out after a rain or thorough watering, cultivate the top inch or so of soil between plants and between rows or beds. With less than half a dozen of these shallow cultivations, weed seeds in the top layer of earth will have germinated and will have been fatally exposed. And don't forget to continue weeding even after harvest time, because annual weeds will keep trying to produce seeds until cold weather kills the plants.

Perennial weeds are best eliminated by out-and-out attack. Half measures here will avail the gardener nothing. The best method of control involves starving out the root systems by preventing any top growth. Perennials must have at least $1/2''$ of new growth above the ground in order to capture enough sunlight to replenish their root reserves. There are a couple of ways to forestall this essential $1/2''$ of growth: 1) tilling followed by covering with black plastic or a heavy organic mulch and 2) continuous shallow cultivating to keep top growth from developing.

Weather-proofing

Protect your plants from the wind, rain and frost of early spring.

The urge to knead the soil with our hands and tools, to coax and nurse life from the earth, has been fueled by months spent scanning seed catalogues. We are spring's impatient gardeners, anxious to get growing.

March winds won't hear of it. They dry out transplants like laundry on the clothesline. They chill and tear tender stems and roots.

Then April rains drown plants, cool and compact the ground, bruise seedlings and wash out seedbeds.

And, in a final holding action, May frosts pass their cold judgment on early gardening hopes. In one still night, they fell seedlings that represent weeks of nurturing.

Spring gardening is back-yard gambling: The sooner we act, the worse our chances. But while no gardener can eliminate bad weather, everyone can take steps, large and small, that will greatly reduce the misfortune that foul wind, rain and cold bring.

The Right Site

Let's start with the biggest—and primary—decision: where you put your garden. Location is one of the most important factors affecting a plot's weather resistance. Buildings, slopes, bodies of water and surrounding vegetation can alter weather patterns so much that you may have several different microclimates on your property—or even within your garden. It may actually be worthwhile to move an existing garden if doing so would dramatically decrease the energy you expend confronting the elements.

Consider slopes. Generally speaking, the crest of a hill is the windiest spot on it, and both water and cold air flow downhill and accumulate at the bottom. The hillside itself, then, is a better location than either the top or the bottom.

Of course, a southern slope is best. It gets more sun than most and is protected from cold north winds. A westerly exposure heats up later in the morning than a direct southern one, thawing frozen plants more slowly and reducing possible damage. It also reaches higher overall temperatures than an eastern exposure—which makes an east or southeast spot better suited to heat-sensitive plants in summer. Since northern slopes receive the least sunlight, many people use them to raise fruit trees; the postponed

spring there retards early blooms that might get wiped out by a late frost.

Buildings create microclimates of their own. The south side of a home offers shelter from north winds, absorbs solar energy during the day and slowly releases that warmth at night. So a permanent bed along the south wall is a great place for your earliest starts.

Lakes and ponds reflect heat and light to plants grown nearby, but they also allow an unobstructed pathway for winds.

Walls and Fences

Once you've picked the best site, consider building fences to provide protection from the wind—an idea so old that the very word *garden* comes from the Middle English *gardin*, or "enclosure." Remember: Wind increases cold damage (and dehydration in dry weather) as well as inflicting direct punishment. Reducing its effects is essential to early-season growing.

Use a fence with slats or an open weave—such as a picket, panel, woven wattle or bamboo fence (even burlap stretched over chicken wire). It'll allow some airflow and provide better wind protection than a solid wall. (An unbroken barrier creates extra turbulence in its wake—see Fig. 1—while a somewhat permeable one slows wind speed without creating extra currents.) A density of 50% is ideal.

Living Curtains

Shelterbelts consist of one or more rows of trees and shrubs arranged to offer wind protection, while tightly grown walls of shrubs alone are known as *hedgerows*. Both these "living curtains" (a literal translation of the Japanese term for hedgerows) offer erosion control, privacy, snowdrift protection, wildlife habitat, food, bee forage and ornamental value, but their chief value is wind shelter.

A shelterbelt of trees should be perpendicular to the prevailing winds. In most areas, this would mean along the north and west borders. You may have different needs; for instance, you may want protection from hot southern summer winds. Whatever, be careful not to situate a windbreak *below* a sloping garden, or you'll trap a pocket of cold air that would normally move on by.

Two or three rows of trees should make an

adequate—and still somewhat permeable—shelterbelt (Fig. 2). Evergreens are the most popular choices, since they provide year-round protection, but deciduous trees lose only 40% of their effectiveness when bare. Plant shrubs on the windward (upwind) side to protect young trees and to fill in the gaps below mature ones.

You might want to plant deciduous trees on the windward side of your evergreens. They generally mature faster and can be cut for lumber or firewood once the evergreens grow up. Windbreak trees should be planted fairly close together so the branches will just touch when mature to form a living canopy. Evergreens are commonly spaced from 5' to 15' apart, deciduous trees from 5' to 20'—but you can plant them more closely at first and thin them as they grow.

(Your local soil conservation service or county extension agent should be able to give you specific species and spacing information for your area and soil type.)

Many shrubs provide beauty or food as well as shelter. Some good choices are *Rosa rugosa* (rose hips), highbush cranberry, eastern sand cherry, lilac, Russian olive, autumn olive, filberts, holly, tree honeysuckle, forsythia and rose of Sharon.

Diverting Run-off

Once you've done all you can to *gardin* your garden, it's time to provide internal protection. If surface run-off from spring rains washes into your plot, dig a horseshoe-shaped or three-sided moat around the top and sides. Notice we said moat, not ditch. A narrow, steep ditch would deepen with time, washing much of its own soil away. A moat, though, is a wide trench with a gradual slope on its uphill (outer) side and a sharper one on the garden side (Fig. 3). When planted with a thick sod, this moat will resist its own erosion as well as protect your garden.

Suppose your problem isn't surface run-off, but groundwater that turns part of your plot swampy during wet spells. In this case, you'll have to dig a trench, 1' wide and 2' to 3' deep, running from the morass to an area out below your plot. (If you have more than one wet spot, you can build a series of trenches that run into a main one like tributaries feeding into a river.) Put 5" of clean ³/₄" gravel in the trench. Lay a 4"-diameter drainpipe (capped at its top) on this, and cover with soil. The drainpipe can consist of either sections of unglazed clay tiles or corrugated black plastic pipe with precut drain slots.

If your trench-drained water doesn't flow into a natural waterway, you should build a sump: a 4' by 4' pit that's 3' deep (Fig. 4). Line its bottom with a 1' layer of fist-sized stones or brick pieces. Then give it another foot of clean ³/₄" gravel, and cover the area with topsoil.

Terracing

The basis of many ancient agricultural systems (and still in wide use today), terracing is the art of constructing strips of growing area that run horizontally along a slope, contoured to the natural curve of the land. Terraces make it possible to garden on a slope—even a very steep one—with little danger of erosion. The heat stored by the terrace wall above each strip can also provide some thermal protection for the crops below.

Permanent walls of stone (the best heat retainer), timber or (if the slope is gradual enough) sod banks are all good for terraces. In all cases, never leave any of the garden soil bare and exposed to erosion. Replant or mulch an area as soon as it is harvested, grow cover crops in the off-seasons, and mulch between widely spaced plants.

Raised Beds

As our listing of weatherproofing methods moves from large scale to small, it also moves

FIG. 1 Solid Barrier Turbulence

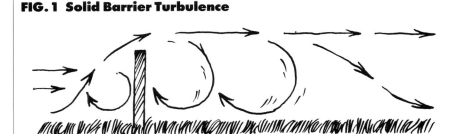

FIG. 2 A Shelterbelt

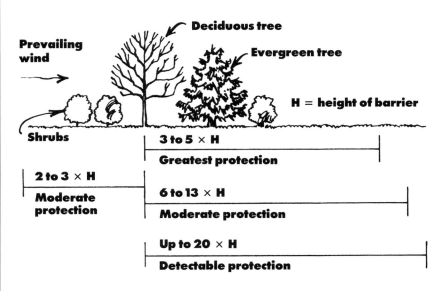

from landscaping techniques to gardening methods. Raised beds incorporate elements of both. The long, 3' to 4'-wide mounds warm more quickly and drain better than flat garden soil. If you use the close plant spacing most often recommended for raised beds—planting on hexagonal centers rather than in straight rows—much less of your garden space will be wasted on erodible pathways. The plants themselves will also form a continuous canopy of leaves as they mature, and this "living mulch" will hold warmth close to the soil surface, help block wind erosion and buffer rainfall.

You'll be better off if you prepare your early-spring growing beds the previous fall. That way you won't have to wait for the soil to dry out when mud month rolls around, but can plant when you like.

Mulch

A thick layer of mulch—straw, leaves, wood chips or other dead plant material laid on your garden—will definitely protect your plot from rain-caused erosion. But this insulating layer can also keep your soil from warming up quickly as well, so don't mulch heavily where you want to grow super-early spring crops. Still, a light mulch over a seedbed will cushion the scattering force of pounding raindrops, and a medium-depth mulch can prevent soil splatter on seedlings.

Cover Cropping

Cover cropping—growing plants to cover idle soil—sharply reduces wind and water damage. It also improves soil tilth, increases organic matter in your plot and helps the soil retain nutrients. Hardy, fall-planted species such as hairy vetch, winter rye and fava beans will help spring plots the most. Such cover crops can even help dry an early-season garden by drawing excess moisture out of the ground.

Individual Plant Protectors

Once you've done all you can to make your entire plot less vulnerable to nature's attacks, you can turn your attention to protecting individual plants or beds. The portable aids we'll talk about here all buffer wind, cold and rain well enough to make a significant differ-

ence in how well your crops weather bad weather.

The highly successful French market gardeners of the early twentieth century used bell-shaped glass jars called *cloches* (the French word for "bells") to protect their early crops. Nowadays, most people use plastic milk jugs for the job. Just cut off the containers' bottoms and put one over each plant you want to shelter. The miniature hothouses are free, durable and—equally important—easy to ventilate on sunny days (just unscrew the cap). If you live in a windy area, be sure to tie them to stakes.

You can also buy or construct cone-shaped plant protectors made of plastic or fiberglass. One such product, the Wall O' Water, has

18"-high, water-filled walls that absorb heat by day and release it at night. Old black tires can be used to shelter and warm seedlings—they work best with space-hungry vining crops like tomatoes and squash. And if you grow your tomato plants in welded-wire

FIG. 3 A Garden Moat

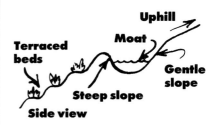

FIG. 4 A Drainage Trench and Sump

FIG. 5 A PVC Tunnel Cloche

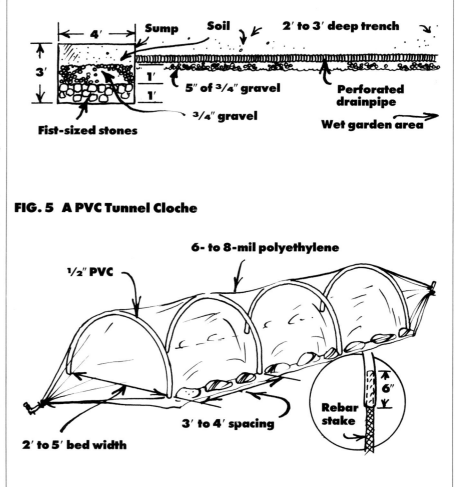

cages, you can wrap those supports with clear polyethylene during the fickle-weather weeks. Anchor them well with stakes. You can also add fiberglass or scrap-wood "lids," but remember to remove them on warm days to avoid overheating.

FIG. 6 A Spunbond Bed Cover

Bed Protectors

Many times it's easier to protect an entire garden bed than to shelter individual plants. While you can make whole-bed cloches out of glass plates or old windowpanes, such structures are heavy and fragile. Portable garden tents are now available that use lightweight polyethylene or fiberglass sheeting. (Or build your own: Just make a framework out of wood or PVC, and cover it.)

You can also take a large piece of fiberglass sheeting, bend it into an inverted U and secure its shape by placing wire crosspieces across the bottom. (Cover the ends with scrap fiberglass or plywood.)

All these bed protectors are wide enough to cover a garden bed, but they're not very long. Tunnel cloches made of six- or eight-mil polyethylene laid over a series of hoops (Fig. 5) can be made any length you'd need. Make the support frames from eight- or nine-gauge wire, PVC (set on rebar stakes), reinforced wire mesh, spring steel and even smooth, supple branches. For the covering, use hardware store polyethylene—or special pre-slit poly for better ventilation. Weight the material at the sides and ends with soil, rocks or lumber. Be sure to open it up as often as necessary to prevent overheating and dampness-induced plant diseases.

Since plastic is not a good insulator, tunnel cloches offer only a few degrees of *direct* frost protection. But they block wind chilling and dehydration and—most especially—help warm the earth. This increases microorganism activity and nutrient availability, as well as helping plants get through cold spells. The cloches fend off invading birds and insects, too. The poly can be replaced by a shading material in summer to cool heat-sensitive crops.

There are other ways to warm spring soil, as well. You can lay black plastic on a bed and poke holes in it for individual trans-

plants. You can even try "solarization": covering a future bed with clear plastic for a few weeks. (Seal the edges tightly.) Tests have shown that this dramatically prewarms soil and even kills some young weeds, yet does not damage most beneficial soil microorganisms.

A recent "space-age" bed cover is spunbond polyester or polypropylene. (Reemay is a popular brand.) Light and rain easily penetrate this white, porous fabric. And it's so lightweight it can be laid loosely right on top of the plants it protects (the ends and sides weighted in place by soil) and then get pushed up by the crops as they grow (Fig. 6). Like plastic, the "floating bed cover" doesn't provide much direct frost protection. But the enhanced, sheltered environment it creates can extend either end of the gardening season by a few weeks.

Since the material breathes well, you don't need to ventilate the bed often. And spunbond covers make excellent insect barriers. (Want to be *sure* those flea beetles don't get on your eggplants?) Indeed, some gardeners use the materials solely for this purpose. On the negative side, you can't weed under a floating bed cover—you have to take it off. You also need to remove it when plants need wind- or insect-pollination.

The creative grower will experiment with all these garden-protecting tactics or, better yet, combine them. Cover a bed with both spunbond material and a poly tunnel cloche to get double frost protection. Lay black plastic as a mulch under your spunbond cover to eliminate that weeding problem. Put both black plastic and old tires out on your pumpkin patch and you can start long-season vines weeks earlier than normal. Build a tunnel cloche against a stone-terraced bed, and trap the heat those rocks give off.

Change the Odds

You can't make your garden invulnerable to the assaults of spring storms, gales and frosts, but you'll be pleased by how well these plot-protecting tactics do work. Let's put it this way: Springtime gardening will always be a gamble—who would really want it any other way?—but you don't have to just set out your plants and take your chances.

You can tilt the odds in your garden's favor.

Sources

Spunbond Row Cover
Gardeners Supply Co.
Johnny's Selected Seeds
Mellinger's
Natural Gardening Research Center
Pinetree Garden Seeds

Polyethylene
A.M. Leonard, Inc.
Mellinger's

Pre-slit Polyethylene
Gardeners Supply Co.
Johnny's Selected Seeds
Mellinger's

Industrial Grade Plastic
Mellinger's

Windbreak Netting
Gardeners Supply Co.

Poly Tape (for use on garden plastics)
A.M. Leonard, Inc.

Bulk Burlap
Mellinger's

Wall O' Water
Henry Field and Co.
Gardeners Supply Co.
Peaceful Valley Farm Supply
Pinetree Garden Seeds

Hotcaps
Burpee Seed Co.
Farmer's Seed & Nursery
Harris Seeds
Mellinger's

Portable Cold Frames
Burpee Seed Co.
Gardeners Supply Co.
Geo. W. Park Seed Co., Inc.
Peaceful Valley Farm Supply

Addresses

Burpee Seed Co.
300 Park Ave.
Warminster, PA 18974
215/674-4900, ext. 222

Farmer's Seed & Nursery
818 NW 4th St.
Faribault, MN 55021
507/334-1623

Henry Field and Co.
407 Sycamore St.
Shenandoah, IA 51602
712/246-2017

Gardeners Supply Co.
128 Intervale Rd.
Burlington, VT 05401
802/863-1700

Harris Seeds
3670 Buffalo Rd.
Rochester, NY 14624
716/594-9411

Johnny's Selected Seeds
Foss Hill Rd.
Albion, ME 04910
207/437-9294

A.M. Leonard, Inc.
6665 Spiker Rd.
Piqua, OH 45356
800/762-8922 (in Ohio)
800/543-8955 (outside Ohio)

Mellinger's
2310 W. South Range
North Lima, OH 44452
216/549-9861

Natural Gardening Research Center
P.O. Box 149
Sunman, IN 47041
812/623-3800

Geo. W. Park Seed Co., Inc.
Box 31
Greenwood, SC 29646
803/223-7333

Peaceful Valley Farm Supply
11173 Peaceful Valley Rd.
Nevada City, CA 95959
916/265-FARM

Pinetree Garden Seeds
New Gloucester, ME 04260
207/926-3400

Companion Planting

Some crops naturally go together.

The best gardens thrive when crops complement rather than compete with each other. Through trial and error, gardeners have learned which "get along" better than others.

Basil

Plant Near:
- Most garden crops.

Keep Away From:
- Rue.

Comments:
- Basil improves the flavor and growth of garden crops (especially tomato and lettuce).
- Basil repels flies and mosquitoes.

Beans, Bush

Plant Near:
- Potatoes, cucumbers, beets, carrots, cabbage, cauliflower, marigolds, corn, savory, catnip, strawberries.

Keep Away From:
- Onions, garlic, shallots, leeks, fennel.

Comments:
- Potatoes and marigolds repel Mexican bean beetles.
- Catnip repels flea beetles.

Beans, Pole

Plant Near:
- Radishes, corn, marigolds, potatoes.

Keep Away From:
- Kohlrabi, beets, leeks, onions, garlic, shallots.

Comments:
- Same as for bush beans.

Beets

Plant Near:
- Bush beans, kohlrabi, onions, cabbage, broccoli, chard, Brussels sprouts, cauliflower.

Keep Away From:
- Pole beans, charlock, field mustard.

Borage

Plant Near:
- Squash, tomatoes, strawberries.

Comments:
- Borage repels tomato worms and improves its companions' flavor and growth.

Broccoli and Brussels Sprouts

Plant Near:
- Beets, onions, rosemary, dill, carrots, hyssop, chamomile, mints, sage, wormwood, thyme, nasturtiums, buckwheat, marigolds, calendula.

Keep Away From:
- Strawberries.

Comments:
- Marigolds repel cabbage moths.
- Nasturtiums repel aphids.

Cabbage and Cauliflower

Plant Near:
- Tomatoes, celery, chard, spinach, Brussels sprouts/broccoli companions.

Keep Away From:
- Strawberries.

Comments:
- Tomatoes and celery repel cabbage worms.

Cantaloupe

Plant Near:
- Corn.

Carrots

Plant Near:
- Lettuce, chives, onions, peas, radishes, cabbage, early potatoes, salsify, leeks, wormwood, sage, rosemary.

Comments:
- Onions, leeks and wormwood repel carrot flies.

Chives

Plant Near:
- Tomatoes, carrots, peas, apples, berries, grapes, roses.

Comments:
- Chives improve their companions' flavor and growth, as well as deterring aphids and Japanese beetles.

Corn

Plant Near:
- Early potatoes, melons, beans, peas, pumpkins, squash, cucumbers, soybeans.

Comments:
- Soybeans deter chinch bugs.

Cucumbers

Plant Near:
- Corn, early potatoes, cabbage, sunflowers, beans, radishes.

Keep Away From:
- Late potatoes.

Comments:
- Radishes deter cucumber beetles.
- Cucumbers encourage blight in late potatoes.

Dill

Plant Near:
- Cabbage, cucumbers, broccoli, cauliflower, Brussels sprouts, onions, lettuce.

Keep Away From:
- Carrots.

Comments:
- Dill improves the flavor and growth of cabbage family plants.

Eggplant

Plant Near:
- Tomatoes, green beans, peppers, potatoes.

Comments:
- Green beans deter Colorado potato beetles.

Garlic

Plant Near:
- Tomatoes, cane fruits, fruit trees, roses, cabbage.

Keep Away From:
- Peas, beans.

Comments:
- Garlic deters Japanese beetles and aphids.
- A garlic oil spray deters onion flies, aphids and ermine moths.
- A garlic tea helps repel late potato blight.

Kale

Plant Near:
- Cabbage family, aromatic herbs, mari-

Eggplant

golds, buckwheat, nasturtiums.

Keep Away From:
- Pole beans, strawberries.

Kohlrabi

Plant Near:
- Cabbage/cauliflower companions (except tomatoes).

Keep Away From:
- Tomatoes, pole beans, fennel.

Comments:
- Kohlrabi stunts tomatoes.

Lettuce

Plant Near:
- Carrots, strawberries, beets, radishes, parsnips.

Keep Away From:
- Cabbage family.

Comments:
- Lettuce tenderizes summer radishes.

Marigolds

Plant Near:
- All garden crops.

Comments:
- Marigolds stimulate vegetable growth and deter bean beetles, aphids, potato bugs, squash bugs, nematodes and maggots.

Marjoram

Plant Near:
- All garden crops.

Comments:
- Marjoram stimulates vegetable growth.

Mustard

Plant Near:
- Grapes, legumes, fruit trees, alfalfa cover crops.

Comments:
- Mustard stimulates its companions' growth.

Nasturtiums

Plant Near:
- Cabbage family, radishes, beans, pumpkins, squash, potatoes, apples, greenhouse crops.

Comments:
- Nasturtiums repel aphids, potato bugs, squash bugs, striped pumpkin beetles, Mexican bean beetles, and destroy whiteflies in greenhouses.

Onions

Plant Near:
- Lettuce, cabbage family, carrots, beets, chamomile, parsnips.

Keep Away From:
- Peas, beans.

Comments:
- Onions deter most pests, especially maggots.

Oregano

Plant Near:
- All garden crops.

Comments:
- Oregano deters many insect pests.

Parsley

Plant Near:
- Tomatoes, corn, roses.

Parsnips

Plant Near:
- Radishes, wormwood, onions.

Comments:
● Onions and wormwood help keep root maggots from parsnips.

Peas

Plant Near:
● Radishes, carrots, corn, turnips, early potatoes, cucumbers, beans.
Keep Away From:
● Garlic, onions, leeks, shallots.

Peppers

Plant Near:
● Tomatoes, eggplant, onions, carrots, basil, parsley.
Keep Away From:
● Kohlrabi, fennel.

Potatoes

Plant Near:
● Beans, cabbage family, eggplant, corn, squash, marigolds, peas, flax, hemp, basil.
Keep Away From:
● Sunflowers, apples, tomatoes, cherries, birch, pumpkins, cucumbers, walnuts, raspberries.
Comments:
● Hemp deters *Phytophthora infestans*.
● Basil deters potato beetles.
● Marigolds (dug into crop soil) deter nematodes.

Radishes

Plant Near:
● Root crops, nasturtiums, peas, chervil, lettuce, cucumbers, melons.
Keep Away From:
● Hyssop.
Comments:
● Radishes deter cucumber beetles.
● Chervil makes radishes hot.
● Lettuce helps make radishes tender.
● Nasturtiums improve radishes' flavor.

Rosemary

Plant Near:
● Tomatoes, beans, sage, cabbage family, carrots, squash.

Strawberry

Comments:
● Rosemary repels bean beetles, cabbage moths and carrot flies.

Sage

Plant Near:
● Cabbage family, carrots, tomatoes.
Keep Away From:
● Cucumbers.
Comments:
● Sage deters cabbage moths and carrot flies, and invigorates tomato plants.

Soybeans

Plant Near:
● Corn, potatoes.
Comments:
● Soybeans choke weeds and enrich soil.

Spinach

Plant Near:
● Celery, eggplant, cauliflower, strawberries.

Strawberries

Plant Near:
● Bush beans, spinach, lettuce, pyrethrum, borage.
Keep Away From:
● Cabbage family.

Sunflowers

Plant Near:
● Cucumbers.
Keep Away From:
● Potatoes.
Comments:
● Sunflowers can provide a trellis and shelter for shade-loving cucumbers.

Swiss Chard

Plant Near:
● Bush beans, kohlrabi, onions.
Keep Away From:
● Pole beans.

Tarragon

Plant Near:
● All garden crops.
Comments:
● Tarragon improves vegetables' flavor and growth.

Thyme

Plant Near:
● All garden crops.
Comments:
● Thyme deters cabbage moths.

Tomatoes

Plant Near:
● Asparagus, parsley, cabbage family, onions, mustard, carrots, basil, sage, rosemary, gooseberries, stinging nettles.
Keep Away From:
● Potatoes, kohlrabi, fennel, walnuts.

Turnips and Rutabagas

Plant Near:
● Peas.
Keep Away From:
● Mustard, knotweed.
Comments:
● Mustard and knotweed inhibit the growth of turnips and rutabagas.

Resistant Plants

Grow varieties that insects would just as soon avoid.

Why look for trouble? You can choose vegetable varieties that are actually resistant to common insect pests. That way you'll save the best eating for yourself.

Beans

Mexican bean beetle:
- Resistant: Wade, Logan and Black Valentine.
- Susceptible: State, Bountiful and Dwarf Horticultural.

Broccoli

Striped flea beetle:
- Resistant: De Cicco, Coastal, Italian Green Sprouting and Atlantic.
- Moderately resistant: Gem.

Cabbage

Cabbage looper and imported cabbageworm:
- Resistant: Mammoth Red Rock, Savoy Chieftain and Savoy Perfection Drumhead.
- Moderately resistant: Special Red Rock, Penn State Ball Head, Early Flat Dutch, Badger Ball Head, Wisconsin Hollander, Red Acre, Danish Ball Head, Charleston Wakefield, Premium Late Flat Dutch, Glory of Enkhuizen, Globe, All Seasons, Midseason Market, Bugner, Succession, Early Round Dutch, Stein's Early Flat Dutch, Badger Market, Large Late Flat Dutch, Jersey Wakefield, Marion Market, Wisconsin Ball Head, Large Charleston Wakefield, Early Glory, Green Acre, Round Dutch, Resistant Detroit and Wisconsin All Season.
- Susceptible: Golden Acre, Elite, Copenhagen Market 86 and Stein's Flat Dutch.

Mexican bean beetle:
- Resistant: Copenhagen Market 86 and Early Jersey Wakefield.
- Susceptible: Michihli Chinese.

Striped flea beetle:
- Resistant: Stein's Early Flat Dutch, Mammoth Red Rock, Savoy Perfection Drumhead, Early Jersey Wakefield, Copenhagen Market 86 and Ferry's Round Dutch.
- Moderately resistant to susceptible: Michihli Chinese.
- Susceptible (Canada): North Star and Northern Belle.

Cantaloupe

Mexican bean beetle: Cantaloupe is generally resistant to this pest, but serious damage was done to Rocky Ford Earliest during an infestation.

Spotted cucumber beetle:
- Resistant (foliage): Edisto 47, Edisto and Harper Hybrid.
- Susceptible (seedlings): Edisto, Edisto 47, Harper Hybrid and Honey Dew.

  Susceptible (foliage): Honey Dew.

Cauliflower

Cabbages

Striped flea beetle:
● Resistant: Snowball A and Early Snowball X.

Cauliflower

Collard

Mexican bean beetle:
● Resistant: Georgia LS, Green Glaze and Vates.
Striped flea beetle:
● Resistant: Vates, Georgia and Georgia LS.
● Moderately resistant: Morris Heading.
● Susceptible: Green Glaze.

Sweet Corn

Corn earworm: Any corn with long, tight husks physically helps to prevent ear penetration by earworms.
● Resistant: Dixie 18 (field corn), Calumet, Country Gentleman, Staygold, Victory Golden, Golden Security, Silver Cross Bantam and Silvergent.
● Susceptible: Ioana, Aristogold Bantam Evergreen, Seneca Chief, Spancross, North Star and Evertender.
Fall armyworm: Late sweet corn crops and second crops are especially vulnerable. Resistance depends on the planting time and tolerance of a variety. The varieties are arranged by survival rates, from best to worst.
● Resistant: Golden Market, Long Chief, Golden Security, Evertender, Marcross, Golden Regent, Silver Cross Bantam, Calumet, Victory Golden, Golden Sensation, Spancross, Golden Cross Bantam, Aristogold Bantam Evergreen, Golden Beauty, Triplegold, Deep Gold and Ioana.

Cucumber

Mexican bean beetle: While not normally a serious pest of cucumbers, this beetle severely damaged these varieties in an outbreak: Arkansas Hybrid No. 4, Colorado, Crispy, Hokus, Marketer, NK804, Nappa 63, Piccadilly, Pico, Pixie and Triumph.
Spotted cucumber beetle:
● Resistant (seedlings): Ashley, Chipper, Crispy, Explorer, Frontier, Gemini, Jet, Princess, Spartan Dawn and White Wonder.
   Resistant (foliage): Ashley, Cherokee, Chipper, Gemini, High Mark II, Ohio MR 17, Poinsett, Stono (Stono is reported resistant to both striped and spotted cucumber beetles, and Fletcher and Niagra are moderately resistant to the two pests) and Southern Cross.
● Moderately resistant (seedlings): Cubit, High Mark II, Hokus, Nappa 63, Pixie, Poinsett and SMR 58.
   Moderately resistant (foliage): Colorado, Crispy, Explorer, Frontier, Long Ashley, Nappa 61, Pixie and Table Green.

Cucumbers

● Susceptible (seedlings): Cherokee, Coolgreen, Model, Nappa 61, Packer, Pioneer, Southern Cross and Table Green.
   Susceptible (foliage): Coolgreen, Cubit, Hokus, Jet, Model, Nappa 63, Packer, Pioneer, Spartan Dawn and SMR 58.

Kale

Mexican bean beetle:
● Resistant: Dwarf Siberian.
Striped flea beetle:
● Resistant: Vates, Dwarf Siberian, Dwarf Green Curled Scotch and Early Siberian.

Muskmelon

Striped and spotted cucumber beetle:
● Resistant: Hearts of Gold.
● Susceptible: Smith Perfect and Crenshaw.

Mustard

Mexican bean beetle:
● Resistant: Green Wave.
● Susceptible: Southern Giant Curled.
Striped flea beetle:
● Resistant: Florida Broadleaf.
● Moderately resistant: Southern Giant Curled and Green Wave.

Potato

Aphids:
● Resistant: British Queen, DeSota, Early Pinkeye, Houma, Irish Daisy and La-Salle.
● Tolerant: Red Warba, Triumph, President, Peach Blow and Early Rose.
● Susceptible: Katahdin, Irish Cobbler, Idaho Russet, Sebago and Sequoia.
Colorado potato beetle:
● Resistant: Sequoia and Katahdin.
● Susceptible: Fundy, Plymouth and Catoosa.
Potato leafhopper:
● Resistant: Delus.
● Moderately resistant: Sebago, Pungo and Plymouth.
● Susceptible: Cobbler.

Pumpkin

Serpentine leaf miner (only four varieties were tested):
● Resistant: Mammoth Chili and Small Sugar.
● Susceptible: King of the Mammoth and Green Striped Cushaw.
Spotted cucumber beetle:
● Resistant (foliage): King of the Mammoth, Mammoth Chili and Dickinson Field.
● Susceptible (seedlings): Green Striped Cushaw, King of the Mammoth, Mammoth Chili and Small Sugar.
   Susceptible (foliage): Connecticut Field, Green Striped Cushaw and Small Sugar.

Radish

Mexican bean beetle:
● Susceptible: Sparkler, Champion and White Icicle.
Striped flea beetle:

● Moderately resistant: Champion and Sparkler.
● Susceptible: Globemaster, Cherry Belle and White Icicle.

Squash

Mexican bean beetle: Although this beetle is not normally a serious pest of squash, White Bush Scallop was damaged severely in an outbreak.
Serpentine leaf miner:
● Resistant: Butternut 23 and Cozella.
● Moderately resistant: Blue Hubbard, Green Hubbard, Zucchini, Benning's Green Tint Scallop, Summer Straightneck, Boston Marrow, Buttercup and Pink Banana.
● Susceptible: Seneca Prolific, Green Hubbard, Seneca Zucchini, Summer Crookneck, Black Zucchini, Cozini and Long Cozella.
Spotted cucumber beetle: These beetles are attracted to the odor of some germinating seeds, and often dig through soil to eat seedlings before they've grown to the surface. They're also attracted to mature flowering varieties with a strong, sweet smell.
● Resistant (seedlings): Blue Hubbard, Long Cozella, Seneca Prolific, Summer Crookneck and Summer Straightneck.

Resistant (foliage): Black Zucchini, Ben-

ning's Green Tint Scallop and Blue Hubbard. (Royal Acorn and Early Golden Bush Scallop were found to be resistant to both the striped and spotted cucumber beetles.)
● Moderately resistant (seedlings): Boston Marrow, Buttercup and Pink Banana

Moderately resistant (foliage): Green Hubbard, Pink Banana, Seneca Zucchini, Summer Crookneck and Summer Straightneck.
● Susceptible (seedlings): Benning's Green Tint Scallop, Black Zucchini, Cozella, Cozini, Seneca Zucchini and Zucchini.

Susceptible (foliage): Boston Marrow, Buttercup, Cozella, Cozini, Long Cocozelle, Seneca Prolific and Zucchini.
Squash bug:
● Resistant: Butternut, Table Queen, Royal Acorn, Sweet Cheese, Early Golden Bush Scallop, Early Summer Crookneck, Early Prolific Straightneck and Improved Green Hubbard.
● Susceptible: Striped Green Cushaw, Pink Banana and Black Zucchini.
Striped cucumber beetle:
● Resistant: Early Prolific Straightneck, U Conn, Long Cocozelle, White Bush Scallop, Benning's Green Tint Scallop, Early Yellow Summer Crookneck, Cozella Hybrid, Marine Black Zucchini, Butternut 23, Short

Cocozelle, Summer Crookneck and Zucchini. (Royal Acorn and Early Golden Bush Scallop were found to be resistant to both the striped and spotted cucumber beetles.)
● Susceptible: Black Zucchini, Cozini, Caserta and Black Beauty.

Sweet Potato

Southern potato wireworm:
● Resistant: Nugget and All Gold.
● Moderately resistant: Porto Rico, Centennial, Georgia Red and Gold Rush.
Sweet potato flea beetle:
● Resistant: Jewel.

Sweet potato

● Moderately resistant: Centennial, All Gold, Georgia Red, Porto Rico and Gem.
● Susceptible: Nugget, Red Jewel, Georgia 41, Nemagold and Jullian.

Tomato

Two-spotted mite:
● Resistant: Campbell 135.
● Moderately resistant: Campbell 146.
● Susceptible: Homestead 24.

Turnip

Mexican bean beetle:
● Susceptible: Amber Globe and Purple Top White Globe.
Striped flea beetle:
● Moderately resistant: Seven Top.
● Susceptible: Purple Top White Globe and Amber Globe.

Watermelon

Spotted cucumber beetle:
● Resistant (foliage): Crimson Sweet and Sweet Princess.
● Susceptible (seedlings): Blue Ribbon, Charleston Gray, Crimson Sweet, Sugar Baby and Sweet Princess.

Tomato

Crop Rotation

Follow takers with givers.

Crop rotation is a long-term soil conditioning technique that can help to balance such nutrients as nitrogen, potassium and potash in the garden and to control bacterial diseases.

Most gardeners would agree that the ideal planting sequence would be to start off with a nitrogen-fixing legume, follow it with a nitrogen-loving leaf crop, then raise a root crop, and finally, after dressing the bed heavily with compost, grow a heavy-feeding fruit crop. This crop rotation cycle would be a three- to four-year one. If you're rarely able to achieve that optimal sequence, you might try operating by this simple formula: Divide everything you plant into four groups—legume, root, leaf and fruiting crops—and refuse to plant two of the same type consecutively in the same place. Another uncomplicated rotational sequence can be devised by dividing your crops into three groups based on how they take from, and give back to, the soil. Heavy takers are followed by lighter takers, which are followed by givers (these replenish the soil). A variation is permissible: A heavy taker may be followed by a replenisher, which would then be followed by a light taker, but a light taker shouldn't be followed by a heavy taker without replenishment.

Crop rotation does help prevent the spread of soilborne diseases, so make an effort not to raise different vegetables from the same family successively in a growing space. Focus on these three vegetable groups, which are especially susceptible to bacterial infection: the *cucurbits* (squash, cucumbers and melons), the *brassicas* (broccoli, cauliflower, cabbage, Brussels sprouts, turnips, mustards, collards and kale) and the *nightshades* (potatoes, peppers, tomatoes and eggplant). It's also wise to avoid back-to-back plantings of members of the *Umbelliferae* family (carrots, parsley, parsnips and dill) and the *Chenopodiaceae*, or goosefoot, family (beets, spinach, chard and lamb's-quarters).

GIVE-AND-TAKE CROP ROTATION CHART

Heavy Takers
Asparagus
Beets
Broccoli
Brussels sprouts
Cabbages
Cauliflower
Celery
Collards
Corn
Cucumbers
Eggplant
Endive and Escarole
Kale
Kohlrabi
Lettuce
Okra
Parsley
Pumpkins
Radishes
Rhubarb
Spinach
Squash, summer
Squash, winter
Tomatoes

Light Takers
Carrots
Garlic
Leeks
Mustard
Onions
Parsnips
Peppers
Potatoes
Rutabaga
Shallots
Sweet potatoes
Swiss chard
Turnips

Givers
Alfalfa
Beans, broad
Beans, lima
Beans, snap
Clover
Peanuts
Peas
Soybeans

Coping With Garden Pests

How to control everything
from aphids, loopers and borers to
rabbits, woodchucks and crows

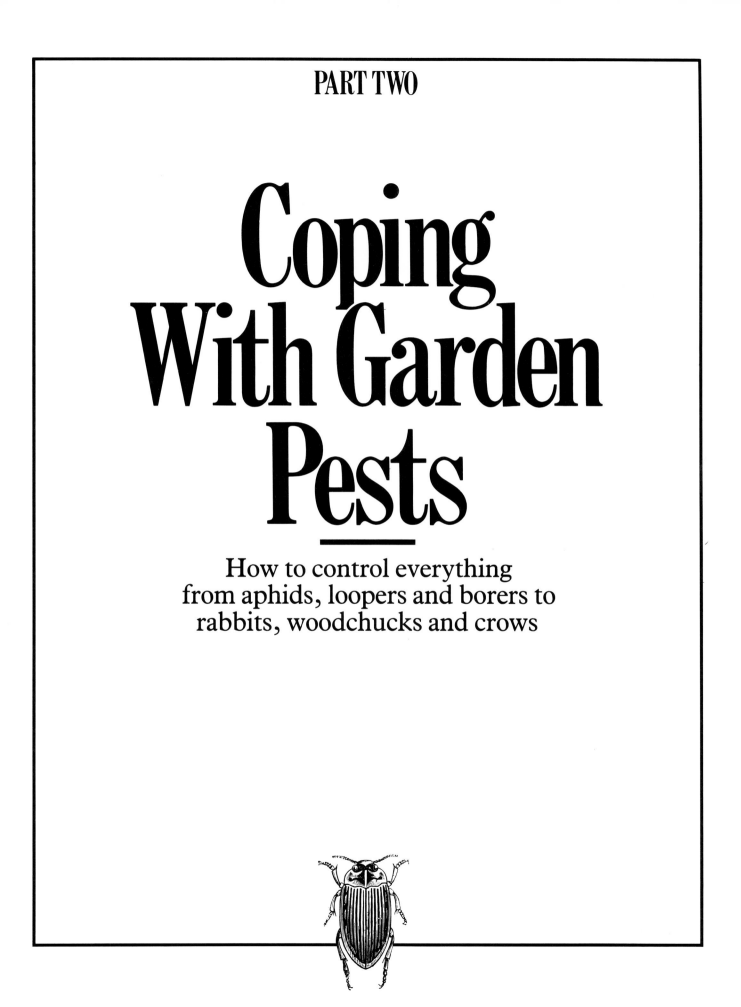

"Bad bug" Japanese beetle (this page) and "good bug" praying mantis (opposite): In fact, their interaction makes for the most effective insect control of all.

Never Cry Bug

What we don't know *can* hurt us.

It was late morning during my summer as an apprentice at the *Mother Earth News* research gardens when someone spotted a praying mantis in one of the flower beds. Soon we gardeners were all drawn to watch. The female mantis had captured a spider. She carried the victim over her forelimb like a basket—spidery legs rounded into a handle, plump body the precious contents.

For over an hour we sat watching the mantis. We shifted our weight countless times and made repeated motions to leave, but kept feeling pulled back to the sight, as if by a thread of spider's silk. By the time the gathering finally dispersed, we had all concluded that sitting and watching a praying mantis at work was just as essential to good gardening as turning compost or weeding.

Beginning gardeners, like new parents, are constantly besieged with advice, and a good portion of that counsel has to do with insects—often put in highly aggressive, pejorative terms: "Better wipe out those damned bugs or there won't be anything left to eat." Such fears come from ignorance, and they encourage us to use poisons almost indiscriminately. But what is the truth? Are all bugs bad? How should we deal with them?

Let's look at a few facts. The average square yard of a garden contains over a thousand insects; the average acre, 4 million. Those simple numbers alone suggest that the vast majority of insects must *not* be eating our crops, since otherwise there would be no crops left.

But if the insects are not ravaging everything that grows, then what are they doing? They are fertilizing and helping create soil by breaking down dead organic matter. They pollinate most all food crops and flowers. They produce honey, silk and other valuable products. They eat weeds. They themselves are eaten by (and serve as a food source for) birds, mammals and reptiles. They also control each other's populations.

Some insects obviously cause genuine harm to garden crops. But even that action is not an unqualified evil. It's now fairly common knowledge, for example, that insects prefer to feed on weak and sickly plants, helping to ensure that the fittest plants survive. Agricultural scientists have noted that insect infestations sometimes actually increase crop yields. I saw this firsthand one year when half my pea seedlings were

defoliated by a still undetermined culprit. I gave up the gnawed ones for lost. But four weeks later, all the pea plants had reached the same height, and the "insect-pruned" vines were stockier and more productive than the unmolested ones.

In one of my favorite books, *Never Cry Wolf*, Farley Mowat describes how hunters in northern Canada blamed wolves for the decline in caribou, when it was the hunters' own greed and wastefulness that actually caused the problem. The Ihalmiut Indians of the area were closer to the truth. They felt the wolf was a gift from God sent to cull the weak and sickly caribou. To those native people, the wolf ensured that the caribou would always remain a strong species.

Too often we gardeners are quick to point the finger and "cry bug," forgetting that destructive insects play important roles in maintaining the checks and balances of the natural world. Not only do they "cull the weak and sickly," they themselves are food for beneficial insects and animals. Indeed, many times one of the surest ways to worsen an infestation is to temporarily wipe out the offending insect. By doing so, we may drive away or poison off the other insects or animals that help keep the offender's numbers down. Then, when that insect returns, it faces no natural enemies and can multiply and cause more havoc than ever.

There are, then, two keys to properly dealing with insect problems in the garden. One is to realize there are no clear-cut distinctions. In reality, there are no good bugs and no bad bugs. Destructive insects have their useful functions, and beneficial insects sometimes do things we might consider harmful. (That praying mantis was eating a spider—a predator that's fully as useful to gardeners as the mantis itself.) So even though this field guide employs the simplistic concepts of "beneficial" and "harmful" to help

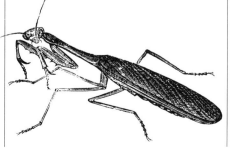

gardeners deal with specific problems, one of its main purposes is to help us all think beyond such labels. Let's take the white hats and black hats off our images of the creatures in our gardens and remember that their own interactions make for the most effective insect control of all.

Acknowledging this first key should convince us that spraying strong chemical pesticides is counterproductive to good gardening. We don't need to do it, and, in the long run, it can make matters worse.

Clearly, however, there *are* times when some insect or animal begins to cause intolerable damage to a garden crop, times when we will want to intervene directly. That's where the second key comes in: knowledge. We need to be sure we know precisely what creatures are causing the damage and what appropriate control measures to take—actions that will solve the specific problem without producing damaging side effects.

It's that kind of precision in diagnosis and treatment that this guide seeks to offer. It covers more than 60 of the insects and animals most commonly encountered in the garden. It provides clear color-identification photos and detailed descriptions. And it has a thorough listing of natural controls. To my knowledge, it represents the first time that good identifying photos and solid control advice have been assembled in the same publication.

In dealing with insect control in the garden, what we don't know *can* hurt us. It may be tempting to squash that fierce-jawed, little black-and-red "thing" on a perforated leaf of Swiss chard, while never realizing the "thing," a ladybug larva, is busily scarfing down the aphids causing the real damage. Or easy to blame a creepy-looking (but quite helpful) assassin bug we see near our lettuce during the day for the damage slugs are causing at night.

It's my opinion that if every gardener could identify and know the habits of, say, 15 of the most common insect pests and 10 of the most common beneficial insects, there'd be a revolution in the way such people approach all insects. There'd be more awe and less fear, more patience and less anger, more peace of mind and less poisons of any kind.
—*Susan Sides*
Head Gardener
Mother Earth News

Intervention
When it's time to act

If necessity is the mother of invention, then desperation is the father. Ask any gardener whose cherished plants start falling prey to pests. Anything short of agent orange and other dangerous chemicals seems worth a try to stop the invasion.

Little wonder that over the centuries gardeners of every stripe and persuasion have contributed to a ponderous list of antipest measures. Some, like the Victorian prescription for soaking seeds in whiskey to make them unpalatable to God-fearing birds, are plainly ludicrous. Others are only marginally useful, giving gardeners little more than a sense of doing *something* about a problem—rather than arming them with a genuinely efficacious means for solving it. And still others work too well, destroying not only the target creatures but virtually everything else living nearby.

The following controls are among the handful that seem, in relative terms at least, to be both effective and safe. Keep in mind, however, that these are only controls, helpful for reducing or discouraging an infestation or for minimizing damage, but not for curing conditions that lead to outbreaks (which are usually related to a garden's general health). Moreover, it should be kept in mind that even the most harmless-seeming "organic" controls can be misused. A garden should always be given a chance to take care of itself before you intervene. A measure as apparently benign, for example, as spraying plants with a forceful jet of water to wash away aphids can also send untold numbers of other small beneficial insects sprawling. Given a few days of grace, the beneficials might have kept the aphids and other pests in check.

Traps & Barriers

Traps

Most gardeners know about the simple, classic trap for slugs: a saucer of stale beer placed strategically at ground level, perhaps with a bit of flour mixed in to keep the victims stuck in place. There are many other kinds of traps, but the principle's the same: Give them bait they can't resist, and put it in a place from which there is no escape.

Yellow sticky traps. Some insects, particularly aphids, whiteflies and leaf miners, are attracted to the color yellow. Yellow traps that lure such pests to a sticky end can either be bought or made at home: Simply coat both sides of yellow-painted panels—pieces of plywood or stiff cardboard—with a tacky substance such as Tanglefoot, Stickem (commercial products available from garden supply companies) or glycerin; then either hang the traps at the height of the foliage or prop them upright among infested plants. Recoat or replace the traps as necessary.

Homemade lures and jar traps. Some of the simplest traps consist of nothing more than bait. An example is the wireworm trap: Cut a potato in half, remove the eyes and shove a 6″ stick into each piece. Bury the spuds an inch or two deep in the problem area, with the sticks protruding above ground. After a couple of days a dozen or more wireworms may be feeding on each piece. Pull the traps up by their "handles" and dispose of them, or remove the worms and rebury the spuds. Another all-in-one trap: a cabbage leaf placed on the ground to draw cutworms and snails.

Many flying and jumping insects can be trapped and drowned in jars containing an enticing liquid—usually water sweetened with sugar, molasses or an aromatic oil such as that of citronella, sassafras, anise or fennel. Lemon and vanilla extract, pine tar oil and vinegar have also been used with success. A recipe that's said to draw hordes of moth-stage pests, including cabbage loopers and fruit worms: Put a banana peel and a cup each of sugar and vinegar in a gallon milk jug; fill the container almost to the top with water, shake well and hang the open jug from a tree. And here's a jug trap baited with a wine that's said to be fatally popular among Japanese beetles: Ferment together a cup or two of sugar, some mashed fruit and enough water to almost fill a gallon jar (add a little yeast to speed up the process); then hang the container upwind from the plants to be protected. (Never put an aromatic trap right next to the plants. Insects follow scents upwind, so it's best to place such traps upwind of garden or orchard.)

Virtually all garden-supply companies offer ready-made versions of most of the traps described, as well as scented lures and baits formulated specifically for slugs, Japanese beetles and most other major insect pests (see the chapter "Shopping for Insects" on page 136). A variety of comparatively high-tech traps are also available to the adventurous gardener.

Pheromone traps. Pheromones are complex compounds secreted by insects (and animals too) to communicate with others of the same species. Pheromones can signal alarm, location of food, desire for mating, etc. Scientists have isolated many of these substances—concentrating primarily on sex attractants—and synthesized them for use as bait. Most of the pheromone traps available to gardeners are cardboard structures coated with a sticky substance and baited with an attractant for a specific pest. Traps for Japanese beetles, corn earworms, tomato pinworms, cucumber beetles, codling moths, black cutworms, peach twig borers and about a dozen others are currently on the market. It is also possible to buy the pheromone bait alone for use in homemade traps.

Black light traps and bug zappers. Insects are drawn to light like, well, like moths

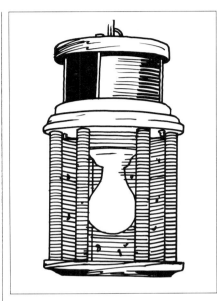

to a flame. Even an ordinary light bulb left on outside overnight above a bucket of water will attract and drown hundreds of bugs. But night fliers (including the adult moths of dozens of major pest species like tomato hornworms, corn earworms, European corn borers and cabbage loopers) seem particularly drawn to the ultraviolet spectrum emitted by a black light. When used to attract insects to a holding trap or electrocuting wire grid, black lights can be extraordinarily effective. There are some drawbacks, however. The lights require an external power source, zappers can be noisy and, most important, the traps can attract large numbers of both harmful and beneficial bugs. This is true of nearly all types of traps to some extent, so it's important to monitor what is caught. If significant numbers of beneficial insects show up in the trap, a different type of control may be in order. Unfortunately, zappers leave little left of their victims, making monitoring difficult.

Mammal traps. Although various methods can be used to discourage animal visitations (see the section on "Barriers" below), sometimes the only effective control short of shooting is trapping. The compassionate gardener may prefer the commercial catch-and-release wire traps, such as Havahart (available in sizes for animals from mice to large raccoons). Deadlier traps are usually necessary to get rid of gophers and moles. Garden suppliers offer a variety of models.

Nettings and Coverings

Single-plant insect barriers for such vegetables as cabbage and broccoli are easy to make: Cut the legs of old nylons or pantyhose into sections, close the tops, slip the "caps" over the plants, and then shut the bottoms. The material will expand as the plant grows.

Row covers or cloches, used primarily to extend the growing season and to protect plants from frost, also make it easy to keep insects off an entire bed or wide row. Tunnellike covers made of polyethylene film supported by a series of wire hoops are the most common type, although these must be vented to prevent overheating and to keep condensed moisture from fostering fungus diseases, and can accommodate only plants shorter than the supports. Cheesecloth is sometimes used as a cover material, but its open mesh allows some small insects to crawl through. Also, the absorbent material becomes plant-crushingly heavy when wet, making it necessary to remove the cover before a rain or to use a supporting framework. Wire hoops can be bought or a simple support system can be made from wire coat hangers. Bend several hangers so that each makes a diamond shape; then straighten their hooks. Drive a stake at each end of the bed to be covered, and suspend the hangers at intervals along a wire or strong cord stretched between the stakes. Stick the straightened

hooks into the ground to anchor the hangers.

Breathable, "floating" row covers made from new, superlightweight textiles offer particular convenience as insect screens and season extenders. One such cover is Reemay, a spunbond polyester that resembles the inner liner of a disposable diaper (though it's heavier-duty and, with care, can be used for several seasons). Reemay allows air, sunlight and moisture in (plants can be watered through it) and needs no support system. The material need only be loosely draped right on top of growing plants and the edges anchored with rocks or earth. The foliage pushes the lightweight cover up as it grows. Reemay comes in 67″-wide rolls, in varying lengths.

Bird netting. Not all birds rob berry bushes and fruit trees, but those that do—starlings, jays and robins among them—can take a heavy toll. Some large-scale growers build huge metal cages around entire rows of trees or bushes. Fabric netting is more practical for home gardeners. Cheesecloth works but tends to snag and tear. Commercial netting, made from plastic, nylon or polypropylene, is easier to put up and take down, and lasts several seasons. It's available in many widths and lengths (even 5,000′ rolls are advertised). For thorough protection, the netting should cover the entire tree or bush. Netting alone, however, isn't effective on blueberries and other plants that produce fruit at the tips of their branches. Birds simply light on the netting and peck at the fruit or knock ripe berries to the ground. In such cases it is necessary to build a framework to support the netting about a foot from the branch tips.

Barriers

Obviously, pests have to get to plants to damage them. Protective barriers can make the trip uncomfortable (for crawling insects, at least) or out-and-out impossible.

Mulches and borders. Some insects, including the Colorado potato beetle, striped cucumber beetle and spotted cucumber beetle, will avoid a deep mulch of straw, hay or leaves. Other pests, notably the squash bug, prefer such a covering, but are put off by a more solid mulch material such as compost or black plastic.

One mulch that's effective against some flying insects—including thrips and aphids —is aluminum foil. The material's reflective quality apparently confuses them; they can't tell up from down, so they go elsewhere. If raccoons are a problem in a corn patch, a layer of black plastic mulch may help; some gardeners report that coons are wary of walking across it (others say the masked foragers get used to it).

To keep squash vine borers away, wrap strips of aluminum foil or pieces of women's stockings around the stems of squash plants. Tanglefoot and Stickem can be spread around the trunks of trees and large plants (such as tomatoes) to create an adhesive "moat" against ants and other crawlers. Another effective commercial barrier is Snail-Barr, a flexible 3″-wide copper strip, usually sold by the foot, that can be placed around tree trunks or used as a border around beds or greenhouses. Copper naturally creates a mild electric current that, though undetectable to humans, gives snails and slugs an unpleasant shock.

Irritants and odor repellents. A sprinkling of wood ashes around plants will discourage many kinds of insects. Other irritants popularly strewn around plants include crushed black pepper, camphor, crushed eggshells, rock phosphate, cedar or oak sawdust (or chips), gravel, powdered charcoal, sharp (builder's) sand, diatomaceous earth or lime.

Odor can be a strong deterrent to pests, particularly mammals. Blood meal or dried blood spread around beds or hung from bushes or low trees in small cloth bags repels deer and rabbits. A spray made from four or five eggs and a gallon of water will keep deer from corn, beans and other crops without exposed edible parts; the rotting-egg odor is strong enough to be noticed by deer, but not by humans. Urine is another effective odor repellent. Some rural gardeners make a habit of occasionally answering the call of nature along the borders of their gardens. A sprinkling of well-used cat litter around beds should deter rabbits.

Fences. In rural areas especially, a fence may be the best way to keep trespassing mammals from vegetable patches. The kind of fence to use depends on the type of animal. A two- or three-foot-high chicken wire fence is enough to bar rabbits, but woodchucks, raccoons and dogs call for something more substantial. With deer, the problem and the solution are bigger still.

Generally, the best (easiest to put up, least expensive, most convenient) choice for the average gardener with an average garden and average-size pests (anything smaller than a goat or deer) is a simple two- or three-strand electric fence powered by a six-volt plug-in or battery-driven pulsed charger. A basic charger will cost about $45 (plus $18 for a battery if needed); 19-gauge steel wire runs under $10 for a 500′ roll. Plastic insulators (under $2 for two dozen) and 3′ stakes are also required—wooden stakes are inexpensive while fiberglass posts cost a dollar or two each (but push into the ground easily and don't require insulators). The first strand of wire should be placed 4″ off the ground, the

second 10″ and the third—if needed—16″. The area under the fence will need to be mowed or cultivated; otherwise, weeds or grass will short out the circuit and render the system useless.

Eight feet is generally considered the minimum height for a nonelectric deer fence, five or six feet for a multistrand electric barrier. Since standard woven-wire farm fence is 4′ tall, some gardeners simply stack one course of woven-wire fence on top of another to produce an eight-footer.

Sprays & Insecticides

Homemade Plant Sprays

Most insects and animals naturally shy away from food that tastes or smells bad or that makes them ill. This behavior has set untold generations of gardeners to work concocting countless homemade repellents. Recipes vary widely, but the vast majority use as ingredients members of the allium family (onion, garlic, chives), hot peppers (jalapeño, cayenne), pungent herbs (basil, nettle, coriander, anise, eucalyptus, wormwood, cedar, peppermint)—or some combination thereof. Generally, the same plants recommended as live repellents (see "Plant Allies" on page 118) are equally, if not more, effective when used as sprays. What works in one garden won't necessarily work in another, however, so individual experimentation may be necessary.

The easiest way to make a spray is to either mix the ingredients together with water in a blender or steep them together for a day or more in hot water. Then strain the liquid, if necessary, through cheesecloth. Some gardeners routinely add a bit of mineral or salad oil, or soap, to help the spray stick to the plants. Since such sprays wash away with rain or heavy dew, they have to be reapplied regularly.

Some sample recipes: "Solar tea" made of chopped hot peppers, onion and garlic cloves left to steep in a large jar of water set in the sun for several days will repel many insects,

including aphids, thrips and grasshoppers. Equal parts of wood ashes and lime diluted in water should chase away cucumber beetles. A spray made of crushed turnips (or parsnips) and corn oil is said to repel or even kill Mexican bean beetles. (The same pest is also averse to a cedar-water spray made by boiling cedar chips or sawdust in water.) And tea made of wormwood (artemisia), an herbal poison, has been used for centuries to repel slugs and many other pests including moles and gophers.

Pathogenic Insecticides

Many insects are host to pathogens, or diseases, that are unique to the infected species or order and harmless to other insects, birds, animals and humans. Some of these diseases have been isolated and serve as highly effective, selective insecticides that attack only the target pest. All such pathogens degrade quickly in sunlight and should be either used as soon as possible or stored in a cool, dark place. They are best applied in early morning or late afternoon; if mixed with water to make a spray, better results occur if the pH of the water is between 5 and 6.

BT, or *Bacillus thuringiensis*. The larvae of more than 60 species of lepidoptera—moths and butterflies—are susceptible to BT, including cabbageworms, leaf miners, cab-

bage loopers, European corn borers and corn earworms. A special strain for the Colorado potato beetle is also available. BT comes in liquid, dust and granular forms sold under such brand names as Dipel, Thuricide and Biotrol. Once pest caterpillars are infected with the store-bought variety, it becomes possible to culture the bacteria, just as yogurt is made by starting a new batch with a bit of the old. Pluck a dozen or so infected—but not yet dead—worms (the larvae will look and act sick), mash or blend them together with about a pint of warm milk and let the concoction stand three days in a warm place. Then strain the mixture through cheesecloth and dilute the liquid with enough water to make a gallon of insecticide. BT is a stomach pathogen and must be ingested by larvae to be effective; it kills within 24 hours. Because of its vulnerability to sunlight and temperature, repeated applications are often necessary.

Milky spore disease, or *Bacillus popillae*, is a slow-acting, long-term control against Japanese beetles. Applied to lawns or soil, the bacteria slowly spread, multiplying and killing any Japanese beetle grubs they encounter. Once all the grubs are destroyed, the milky spores become dormant and prevent future infestations. Milky spore disease won't help turn the tide of an existing outbreak, and Japanese beetles may return the following season; but within two to three years the spore should have spread sufficiently to provide effective control for up to 15 to 20 years. Milky spore is usually sold as a powder consisting of infected, ground-up grubs mixed with a carrier such as chalk. Brand names include Doom and Grub Attack.

NPV, or nuclear polyhedrosis virus. This pathogen isn't available commercially, but if you raise cabbage and can find loopers infected with NPV, you can make your own. Look for cabbage loopers (see page 80) that have turned chalky white and appear nearly dead; they may be lying motionless on top of leaves or hanging from the underside. After finding a dozen or so sick loopers, run them through a blender with a little water, then dilute the mixture to make a sprayable liquid. Effective against cabbage loopers and corn earworms, NPV is longer-lasting but slower-acting than BT. It takes five to six

days to kill, but a single application may be enough for a whole season.

Bug juice. A more haphazard approach to making and using pathogenic insecticides, but often effective nonetheless, is to concoct a batch of what is collectively known as "bug juice." Aficionados gather a number of whichever insects are troublesome, making sure to collect only that species. The insects are ground with water in a blender, strained if necessary, then diluted with more water and finally sprayed on the plants being eaten. (The more insects gathered, the more the mix can be diluted; a quart of caterpillars can make dozens of gallons of spray.) Bug juice has been effective on bean and potato beetles, squash bugs, ants, slugs, grasshoppers and many kinds of caterpillars. The theory is that at least some of the insects harvested carry one or more pathogens that, when liberated as a spray on plants, infect other members of the same species.

Mineral-Based Insecticides

Safer's Insecticidal Soap. Ordinary soap, sprayed in solution with water, discourages such insects as flea beetles and aphids. Safer's, however, is a special soap derived from potassium salts that smothers its victims—whiteflies, aphids, spider mites, leafhoppers, even grasshoppers. One of the

oldest commercial organic insecticides, Safer's contains no petroleum products and is biodegradable and nontoxic to beneficials and plants. It is sold both as a concentrate and in ready-to-use spray bottles.

Diatomaceous earth. From a gardener's perspective, diatomaceous earth is a flourlike dust made by grinding and milling the fossilized shells of tiny sea creatures called diatoms. From a soft-bodied insect's point of view, diatomaceous earth is a mass of razor-sharp silica daggers that kill on contact by scraping or piercing the skin and dehydrating the body. After it is consumed by an insect, DE clogs the respiratory and digestive systems. In addition to controlling such pests as aphids, spider mites, fleas, snails and slugs, DE is rich in trace minerals and supplements soil fertility. Use only DE designed for agricultural use, *not* that intended for swimming pool filters. Diatomaceous earth is applied as a dust or as a water slurry.

Botanic Insecticides

These insecticides come last because that is how they should be viewed: a last resort, to be used only when the garden is suffering intolerable damage and all other measures have failed. Botanic insecticides are made from natural plant materials and break down quickly into harmless substances. They don't accumulate in the environment or the tissues of living creatures, and insect pests apparently don't develop resistance to them (as happens with many nonorganic pesticides). However, these insecticides are not entirely without untoward effects: They're nonselective poisons that kill most insects in the treated area, including, in many cases, beneficials such as ladybugs and honeybees. (It's always best to apply late in the day, when bees have returned to their hives.) Unfortunately, used routinely or as a quick fix for any insect outbreak, botanicals can do more harm than good to a garden, upsetting the relationship of predators, parasites and hosts.

Regardless of which botanical is used, hands and other exposed parts of the skin should be washed after application. Clothing should be laundered. Don't wear contact lenses when spraying or dusting plants. Take care not to get insecticide in eyes or in cuts or sores. In that event, flush those areas im-mediately with water. Gardeners suffering from asthma, hay fever or other respiratory ailments should avoid breathing in the dust.

Pyrethrin. Generally considered among the most effective of botanical insecticides, pyrethrin is made from the crushed dried flowers of a daisylike perennial, *Chrysanthemum cinerariaefolium* (more commonly called pyrethrum). Usually applied as a spray, the insecticide acts quickly; it passes directly through the skin of insects and disrupts nerve centers, agitating the insects and causing them to become disoriented and stunned. For this reason, pyrethrin is known as an exciter and is used not only to kill insects but also to flush them out of hiding places. Some gardeners apply a light dose of pyrethrin—just enough to coax insects out in the open and stun them but not kill them—and then hand-pick the pest species, leaving the beneficials to recover. Pesticide manufacturers often combine pyrethrin with stronger synthesized poisons, using it to bring insects out where they'll be exposed to the more deadly ingredient.

Pyrethrin is effective against aphids, thrips, leafhoppers and many beetles. It should be applied in the evening to avoid killing honeybees. Since it is toxic to fish, it should not be used near streams. Widely available as both a concentrate and ready-to-use spray, pyrethrin is often combined with piperonyl butoxide (PBO), a sassafras extract said to increase the insecticide's effectiveness. However, some researchers suspect PBO of having mutagenic properties. Though harder to find, pyrethrin without PBO can be bought (Raid Tomato and Vegetable Fogger is one such product), as can plain crushed pyrethrum flowers. Some seed companies now offer *C. cinerariaefolium* seeds, so gardeners can grow their own insecticide and sprinkle the crushed dried flowers around infested plants.

Rotenone. Probably the most widely available botanic insecticide, rotenone is also, unfortunately, one of the most toxic. Derived from the roots of tropical plants in the genus *Derris*, it was originally used by tribal fishermen as a fish stunner. Rotenone is primarily a stomach poison and takes a bit longer than pyrethrin to act. It is effective against squash bugs, cucumber and flea beetles, Japanese beetles, mites, leafhoppers, thrips and others. It is available as either a dust or a concentrated extract in varying strengths; the most common and easiest form for gardeners is 1% rotenone dust. It is also found mixed in combination with pyrethrin or ryania. Rotenone dust can irritate breathing passages, so always wear a dust mask when applying.

Ryania. Made from the ground roots and stems of *Ryania speciosa*, a shrub native to Trinidad, ryania is not only harmless to warm-blooded animals but also somewhat selective; it can be used against target pests—particularly codling moths, leaf rollers and corn earworms—without harming as many beneficials as pyrethrin or rotenone. It is not effective, however, against such insects as cabbage maggots, Japanese beetle larvae and spider mites. Ryania's active ingredient, ryanodine, is a stomach and contact poison that kills by paralysis. Unlike other botanicals, this insecticide is highly stable in sunlight (it works best in hot weather) and retains its potency for several years when stored in a cool, dry place. Ryania is sold as a dust, either full-strength or in combination with diatomaceous earth.

Sabadilla. Though little known today, this powerful insecticide has been in use since the sixteenth century. Sabadilla dust is made from the seeds of a lily-family plant native to South America and Mexico; interestingly, scientists have found that the insecticide becomes more powerful in storage. It can be used to control European corn borers, aphids, webworms, squash bugs, cabbage loopers and blister beetles, among others. Sabadilla is said to have little effect on mammals and beneficial insects. It can, however, irritate mucous membranes, so take care not to breathe it in.

Quassia. Probably the most benign of botanical insecticides, this one comes from the quassia tree, which grows in Jamaica. Though effective against aphids, caterpillars and most other soft-bodied pests, it doesn't harm bees, ladybugs or other beneficials. Quassia is sold in the form of wood chips, shavings or bark. To make a spray, the material should be steeped or boiled in water and then strained.

Other Controls

Hand-picking. Removing bugs by hand and destroying them may not be pleasant duty, but it's unquestionably one of the most effective of all pest-control techniques. Hand-picking is especially important early in the season, when overwintered insects lay eggs to produce the next generation. Morning is usually the best time to tackle the task; most species are sluggish in the early hours and can easily be plucked off leaves or knocked off onto the ground or a cloth spread below to catch them. Diligence is essential; look carefully under leaves, at the junctions of stems and branches and around the bases of plants. Some species, such as Mexican bean beetles and their bright yellow larvae and egg clusters, are easy to spot; others, such as pale green cabbage loopers, require a keen eye. Choose your own method of destruction. Squishing them is easiest, but not for

the squeamish. If you have chickens or other poultry that appreciate a good breakfast, drop the bugs into a container of water topped with a bit of salad oil (to keep the insects from escaping) and serve. If extermination is the only motive, drop the insects into kerosene or water topped with kerosene. In any case, take care not to kill beneficial insects in the process, and learn to recognize desirable species and their eggs.

Water sprays. Giving infested plants a good, hard hosing down will dislodge many insect pests, particularly aphids, thrips and various worms. Plants should first be inspected to confirm the target insect.

Irritant dusts. Giving plant leaves a light dusting of slaked lime, wood ashes or diatomaceous earth (see the chapter "New Natural Controls") can chase away many pest species. A sprinkling of bone meal will discourage asparagus beetles, and rock phosphate can expel cucumber beetles. It's usually best to apply the powder in the morning, when the dust will stick to the dew on leaves. Dewy mornings are also good times for shaking rye or wheat flour on cabbage plants; the resulting dough will cling to worms and moths, forming a fatal crust when it dries.

Scare tactics. The old-fashioned scarecrow receives mixed reviews: It works—sometimes. So do the plastic snakes and owls sold by most garden suppliers. All are designed to scare birds, rabbits, rodents and other skittish pests. Moving the decoys occasionally increases their effectiveness, since animals and birds apparently become accustomed to scare devices that remain motionless for days. More elaborate and more expensive (and reportedly more effective) decoys include predator bird kites. Sold in life-size hawk, eagle, falcon and buzzard models, the tethered kites are suspended by a helium balloon and fly up to 200′ above the ground. Their swooping motions are realistic enough to frighten small animals and birds.

Other scare devices range from simple windmills that make a klippety-klop noise (said to be annoying to gophers) to high-priced ultrasonic transmitters that emit high-frequency sound waves inaudible to all but the animals for which the device is tuned. A lower-tech ultrasound device, sold commercially, is plastic tape—resembling the tape in an audio cassette—that, when stretched between two stakes, produces a rabbit-distressing hum. Many gardeners hang aluminum pie pans, strips of tinfoil and other reflective or noisy materials between rows. Some gardeners who have both ripening sweet corn and hungry raccoons claim that leaving at least one transistor radio turned on in the garden at night, set to a 24-hour station, keeps the raiders away.

Gluttony. There's a certain irony in destroying insect pests by feeding them to death. If Colorado potato beetles pose a problem, sprinkle dry wheat bran on potato plants early in the morning; the beetles will eat the bran, drink dew to slake their thirst—and burst from the water-expanded meal. (Some say the same recipe works for Mexican bean beetles.) Cutworms readily eat cornmeal but can't metabolize it, so providing it gives them terminal indigestion. Cabbage worms, too, have a fatal preference: A meal of one part salt to two parts flour.

Peak Infestation Times

Insect emergence times are roughly the same within each of these 18 zones, though actual times will vary with altitude.

Region	Asparagus Beetle	Bean Aphid	Cabbage Looper	Colorado Potato Beetle	Corn Earworm	Flea Beetle
1	Mid-June	NA	July	June	July	June
2	May	NA	June–July	May	August	May–June
3	Late April–May	NA	July–September	May	June–August	April–May
4	Early May	Early June	June	Early May	July–September	Early May
5	April–May	May–June	Late April–May	May	June	April–July
6	NA	October–May	Entire season	March–May	Spring–Fall	April–August
7	NA	March	Early March	NA	June–mid-July	March–April
8	May	Spring	Spring	April–May	Spring	Late May
9	May	June	August	May–June	Late July–August	May–June
10	May–June	NA	July	June	July–August	NA
11	April–May	NA	Spring	April–May	June–September	April–May
12	March–April	NA	Year-round	NA	May–early June	April–August
13	Mid-June	NA	May	June	July	June
14	Late May–June	June–August	June–September	Late June	Late July	June–July
15	May–June	June–August	May–September	Mid-June	July	June
16	NA	Spring–Fall	September–October	NA	NA	NA
17	NA	Spring–Fall	August–October	NA	NA	NA
18	April–June	May–July	April–May	April–June	June–July	Late May–June

NA = not applicable

COPING WITH GARDEN PESTS

Mexican Bean Beetle	Pea Aphid	Spotted Cucumber Beetle	Squash Bug	Squash Vine Borer	Striped Cucumber Beetle	Region
Early June	June	Mid-June	NA	NA	June	1
June	April	Mid-June	June	June–July	June	2
May	April	May–June	May–June	May–June	Late May–June	3
June	April	June	June	June	June	4
May	May	May	May	Late June–July	May	5
NA	Entire season	Entire season	March–August	August–October	NA	6
NA	March	NA	June	June–July	NA	7
March–June	May–June	Spring	June	Entire season	May	8
NA	April–May	May–August	NA	NA	NA	9
NA	May–June	June	NA	June–July	NA	10
NA	April	May	June–August	July	NA	11
NA	March–April	NA	May–June	Late May–June	NA	12
NA	May	May	Late Spring	June	NA	13
June–July	May–September	NA	August–September	NA	NA	14
May–July	May–September	NA	July–August	NA	NA	15
NA	NA	NA	NA	NA	NA	16
NA	NA	NA	NA	NA	NA	17
NA	May–June	NA	April–May	NA	NA	18

What Makes an Insect

Body divisions, legs
and remarkable tenacity

The vast majority of entries in this field guide are insects. Knowing a little about their biology will help the gardener who wants to identify them and discourage, or encourage, their presence.

The Two Proofs

All adult insects have two qualifying characteristics:
● They have three body divisions: the head, the thorax and the abdomen.
● They have three pairs of legs, all attached to the thorax.

The head of an adult insect contains its antennae, mouth and (compound) eyes. The thorax bears the legs and wings (if the insect has wings). The abdomen contains the digestive and reproductive organs. An adult insect also has an exoskeleton, a hard outer shell, instead of an internal backbone. (It's an invertebrate, not a vertebrate.) And it breathes through little holes in its abdomen called spiracles. But the truly defining characteristics—the ones that say this, and only this, is an insect—are those three body parts and the six legs.

Metamorphosis

Identifying an adult insect is relatively easy. What is often more difficult is identifying an *immature* insect. Because insects have exoskeletons, they don't grow gradually the way mammals and other vertebrates do. As they grow, they periodically have to break out of an old shell and develop a new one. This process is called metamorphosis, *meta* meaning "change" and *morphe* meaning "form." And sometimes the new form is

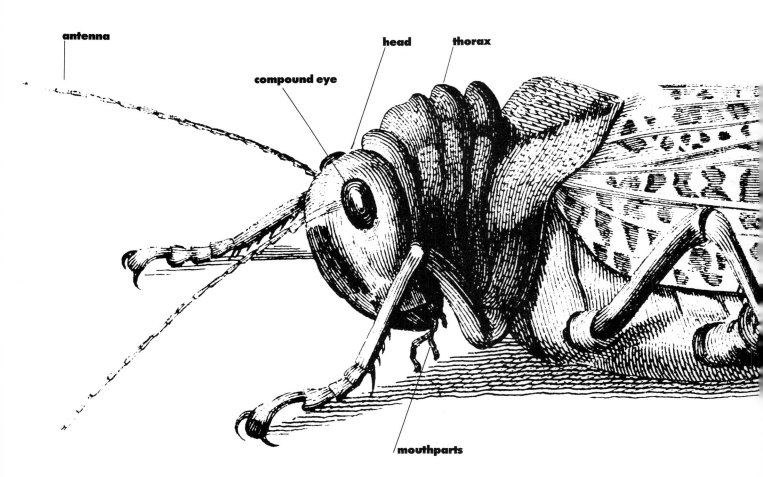

antenna

compound eye

head

thorax

mouthparts

quite different from the old one.

There are two major patterns of insect development: complete metamorphosis and incomplete metamorphosis.

Complete metamorphosis is the type we usually associate with butterflies. The insect starts out as an egg. It hatches into a larva, a soft-skinned and maggotlike, grublike or caterpillarlike creature. This larva will go through several skin-shedding stages, called *molts* or *instars*, as it grows. Most times, the different larval stages are basically similar.

But then comes "insect adolescence," the stage between larva and adult called *pupation*. At this point, the pupa stops eating, becomes inactive and—partly for protection—

Silk moth life cycle shown at right. It goes through complete metamorphosis from larva to pupa to adult.

lets its outer skin harden into a tough casing. Some insects even construct an extra protective covering called a cocoon.

Finally, a radically different creature emerges, an adult with wings and reproductive organs. Many such mature insects live only a short while, essentially existing just to reproduce and then die.

The changes are not so radical in incomplete, or gradual, metamorphosis. In this case, the egg hatches into a young insect called a *nymph*. A nymph doesn't resemble a type of worm the way a larva does; instead, it looks more or less like the adult insect it's going to become. It too will go through various molts, looking more mature after shedding each skin. Finally, after a certain number of molts, it will stop growing, have functional wings and be able to reproduce. It will be an adult.

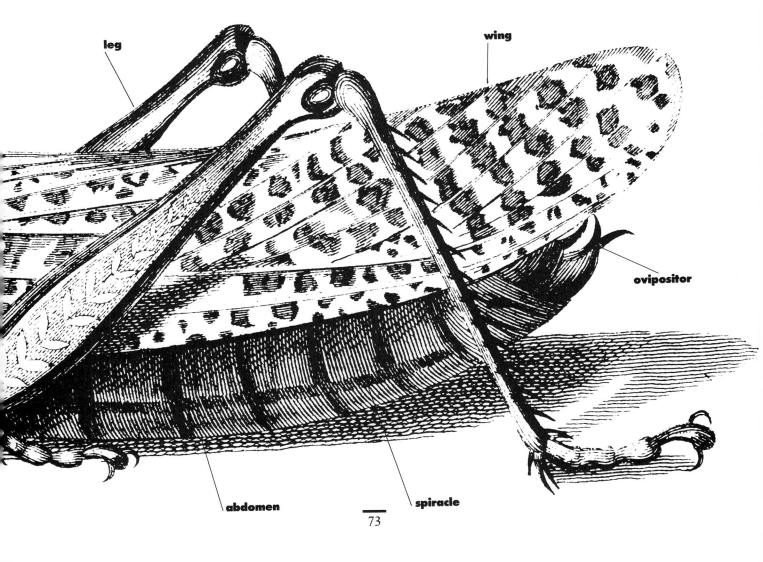

leg

wing

ovipositor

abdomen   spiracle

Shape Guide

Recognizing orders in the garden

To help you identify a particular pest or helper in your plot without having to leaf through all 48 entries, the orders of insects covered in this guide are listed below, along with the main characteristics of each order and the common names of the species they include. Three entries—spiders, nematodes, and slugs and snails—are not insects but are included because of their significance to the gardener.

COLEOPTERA ("sheath wings")

Beetles
● Every beetle has a pair of hardened wings that cover the top of its body and meet in a straight line down its back.
● Beetles have two pairs of wings, but you rarely notice the soft, membranous hind pair, which are often folded under the tough front wings.
● Every beetle goes through its larval stage as a grub, a fat or wormlike larva with a well-developed head and three pairs of legs. In almost every instance in this guide, the grub and the adult are either both harmful or both beneficial. (Grubs, however, are important enough to rate an entry of their own.)
● Beetles go through complete metamorphosis—from egg to larva to pupa to adult.

Harmful Beetles
Asparagus Beetle . . . . .p. 78
Blister Beetle . . . . .p. 80
Colorado Potato Beetle . . . . .p. 82
Flea Beetle . . . . .p. 86
Grub . . . . .p. 88
Japanese Beetle . . . . .p. 90
Mexican Bean Beetle . . . . .p. 92
Spotted Cucumber Beetle . . . . .p. 96
Striped Cucumber Beetle . . . . .p. 98
Wireworm . . . . p. 100

Beneficial Beetles
Firefly . . . . p. 104
Ground Beetle . . . . p. 106
Ladybug . . . . p. 108
Rove Beetle . . . . p. 112
Soldier Beetle . . . . p. 112
Tiger Beetle . . . . p. 116

LEPIDOPTERA ("scaly wings")

Moths and Butterflies
● Every moth or butterfly has two pairs of highly visible wings.
● The wings are covered with small scales that can easily be rubbed off.
● Moths generally fly at night, butterflies by day.
● All lepidoptera go through a larval stage as a caterpillar. Indeed, *in every case* in this guide, it is the caterpillar and not the winged adult that causes harm in the garden. Caterpillars have segmented, wormlike bodies with distinct heads, eyes and legs. Some caterpillars bore inside plants and are called borers.
● All lepidoptera go through complete metamorphosis—from egg to larva (caterpillar) to pupa (often a cocoon or chrysalis) to adult.

Harmful Lepidoptera
Cabbage Looper . . . . .p. 80
Corn Earworm . . . . .p. 82
Cutworm . . . . p. 84
European Corn Borer . . . . .p. 84
Fall Armyworm . . . . .p. 86
Hornworm . . . . .p. 88
Imported Cabbageworm . . . . .p. 88
Squash Vine Borer . . . . .p. 98

DIPTERA ("two wings")

Flies, Mosquitoes and Gnats
● Diptera are the only insects with just one pair of wings. The wings are transparent.
● All the diptera covered in this guide are types of flies.
● All flies go through a larval stage as a maggot. In many cases, the maggot does more harm or good than the adult.
● Diptera go through complete metamorphosis—from egg to maggot to pupa to adult.

Harmful Flies
Carrot Rust Fly . . . . .p. 80
Leaf Miner . . . . .p. 92

Beneficial Flies
Robber Fly . . . . p. 110
Syrphid Fly . . . . p. 114
Tachinid Fly . . . . p. 116

HEMIPTERA ("half wings")

Bugs
- All true bugs have a triangle on their backs just behind their heads.
- Hemiptera have two pairs of wings: the back pair membranous, the front pair partly hardened.
- Some bugs look like beetles, but beetles' wings form a straight line on their backs and bugs' wings form triangles.
- Bugs go through gradual metamorphosis—from egg to wingless nymph to adult. Both nymphs and adults have the same diet.

Harmful Bugs
Squash Bug..................p. 96
Tarnished Plant Bug...........p. 98

Beneficial Bugs
Assassin Bug.................. p. 102
Minute Pirate Bug............ p. 108

HOMOPTERA ("same wings")

Aphids, Cicadas and Leafhoppers
- Homoptera have two pairs of membranous wings.
- The wings are held up like a tent over the insect's body when it's at rest. Consequently, most homoptera look somewhat wedge-shaped.
- Homoptera go through gradual metamorphosis—from egg to wingless nymph to adult. Both nymphs and adults have the same diet.

Harmful Homoptera
Aphid........................p. 78
Leafhopper...................p. 90
Whitefly.....................p. 100

HYMENOPTERA ("membrane-winged")

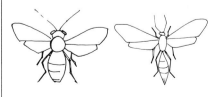

Bees, Wasps and Ants
- All hymenoptera have two pairs of clear, thin, membranous wings.
- Hymenoptera females have stingers and/or protruding egg-laying organs (ovipositors) at the end of their abdomens.
- Almost all hymenoptera are beneficial insects.
- All the hymenoptera in this guide are wasps. None of the wasps listed here is at all likely to sting humans.
- Hymenoptera go through complete metamorphosis—from egg to larva to pupa to adult.

Beneficial Wasps
Braconid.....................p. 102
Chalcid......................p. 102
Encarsia formosa ....p. 104
Ichneumon....................p. 106
Trichogramma................p. 116

ORTHOPTERA ("straight wings")

Grasshoppers, Crickets and Mantises
- All orthoptera have large back wings covered by thin, leathery front wings.
- Orthoptera go through gradual metamorphosis—from egg to nymph to adult. Both nymphs and adults have the same diet.

Harmful Orthoptera
Grasshopper...................p. 86

Beneficial Orthoptera
Praying Mantis...............p. 110

NEUROPTERA ("nerve wings")

Lacewings ....p. 106
- Lacewings possess transparent wings with many veins. (The resemblance of veins to nerves gives the order its name.) They go through complete metamorphosis—from egg to larva to pupa to adult—and are beneficial insects.

THYSANOPTERA ("fringed wings")

Thrips ....p. 100
- Thrips are tiny insects with slender bodies, short antennae and short legs. Winged species (some are wingless) have fringes of hair on the wings. They go through gradual metamorphosis—from egg to nymph to adult—and are harmful insects.

ARANEAE ("spider")

Spiders ....p. 114
- Spiders are not insects. They have eight legs instead of six, and two body sections instead of three. They also do not have antennae or wings. They are considered beneficial.

Phylum MOLLUSCA ("soft")

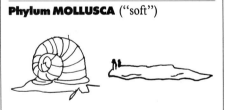

Slugs and Snails ....p. 94
- Slugs and snails—as well as their aquatic kin: clams, mussels and scallops—have soft unsegmented bodies. Most species are protected by hard shells; slugs are not. They are considered harmful to gardens.

Phylum NEMATODA ("thread")

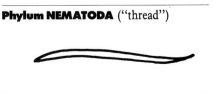

Nematodes...................p. 94
- Nematodes are miniature cylindrical worms that live in the soil. They are too small to be seen. Although some species are beneficial, many are harmful.

Key Players

The lively cast of characters on the garden stage

Growing a garden sets the stage for several life forms besides crops. Here are the characters with important roles.

Harmful Insects

This is the largest section of the guide, covering 29 pests. Any one of them may, at one time or another (or at one stage or another of its life cycle), damage garden crops. Two entries—nematodes, and slugs and snails—concern creatures that are not insects at all. Nevertheless, they come readily to mind when the subject of garden pests is raised and have been included as a result.

It is difficult, in light of this section, not to wonder how anyone ever grows anything, because the variety of pests is great and their appetites are legend. However, people who garden know that serious insect infestations are relatively rare. Indeed, most gardeners will never have to deal with any but a few of the pests listed here. Even so, since different troublemakers home in on different plants, the entire range of common garden pests is included.

To make this guide as handy as possible, it is designed to address only those insects that damage vegetable gardens. Omitted are pests that primarily plague fruits, flowers or greenhouse plants. All reasonable controls are listed for each pest. Granted, each control may not be universally effective, yet each

one has worked in some situation for some gardener. In general, the remedies that appear to work best are listed first, followed by the "iffier" ones.

In order to provide more information about some of the controls listed, many of the remedies are covered in greater detail in the chapter "Intervention" on page 64. The "Peak Infestation Times" chart on page 70 shows how to plant around the worst insect outbreaks. And "Resistant Plants" on page 56 details which plant varieties are less likely to be harmed by which pests. For information on where to find commercially available organic remedies, see page 135.

Last, to positively identify any given pest requires that the gardener become something of an insect detective. A flashlight to examine the plants at night and a small magnifying hand lens (10X or better) are essential for such entomological sleuthing.

Helpful Insects

The second section of the field guide covers 19 species that prey on harmful insects. (It also includes spiders, which are not insects but arachnids.) These are only a few of the many insects that play a role in keeping the numbers of other insects in check. Those that are discussed are either exceptionally common in gardens or exceptionally useful.

The helpful insects can be broken down into two groups: predators and parasites. Predators are the hunters that capture and eat their prey. Parasites are less direct. They lay their eggs (or set their larvae) within the body of a host, where the offspring can then slowly consume their larger victims. Often the parasites live off the fat and spare tissue of their hosts, avoiding vital organs so as to prolong the meal.

The category of helpful insects can be divided in yet another way: those insects that can be mail-ordered and those that cannot. The vast majority of helpful insects that occur naturally are widespread and don't need to be purchased. To encourage them, toxins (organic or chemical) should not be sprayed or dusted on the garden unless it's absolutely necessary, since helpful insects are often more vulnerable to such potions than harmful insects. Furthermore, because many predators and parasites attack when in the

The adult lacewing may be delicate, but its larva is a voracious predator.

larval or nymph stages but feed on nectar and pollen as adults, such beneficial insects can be enticed by the presence of flowers and weeds that are rich in pollen and nectar. Goldenrod, Queen Anne's lace, evening primroses, dandelions and lamb's-quarters are a few good attractants.

Five of the common helpful insects can be easily mail-ordered (see page 136 for suppliers): ladybugs, praying mantises, lacewings, trichogramma wasps and *Encarsia formosa*. Only the last two should be considered insects unlikely to appear naturally in gardens. But fair warning, dealing with imported beneficial insects can be tricky. If released too early, not enough victims may be available for them to prey on and they may leave or die out. (Ladybugs, in particular, have a reputation for flying away if conditions aren't just right.) Released too late, they simply may not be able to keep up with the expanding infestation. Also, some predators or parasites are highly specific about which stage of a pest's life cycle they'll attack. *Encarsia formosa*, for example, only parasitize the third and fourth instars (molts) of whiteflies.

Ideally, a parasite or predator will keep its food supply in check without wiping it—and therefore itself—out. A good supplier (or county extension agent or state entomology department) will be able to help pin down just when and how often mail-ordered insects should be released.

Several of the parasites listed are wasps. These often small insects are not interested in stinging gardeners. Indeed, the long "needles" protruding from the abdomen are used for laying eggs rather than for defense or aggression.

Plant Allies

The third section of the field guide covers flowers and herbs that repel or otherwise combat pests. All common plants, the 10 main entries serve as useful botanical controls and are easy to grow. Several others are also briefly listed that deal with specific insect problems.

Many of these flowers and herbs will work well as companions; their powerful fragrance or flavor will help keep pests away if the plants are placed near or among a crop requiring protection. (Most insects can smell and taste better than they see.) That may not always do the trick, however. Such plants will often be more effective if their foliage is pinched or broken to better release their fragrance. They will be even more effective if a tea or potion is made from their foliage or blossoms and sprayed over vulnerable crops.

Harmful Animals

Insects aren't the only creatures that will damage a garden. Gophers can't resist pole beans, and raccoons are partial to sweet corn. Add mice, obnoxious house cats and hungry deer, and it becomes clear why such animals belong in this field guide. Eleven such pests are included, as are sketches of tracks and scat (droppings) to help in identification.

Colorado potato beetles also chew eggplant, tomatoes and peppers.

Helpful Animals

As with certain insects, certain animals and birds help keep garden-harming creatures in check. Six of these are covered, with descriptions of just what they can do and how they can be attracted.

Harmful Insects

Aphid 78
Asparagus Beetle 78
Blister Beetle 80
Cabbage Looper 80
Carrot Rust Fly 80
Colorado Potato Beetle 82
Corn Earworm 82
Cutworm 84
European Corn Borer 84
Fall Armyworm 86
Flea Beetle 86
Grasshopper 86
Grub 88
Hornworm 88
Imported Cabbageworm 88
Japanese Beetle 90
Leafhopper 90
Leaf Miner 92
Mexican Bean Beetle 92
Nematode 94
Slug 94
Snail 94
Spotted Cucumber Beetle 96
Squash Bug 96
Squash Vine Borer 98
Striped Cucumber Beetle 98
Tarnished Plant Bug 98
Thrips 100
Whitefly 100
Wireworm 100

Helpful Insects

Assassin Bug 102
Braconid Wasp 102
Chalcid Wasp 102
Encarsia formosa 104
Firefly 104
Ground Beetle 106
Ichneumon Wasp 106
Lacewing 106
Ladybug 108
Minute Pirate Bug 108

Wild birds fall under both helpful and harmful animal categories because they're classic examples of the fact that nothing in nature is all good or all bad. When a robin swoops up your hornworms, it's a blessing; when it turns around and pecks at a strawberry, it's less welcome. Which to invite and which to exclude is the heart of the matter.

Praying Mantis 110
Robber Fly 110
Rove Beetle 112
Soldier Beetle 112
Spider 114
Syrphid Fly 114
Tachinid Fly 116
Tiger Beetle 116
Trichogramma Wasp 116

Plant Allies

Feverfew 118
Four-O'Clock 118
Garlic 118
Marigold 120
Mint 120
Nasturtium 120
Pyrethrum 122
Rue 122
Tansy 122
Wormwood 124
Others 124

Harmful Animals

Bird 128
Cat 129
Deer 128
Dog 129
Gopher 129
Groundhog 130
Mole 129
Mouse 130
Rabbit 131
Raccoon 131
Skunk 131

Helpful Animals

Bat 132
Bird 132
Domestic Fowl 133
Owl 133
Snake 134
Toad 134

Harmful Insects

Pea aphid

Woolly aphids

Adult laying eggs

Pea aphids. Dead, parasitized shells are brown.

Aphid giving birth to live young

Larva

Bean aphid

Ants tending aphids

Adults

Aphid Order Homoptera		**Asparagus Beetle** *Crioceris asparagi*

Alias: Aphis, greenfly, blackfly, whitefly, plant louse.

Favorite Victims: Almost all garden plants. Aphids love warm, moist conditions, so they frequently attack indoor and greenhouse plants.

Range: Throughout North America.

Description: Soft-bodied, tear-shaped, sucking insects, winged or wingless, less than $1/10''$ long. Come in different colors—black, green and white are most common. All have cornicles (small extensions) at rear of body.

Aphids are considered the insects with the highest potential capacity to reproduce; under ideal conditions, a single female could bear 5 billion offspring in one growing season. Why are they so prolific? The females reproduce parthenogenetically (without being fertilized by males) and bear all-female offspring that are ready to bear another generation of females in only six days. (The original mother creates the embryos of both her children *and* grandchildren.) Sexually reproductive male and female aphids appear only in the fall to produce overwintering eggs.

Aphids often serve as "ant cows," tended and milked by ants for their honeydew, a sweet, sticky "milk" excreted by the aphids.

Modus Operandi: The aphid injects a slender, hollow proboscis into leaves, buds and stems and sucks out the plant sap, secreting as honeydew what it doesn't consume. Curled, mottled leaves are a first sign of an aphid attack—which can involve hundreds of the sap sippers. Afflicted plants grow poorly or even die. Aphids also spread many viral diseases, and the sugary honeydew they excrete encourages sooty mold, a damaging black fungus that can cover a plant's surface. Aphids sometimes avoid indictment for their crimes, since they like to hide on the undersides of leaves and in the tight folds of new growth.

Controls:

● The force of a strong water spray can knock the weak-legged insects off the plants. Drenched and stunned, the aphids often cannot recover. Both sides of infested leaves should be sprayed.

● A little dishwashing soap added to a water spray (one or two tablespoons per gallon of water) will act to remove the aphids' waxy surface coating and cause their bodies to dry out. Let the spray work overnight, but rinse the plants well the next day with clear water.

● Yellow sticky traps (homemade or commercial) work well.

● Ladybugs and their larvae, green lacewing adults and larvae, and syrphid fly larvae all prey on aphids. One ladybug larva can consume 40 aphids in just an hour.

● Diatomaceous earth dusted on affected plants will dry the pests up.

● Garlic, onions, chives, petunias, coriander and anise all repel aphids. Nasturtiums and radishes are said to deter them, as well.

● Too much nitrogen fertilizer makes for succulent growth, which attracts aphids.

● A tea spray made from rhubarb or elderberry leaves contains oxalic acid, which deters aphids.

● Sprays made from tobacco stems or leaves and water or by mixing lime and water are also effective.

● An aluminum foil mulch laid around low-growing plants will reflect light and confuse flying aphids so they won't know where to land.

● If you see ants traveling up and down a plant (a sign of probable aphid activity), spread Tanglefoot or some other sticky substance around the plant's base to stop them; ants protect aphids and also transport them from one plant to another. Fine calcium dust is also reputed to control ants.

Favorite Victim: Asparagus.

Range: Throughout North America.

Description: *Adult* is a $1/4''$-long beetle with bluish black head and legs, and rust-colored thorax with two black spots. Wing covers look white or yellowish orange, with a black cross and rust-colored edges. *Larva* is plump and soft-looking, with black head and legs and gray or greenish body. *Eggs* are shiny, black and about $1/8''$ long each. They stick out horizontally and are quite noticeable on young asparagus spears.

Modus Operandi: Adults and larvae chew spring spears and attack summer foliage. A mild influx will cause cosmetic—but otherwise harmless—damage to young spears.

Controls:

● Clean up garden debris in the fall. This is very important since the beetle hibernates over the winter in plant refuse.

● Tomatoes and asparagus are good companion plants. Asparagus helps eradicate the nematodes that plague tomatoes, and tomatoes seem to repel the asparagus beetle.

● Aromatic marigolds and nasturtiums repel the beetle and make attractive asparagus borders.

● Ladybugs, trichogramma wasps and *Encarsia formosa* are natural predators.

● Cheesecloth or a spunbond row cover such as Reemay can be laid over a bed of new shoots in spring to provide a protective barrier.

● Bone meal deters the beetle and helps fertilize the asparagus with phosphorus.

● Chickens, guineas and other fowl love to eat asparagus beetles. They can help clean up a patch in fall so it will be beetle-free the following spring.

● Wild birds also like dining on the beetles.

● Dust with rotenone (only for serious problems).

Blister Beetle–Margined and Striped	Cabbage Looper	Carrot Rust Fly
Epicauta pestifera and *E. vittata*	*Trichoplusia ni*	*Psila rosae*

Alias: Black blister beetle, old-fashioned potato bug, Yankee bug.

Favorite Victims: Beets, melons, beans, peas, potatoes and tomatoes. Will eat other garden crops, as well.

Range: *Margined* in central and northern U.S., eastern Canada. *Striped* in eastern North America and parts of central U.S.

Description: *Margined adult* is $1/2$"-long, soft-bodied beetle with hard, black wing covers. A gray or white band outlines each wing cover. *Larva* goes through various molts (instars) from yellow and long-legged to white and grublike. *Eggs* are cylindrical, laid in the soil in clusters.

Striped adult is $1/2$" long. Head, thorax and abdomen are yellow with black stripes. *Larva* goes through various molts, starting off yellowish white and getting much darker. *Eggs* are cylindrical, laid in the soil in shallow cells.

Modus Operandi: Both margined and striped blister beetles cause the same havoc in the garden. The adults feed on foliage, fruit and flowers, sometimes flying in and invading a garden en masse. But (just to show the balance of nature—no bug is all bad, remember) the larvae make their way through the soil eating grasshopper eggs.

Controls:

● Handpick, but *wear gloves*; the beetles secrete a caustic fluid that can raise blisters on the skin.

● Commercially available sabadilla seeds can be used to make a powerful but short-lived organic insecticide. Caution: Sabadilla can harm many insects, including honeybees, and irritate human mucous membranes.

● If you suffer a large-scale invasion of blister beetles, rally some people to help you. Waving branches or clothes and shouting boldly, advance on the pests and drive them out of the garden. It works—and once out, the frustrated attackers tend to stay out.

Favorite Victims: Cole crops such as broccoli, cabbage, cauliflower and kale. Also enjoys beans, celery, lettuce, parsley, peas, potatoes, radishes, spinach and tomatoes.

Range: Throughout the U.S. and southern Canada.

Description: *Larva* is a green, $1^{1}/2$"-long caterpillar with pale stripes down its back. Lacks two of the five pairs of legs common to most caterpillars, so it has to "loop" its body like an inchworm as it crawls. *Adult* is a brownish, nocturnal moth with a $1^{1}/2$" wingspan and a silvery splotch in the middle of each forewing. *Eggs* are round and greenish white, laid singly on the upper surface of leaves.

Cabbage loopers have several broods per year. Pupae overwinter by attaching themselves to leaves, except in the extreme north, where the moths migrate south during the cold months.

Modus Operandi: The caterpillars chew jagged and rather large holes in leaves. Seedlings can easily be wiped out or stunted beyond hope.

Controls:

● Handpick individual caterpillars.

● *Bacillus thuringiensis* is very effective. You can further spread this bacteria by blending a handful of BT-stricken loopers in water and spraying that over your plants.

● Trichogramma wasps are natural enemies of cabbage loopers.

● Some crop varieties resist infestation.

● Time the planting of your cole crops to miss periods of peak looper activity.

● Cover rows or beds of vulnerable crops with cheesecloth or spunbond row covers such as Reemay.

● Cover individual plants with cutoff sections of pantyhose tied at the top and bottom. The hose will stretch as the plant grows.

● Let chickens forage for loopers, but only among crops the fowl normally don't eat.

● If you can find 10 loopers that are chalky white and obviously sick, you're in luck. Those loopers are infected with nuclear polyhedrosis virus (NPV). Blend them in water and spray the solution over as much as an acre of crops. Infected loopers will die in three or four days.

Favorite Victims: Carrots, parsnips, parsley and celery.

Range: Throughout North America, but most common in northern U.S.

Description: *Larva* is a yellowish white, $1/3$"-long, legless maggot. *Adult* is a shiny green or black fly, slender, with yellow head, legs and body hairs. Only $1/5$" long.

Modus Operandi: Eggs are laid in the crowns of afflicted plants. The larvae hatch and burrow down into the roots, creating tunnels that are rust-colored from the maggots' excrement (hence, the name). Maggots can also overwinter in the soil. Infected plants become stunted and vulnerable to soft-rot bacteria.

Controls:

● Sprinkle rock phosphate, crushed wormwood or dry wood ashes around each plant's base and crown to repel the egg-laying flies.

● Cultivate the soil in the fall and early spring to expose overwintering maggots.

● Rotate plantings of vulnerable crops with unaffected ones to avoid maggots.

● Delay planting susceptible crops until late spring or early summer so the larvae will die of starvation.

● Onions, leeks, pennyroyal, rosemary, sage, coriander and black salsify (also known as oyster plant) are known repellents.

● Some gardeners say that putting used tea leaves in with crop seed when planting keeps the carrot rust fly away.

Blister Beetle–Margined and Striped	**Cabbage Looper**	**Carrot Rust Fly**
Epicauta pestifera and *E. vittata*	*Trichoplusia ni*	*Psila rosae*

Margined blister beetle

Larva

Maggots

Striped blister beetle

Adult

Adult

Colorado Potato Beetle *Leptinotarsa decemlineata*	**Corn Earworm** *Heliothis zea*	

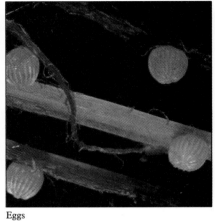

Eggs

Eggs

Adult

Larvae

Larvae

Adult

Pupa

Colorado Potato Beetle	**Corn Earworm**	
Leptinotarsa decemlineata	*Heliothis zea*	

Alias: Potato bug.

Favorite Victims: Potatoes, eggplants, tomatoes, peppers.

Range: Upper two-thirds of the U.S. and Canada.

Description: *Adult* is a striking, $1/3$"-long, hard-shelled, round beetle. Head is orange with black dots. Body has black and yellow stripes. *Larva* is a plump, red or pink-orange maggot with two distinctive rows of black dots down each side. *Eggs* are orange, laid in rows on undersides of leaves.

Colorado potato beetles can go through one to three generations a year. The adults overwinter in the soil.

Modus Operandi: Both larvae and adults devour leaves.

Controls:
- Handpick. Remember to search the undersides of leaves when looking for eggs.
- Interplant green beans and potatoes: Each crop repels the other's main pest.
- Horseradish (especially), flax, aromatic marigolds and garlic are repellent plants.
- A deep mulch around victim crops makes it hard for the larvae to move between plants. In fact, growing potatoes *on top of* the ground by planting them in a thick layer of leaves and straw is an effective tactic.
- Toads, ground beetles, ladybugs and the two-spotted stinkbug (*Perillus bioculatus*) are natural predators.
- Dust damp foliage with wheat bran. The beetles will eat it, the bran will swell and the bugs will burst.
- Grow resistant varieties.
- Time plantings to avoid peak infestations.
- There is now a strain of *Bacillus thuringiensis* that kills the beetles.
- Sprays made from basil, eucalyptus and peppermint oil have been used successfully by some folks.
- An old-timey remedy is to boil cedar boughs until the water turns an amber color. Cool, and sprinkle or spray on potato foliage.
- Pyrethrum, or pyrethrum and rotenone mixed, should kill the potato bug.
- Diatomaceous earth can destroy the larvae.
- Well-fed chickens enclosed in a potato patch will supplement their diet by eating the pests.
- The commercially available *Edovum puttleri* wasp (imported from Peru) parasitizes Colorado potato beetles.

Alias: Tomato fruitworm, cotton bollworm.

Favorite Victims: Corn, tomatoes, potatoes, beans, peas, peppers and squash.

Range: Throughout North America.

Description: *Larva* is a $1^1/2$" caterpillar with dark stripes down either side. Usually green or white, but may be light yellow, brown or even reddish. *Pupa* is a rust-colored capsule. *Adult* is a strong-flying nocturnal moth that feeds on flower nectar. Greenish gray or brown with black dots or marks on its forewings. *Eggs* are off-white, ribbed domes, laid singly.

Corn earworms go through as many as seven generations a year in warm areas. The pupa overwinters in the soil.

Modus Operandi: Earworm larvae chew the foliage of several crops and like to dig in the stem ends of tomatoes, as well. But they're most famous for spoiling corn. A female moth lays an average of 1,000 eggs in her lifetime. The newly hatched caterpillar eats fresh silk tassels; then, when the silk withers, it burrows in to gnaw down on kernels. The pest spoils the ear's end, inhibits full pollination and invites mold and other diseases. Luckily, earworms are very cannibalistic, so you'll rarely find more than one or two in an ear.

Controls:
- Handpick larvae by pulling back corn tips and removing worms. Do this only after silks begin to brown, indicating pollination has occurred.
- *Bacillus thuringiensis* kills the larvae. This works best before the larvae have burrowed into fruit or ears.
- Apply mineral oil to corn ears to suffocate the worms—again, after silks have withered and begun to brown. Squirt it just inside the ears, applying $1/2$ dropperful for small ears and $3/4$ dropperful for large ones. (You may want to use an oilcan to speed the process if you have a large corn patch.) Red pepper, pyrethrum or BT can be added to the mineral oil. Make two follow-up applications spaced one week apart.
- Tachinid flies and trichogramma wasps parasitize earworm eggs.
- Electronic bug zappers can reduce moth numbers.
- Time plantings to miss peak infestations. Caterpillars are most abundant at a new moon, so plantings that silk during a full moon will be better off.

Cutworm Family Noctuidae		European Corn Borer *Ostrinia nubilalis*

Favorite Victims: Your carefully nurtured garden seedlings.

Range: Throughout North America.

Description: Grayish brown, 1"-long caterpillars, some with spots or stripes. Nocturnal—rarely seen in daytime. Curls up when disturbed. *Adult*, or Miller's moth, is gray or brown with paler hind wings and a 1" to 1½" wingspan.

The name *cutworm* is justifiably foreboding—you won't know you've got cutworms in your garden until they've performed their guillotine act and decapitated several of your plants. Actually, there are approximately 20,000 kinds of cutworms, including tunneling, subterranean and climbing species (such as the armyworm), but the surface feeders are the most common. These spend two summers as destructive larvae (overwintering in the soil) before they mature into harmless moths.

Modus Operandi: Fells young plants by cutting off stems at or just below soil surface.

Controls:

● The traditional—and very effective—control is to set a small 2" to 3" collar, pressed 1" into the soil, around each vulnerable plant. Collars can be made of paper, cardboard, PVC, metal cans, paper cups or toilet tissue tubes.

● *Bacillus thuringiensis*, a widely available caterpillar-killing bacterium, is a very good control for climbing cutworms as well as the surface feeders.

● Handpick larvae at night by flashlight.

● Mulch plants with oak leaves, crushed egg shells, damp wood ashes or other irritating physical barriers.

● Deep plowing, digging or tilling in fall and again in spring will expose and kill soil-laid eggs and overwintering larvae. Chickens let into the plot after these cultivations will improve the effectiveness of this technique.

● Tachinid flies, trichogramma wasps, braconid wasps and insect-killing nematodes parasitize cutworms.

● Toads, moles, shrews, blackbirds, meadowlarks and firefly larvae are all natural predators.

● The adult moths can be attracted to, and killed by, electronic bug zappers.

● Sprinkle cornmeal around your garden. Cutworms love it but can't digest it. Some will die from overeating the treat.

● Make a mixture of molasses (another vice), water, wheat bran and hardwood sawdust. Circle plants with this glop. It dries on the cutworms' bodies and immobilizes them.

● It's said that if you push a small twig, nail or toothpick into the earth right next to a seedling, the cutworm cannot wrap around the stem and fell the plant.

● According to University of British Columbia student Greg Salloum, cutworms would rather starve than eat plants treated with extracts of pineapple weed or sagebrush.

Favorite Victims: Corn, but can attack foliage, fruit and stems of over 260 plants.

Range: Northern and central U.S. (east of the Rockies and north of Tennessee) and southern Canada.

Description: *Larva* is a 1"-long, grayish pink caterpillar with dark head and with spots at each segment. *Adult* is a yellow-brown, nocturnal moth with ½" wings with dark bands. *Eggs* are white, laid in clumps on undersides of leaves. *Pupa* is a plump, reddish brown grub.

The corn borer goes through one to three generations per year. The pupa overwinters in dead stalks.

Modus Operandi: Larvae chew into corn plants, starting at the whorl (the funnel of leaves at the top of the plant) and tassels. Several can attack each plant, causing extensive damage. When you see small, shotlike holes in upper foliage, or holes with plant "sawdust" at their edges in stalks or ears, you've got borer troubles.

Controls:

● Plant corn early, using early or midseason varieties that mature in 80 days or less. This way you may be able to avoid the second, more numerous, generation of corn borers.

● Grow resistant varieties. Apache, Stowell's Evergreen, Butter & Sugar, Bellringer, Wonderful, Calumet, Country Gentleman, Burgundy Delight, Quicksilver, Sweet Sue and Tablevee all show some resistance to borer damage. Spring White, Seneca 60, Beacon and Polar Vee are more likely to be attacked.

● Use good garden hygiene. Immediately after harvest, shred, chop, mow or rototill in an affected crop to destroy the borers' winter home. That should greatly reduce future populations. (You must destroy the plants to within 1" of the ground.)

● Handpick. Slit stalks or ears right under obvious borer holes with a fingernail or knife and pluck out the invaders.

● Kill moths in the corn patch with an electronic bug zapper.

● Braconid wasps, tachinid flies and ladybugs all prey on borers.

| **Cutworm**
Family Noctuidae | **European Corn Borer**
Ostrinia nubilalis | |

Larva

Eggs

Adults

Moths

Larva

Pupa

Fall Armyworm *Spodoptera frugiperda*	**Flea Beetle** *Phyllotreta striolata* and *Epitrix* spp.	**Grasshopper** Family Acrididae

Larva

Adult

Adult

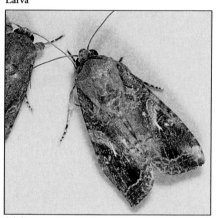

Adult

Fall Armyworm	Flea Beetle	Grasshopper
Spodoptera frugiperda	*Phyllotreta striolata* and *Epitrix* spp.	Family Acrididae

Alias: Budworm.

Favorite Victim: Probably corn, but they'll eat most anything.

Range: Most of the U.S., excluding the northernmost areas.

Description: *Larva* is a 1½"-long, brown and yellow striped caterpillar. Black head has a V- or Y-shaped white marking. Younger larvae are white and can be found curled up in leaves or hanging from threads. *Adult* is a gray, mottled, 1¾"-long moth. Females have pink or white on wing margins. *Eggs* are hairy, laid in large groups on victim plant.

The fall armyworm goes through from one to six generations per year. Adult moths migrate south for the winter.

Modus Operandi: Larvae devour what's in their path, earning their name from the fact that they appear in the North during the fall and may travel in large hordes. They usually feed at night.

Controls:

● *Bacillus thuringiensis* works well on the larvae.

● Interplant rows of corn and sunflowers.

● Trichogramma wasps, braconid wasps, tachinid flies, ground beetles, toads, birds and skunks all attack fall armyworms.

● A beneficial nematode, *Neoaplectana carpocapsae*, parasitizes fall armyworms and is commercially available.

● If you suffer a serious mass invasion, you can dig a steep ditch around your garden. The armyworms will fall in and be unable to climb out. You can then bury, burn or otherwise destroy them.

Favorite Victims: Eggplants, brassicas (broccoli, cabbage, etc.), radishes, potatoes.

Range: Throughout North America.

Description: *Adult* is a ¹/₁₀"-long, black or brown beetle, some species with yellow body stripes. Hops like a flea when disturbed. *Eggs* are tiny, laid in soil.

The flea beetle goes through one or two generations a year. Adults spend the winter in garden debris or weeds.

Modus Operandi: Chews tiny holes in leaves and hops away when you try to catch it. Likes to destroy tender spring seedlings.

Controls:

● If flea beetles are a chronic spring problem, you may want to skip all the other remedies and go right to the physical barrier approach. Cover all vulnerable seedlings as early as possible with a spunbond row cover such as Reemay. (If the beetles can't get to your crops, they can't eat them.) Remove the row cover when your plants reach about midsize growth and are no longer susceptible to attack.

● Sprinkle wood ashes or slaked lime on damp plants. Replenish after rains.

● Sprinkle crushed elderberry or tomato leaves on vulnerable plants.

● Cultivate soil frequently around crops to destroy eggs.

● Clean up garden and weed debris in fall to destroy the pest's winter home.

● Provide shade and moisture—which the beetles hate—while crops are vulnerable.

● Use garlic, catnip, mint or wormwood as repellent plants or sprays.

● Use diatomaceous earth or rotenone.

● Plant a trap crop for the beetles to enjoy while they leave your main ones alone. Radishes are often recruited for this purpose. Some gardeners interplant pak choi in their garden. The flea beetles devour it, avoiding the other crops. And although the pak choi leaves are ruined beyond use, the plants' stalks can still be harvested and enjoyed.

● Cover small cabbages with sections of pantyhose tied at the top and bottom. They'll expand as the plants grow.

● Cover a white board with something sticky, such as Tanglefoot or petroleum jelly, and set it near crops to trap flea beetles.

● Admit defeat; i.e., skip your spring plantings of vulnerable crops. Plant them later when the beetles are less abundant.

Alias: Locust.

Favorite Victims: Just about everything.

Range: Throughout North America.

Description: *Adult* is large (1" to 2" long), "armor-plated" insect with big hind legs for jumping, good-sized jaws and short antennae. Generally green, but also brown, yellow, black, gray and even a reddish shade. *Eggs* are laid in soil or weeds.

The grasshopper goes through only one generation a year. The eggs overwinter in the soil.

Modus Operandi: Those munching mandibles chew leaves and stems. Grasshoppers feed during the day.

Controls:

● Fill jars with molasses and water, then bury them so their mouths are level with the ground.

● Cultivate the soil frequently in the fall to discourage egg laying and to expose eggs already in the soil.

● Cover seedlings with cheesecloth or a spunbond row cover such as Reemay.

● Chickens and guinea fowl relish the insects.

● Crows, sparrows, bluebirds, mockingbirds, catbirds, meadowlarks, hawks and brown thrashers also enjoy dining on locusts. Skunks, snakes, toads, spiders and cats will dent their numbers. Ground squirrels, field mice and several other rodents not only eat the adults but dig for their eggs, as well.

● Blister beetles and ground beetles like to lay their eggs near those of grasshoppers so the beetle offspring can consume the hoppers' eggs. Those beetle larvae are capable of consuming 40% to 60% of an area's grasshopper eggs.

● The one-cell parasite *Nosema locustae* infects 58 species of grasshoppers. Some species die within a few hours of infestation, others within four to six weeks. The spores are quite long-lived, so a single treatment may last for several years. *Nosema* is best applied in the spring as a preventive measure for curbing grasshopper outbreaks *before* they occur.

● A spray of hot pepper, soap and water *may* repel the adults.

Grub Order Coleoptera	Hornworm—Tomato and Tobacco *Manduca quinquemaculata* and *M. sexta*	Imported Cabbageworm *Pieris rapae*

Favorite Victims: Corn, strawberries, onions, small grains, potatoes and lawn grasses.

Range: Throughout North America.

Description: Grubs are the larval stage of beetles. They are generally $3/4$" to 1" long, with three pairs of legs, and are found lying curled in the soil. June beetle and Japanese beetle grubs are white with dark heads. Grubs may live underground from 10 months to two years.

Modus Operandi: Grubs eat roots and plant bases, so they can cripple or ruin plants without ever being detected. Since many beetles love to lay their eggs in sod or weeds, grubs are often most prevalent in new gardens that have just been converted from sod to plot.

Controls:

• Cultivate the soil frequently in the fall and early spring to expose grubs (especially in a new garden site). Squash any you see. Native birds will dine on the tilled-up larvae, as well.

• Hens and other back-yard fowl love to probe recently dug soil for grubs.

• Apply milky spore disease (*Bacillus popilliae*) to your soil. This takes a few years to spread enough to be fully effective.

• If possible, avoid planting corn and other grub-favored crops in garden areas that were just converted from sod.

Favorite Victims: Plants in the Solanaceae (nightshade) family, including tomatoes, potatoes, eggplants, peppers and tobacco.

Range: Throughout North America.

Description: *Larva* is a large, 3" to 4" caterpillar. Lime green with seven or eight white diagonal stripes and a thornlike horn on its tail. Tomato larva has a black horn; tobacco larva a red horn. *Adult* is a large (4" to 5" wingspan), gray or brown moth with white zigzag lines on rear wings. Often called sphinx, hummingbird or hawk moth. Appears in late spring and feeds at twilight on the nectar in deep-throated flowers. *Eggs* are yellow-green, laid singly on the underside of leaves. Hatch in three to eight days.

The caterpillar feeds voraciously after it is hatched. In little over two weeks, it grows to its imposing full size. Then it crawls down into the soil, where it overwinters as a hard-shelled pupa with a pitcherlike "handle."

Modus Operandi: Larvae chew on leaves and sometimes fruit. Tomato and tobacco hornworms attack the same plants.

Controls:

• Handpick the larvae. Their green coloration provides surprisingly good camouflage for such large caterpillars, so you may have to hunt through the foliage to spot them. (If you see dark green droppings directly under a tomato plant in the morning, you can be sure a hornworm's at work.)

• Apply *Bacillus thuringiensis*.

• Braconid wasps parasitize the larvae, laying eggs inside that later develop into cocoons on the hornworms' backs. So *don't* pick any cocoon-covered hornworms: Let them serve as hosts for the useful wasps.

• Trichogramma wasps parasitize the eggs. If you see any hornworm eggs with dark streaks, leave them alone. They've already been raided by trichogrammas.

• Time your plantings to avoid peak infestations of hornworms.

• Marigolds and opal basil are said to repel hornworms.

• Dill and borage are reputed to be good trap crops.

• An electronic bug zapper will kill many of the moths.

• Cultivate the soil deeply in the fall to destroy the pupae.

• The Peron tomato is said to be immune to hornworms.

Favorite Victims: All members of the cabbage family, including cabbage, broccoli, cauliflower, kale, mustard, radishes, turnips and kohlrabi.

Range: Throughout North America.

Description: *Larva* is a pale green caterpillar, 1" to $1^1/4$" long, with a thin yellow stripe down its back. Leaves behind dark green telltale droppings. *Adult* is a white or yellowish, powdery-looking butterfly with a 1" to 2" wingspan. Three to four black spots on wings, and black or gray tips on all four wings.

The cabbageworm goes through two or three generations a year. It overwinters as a pupa in the soil.

Modus Operandi: The butterflies flit delicately among your crops, laying eggs all the while. Then the caterpillars hatch and attack the leaves.

Controls:

• *Bacillus thuringiensis* is very effective.

• Sprinkle damp leaves with rye flour or a mixture of one part salt to two parts flour. Cabbageworms that eat this coating will bloat and die.

• Onions, garlic, tomatoes, sage, tansy, rosemary, southernwood, nasturtium, mints and hyssop are all repellent plants. You can grow them as companions, lay boughs of them over vulnerable crops or use them in sprays.

• Cover plants with cheesecloth or a spunbond row cover such as Reemay to protect them from the egg-laying moth.

• Rotate your cole crops (particularly with the listed repellent plants).

• Cover individual plants with sections of pantyhose tied at the top and bottom.

• Cultivate the soil frequently in the fall and early spring to expose and kill pupae.

• The trichogramma wasp parasitizes cabbageworms.

• Rid your plot of weeds in the cabbage family, such as wild radish, wild mustard and winter cress.

• If you can find 10 cabbageworms that are chalky white and obviously sick, you can use them to make your own nuclear polyhedrosis (NPV) spray. Blend them in water, and spray the solution over as much as an acre of crops. Infected cabbageworms will die in three or four days.

| **Grub**
Order Coleoptera | **Hornworm—Tomato and Tobacco**
Manduca quinquemaculata and *M. sexta* | **Imported Cabbageworm**
Pieris rapae |

June beetle grub

M. sexta larva

Larvae and droppings

Scarab beetle grubs

M. sexta larva parasitized by braconid wasp

Adult

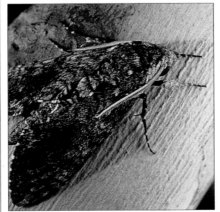

M. sexta adult

Japanese Beetle *Popillia japonica*	**Leafhopper** Order Homoptera	

Pupa and larva

Potato leafhopper adult

Adults

Beet leafhopper adult

Japanese Beetle *Popillia japonica*	Leafhopper Order Homoptera	

Favorite Victims: Loves raspberries, roses, most fruit trees, but is hardly a fussy eater, feeding on at least 275 different plants.

Range: Eastern U.S. (but moving westward).

Description: *Adult* is a 1/2"-long beetle with shiny, blue-green head and copper-colored wing covers. Often seen mating. *Larva* is a fat, 3/4"- to 1"-long, gray-white grub with brown head. Overwinters deep in the soil, moving upward as spring approaches.

The grubs pupate in early summer, and the emerged adults feed from midsummer until fall.

Modus Operandi: Adults devour leaves (leaving veiny skeletons), fruit and flowers. They do most of their damage on warm, sunny days. The grub chews on plant roots.

Controls:

● Handpick. The easiest way is to shake clusters of beetles onto tarps in the early morning when the dew is still on their wings and they're not likely to fly.

● Tachinid flies and spring and fall tiphia wasps prey on Japanese beetles.

● The leaves of castor beans and the flowers of white geraniums, dwarf and red buckeyes and four-o'clocks all attract and poison the beetles. Four-o'clocks are a favorite choice: They're pretty, easy to grow, self-seed abundantly and smell great. But the plants *are* poisonous to humans.

● Time plantings of susceptible crops to miss peak infestations.

● Trap crops include borage (the most popular), African marigolds, evening primroses, soybeans, knotweed, white roses, white or pastel zinnias, wild grapes and wild blackberries.

● Commercial Japanese beetle pheromone traps are not recommended unless they're placed a considerable distance from your plot. They may work *too* well, luring pests from miles around to your garden.

● Use milky spore disease to infect the grubs. This is commercially available but takes a few years to be fully effective and is best done on a community-wide basis.

● Cultivate the soil frequently in the fall and early spring to expose grubs. Native birds and back-yard fowl love to dine on these larvae.

Alias: The beet leafhopper is also called the whitefly, the potato leafhopper is sometimes called the bean jassid, and the six-spotted leafhopper is also called the aster leafhopper.

Favorite Victims: Potatoes, beans, tomatoes, lettuce, carrots, asters.

Range: Western North America (beet leafhopper), eastern North America (potato leafhopper) and throughout North America (six-spotted leafhopper).

Description: *Adult* is a very active (hence the name), long-winged, small-headed insect. The beet leafhopper is 1/3" long and has a yellow-green body. The potato leafhopper is 1/3" long and green with white spots. The 1/8"-long six-spotted leafhopper has six black spots on its greenish yellow body. Some adults can leap surprisingly far. *Nymphs* resemble the adults, and step sideways when disturbed.

Modus Operandi: Leafhoppers suck juices from plant tissues. They inject salivary fluids that start predigesting their victims. These fluids restrict nutrient flow and spread disease. Young plants are most vulnerable and may become stunted and deformed.

Victimized leaves often curl, dry and become discolored (yellow, white or brown) at the edges. These symptoms are known by various names, depending upon the plants that are afflicted. *Tomato yellows* is caused by the beet leafhopper, *potato hopperburn* is brought by the potato leafhopper, and *aster yellows* (which strikes carrots and lettuce as well as asters) is transmitted by the six-spotted leafhopper. Beet leafhoppers also afflict beans in a similar manner with the *curly top virus*. Indeed, this insect is the only known carrier of the disease.

Controls:

● Cover young plants with cheesecloth or a spunbond row cover such as Reemay.

● Plant petunias and geraniums to repel leafhoppers.

● Swallows and lacewing larvae enjoy dining on leafhopper nymphs.

● Black-light traps attract the adults.

● Pyrethrum or diatomaceous earth may control a serious infestation.

● An "old-timey" remedy (cited in John B. Smith's 1906 text, *Economic Entomology*) is to use a spray made by boiling one pound of tobacco in a gallon of water. It may, however, spot delicate leaves and flowers.

● Adults like to hibernate in weeds but dis-

like perennial grasses. So keep the winter garden clean and raise grass, not weeds, around your garden.

● Leafhoppers seem to prefer open spaces, so grow susceptible crops near your house or in another sheltered location.

● Don't plant carrots, lettuce and asters together if you have problems with the six-spotted leafhopper.

● Sequoia, Delus, Sebago, Pungo and Plymouth potatoes resist the potato leafhopper. (Sequoia, however, is susceptible to aphids.)

● Great Northern, Red Mexican and University of Idaho beans resist the beet leafhopper.

Leaf Miner *Liriomyza* species	**Mexican Bean Beetle** *Epilachna varivestis*	

Favorite Victims: Spinach, Swiss chard, beet greens and lamb's-quarters.

Range: Throughout North America.

Description: *Larva* is a pale green or whitish maggot approximately $1/3''$ long. *Adult* is a tiny, $1/10''$ black fly with yellow stripes. *Eggs* are white, cylindrical, laid on the undersides of leaves.

The leaf miner can go through several generations a year but overwinters as a cocoon in the soil.

Modus Operandi: Larvae tunnel inside leaves, leaving white trails or creating gray-white blotches. Damage is often mostly cosmetic.

Controls:

● Crush the small eggs or tunneling miners between your fingers.

● Rotate plantings of susceptible crops with nonsusceptible ones.

● Cultivate the soil well in the fall and early spring to destroy cocoons or expose them to birds.

● Protect plants with a cheesecloth covering or a spunbond row cover such as Reemay.

● Gather and burn infested leaves.

● Clear out wild lamb's-quarters in and around your garden, or use as a trap crop.

● Plant vulnerable crops for fall harvest, when leaf miners cause less damage.

Favorite Victims: Beans.

Range: Eastern U.S. and portions of the Southwest.

Description: *Adult* is a $1/3''$-long, round beetle with 16 black spots on its wings. It looks a lot like an orange ladybug; however, unlike that beneficial insect, the bean beetle has no markings on its thorax (the segment between the head and the body). *Larva* is a $1/3''$-long, yellow, soft-bodied (squishy-looking) but very spiny grub. *Eggs* are also yellow, laid in clusters on the undersides of leaves.

The bean beetle goes through from one to three generations a year. The adult hibernates in woods or fields.

Modus Operandi: Both adults and larvae chew leaves, operating from the undersides and leaving little more than skeletonized foliage.

Controls:

● Handpick adults and larvae (you can drop them in a bucket of water topped by a film of kerosene). Squashing the egg clusters on the leaves is a very effective way of limiting larvae and beetle numbers—you can destroy 50 to 60 eggs at a time. If you're not too squeamish, you can thumb-squash the larvae, as well.

● Interplant rows of beans and potatoes. Each repels the other's main insect pest.

● Savory, garlic, marigolds, rosemary, petunias and nasturtiums are repellent plants.

● Clean up bean debris right after harvest. Compost it, or put it in plastic bags and bake it in the sun for a week or so to destroy remaining beetles.

● Plant early to avoid heaviest outbreaks.

● Assassin bugs and the tiny wasp *Pediobius foveolatus* prey on the bean beetle.

● As a last resort, use rotenone or pyrethrum to wipe out a serious infestation.

Leaf Miner *Liriomyza* species	**Mexican Bean Beetle** *Epilachna varivestis*	

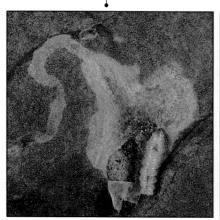

Larva and leaf damage

Eggs and larvae

Adult

Larvae

Adult

Nematode Phylum Nematoda	**Slugs and Snails** Phylum Mollusca	

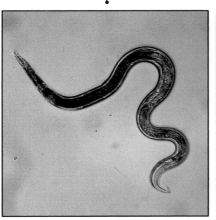

Adult

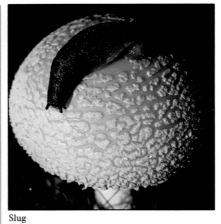

Slug

Nematode potato damage

Snail

Nematode Phylum Nematoda		95	**Slugs and Snails** Phylum Mollusca

Alias: Eelworm, roundworm.

Favorite Victims: Most crops, but seems to have a special fondness for tomatoes, cucumbers, mustard, dill, celery, peas, beans, raspberries and apples.

Range: All soils, even those on the ocean floor. There are over a half million nematode species, including one that lives in whale placentas.

Description: Blind, usually microscopic (a mere $^1/_{125}''$), threadlike soil creature.

Modus Operandi: Feeds on roots, reducing plant vigor and stunting growth. Wilting, yellowing and dieback may be signs of nematode damage. Root-knot nematodes cause nutrient-blocking galls to form on the roots of many vegetables. Nematodes are most damaging during hot weather.

Not all nematodes are harmful. Many don't hurt plants a bit, and some are even parasites of other insect pests. If you suspect nematodes *are* damaging your crops, you can have your soil tested professionally to make sure. Or you can try growing a test crop, such as radishes, in pots. Use your garden soil, half of which you've frozen for a few days first to kill any nematodes. If the plants grown in regular soil do worse than those in the prefrozen soil, you've got nematode troubles.

Controls:

● The best tactic is to use lots of compost or heavy mulch in your garden to encourage predacious fungi. A garden with a high organic-matter content has a low nematode content.

● Plant nematode-resistant varieties.

● Grow French or African marigolds, hairy indigo, white or black mustard, velvet beans or garlic as repellent crops. Marigolds are the most effective crop. They should be grown the whole season to maximize the benefits from their slowly released soil toxin. Several successive years of marigold growing can make a big dent in nematode populations.

● Certain cover crops can greatly reduce nematode populations if the plant matter is mashed and tilled under at the end of the growing season. Rye, barley, corn, wheat and millet are most effective. Chicory, timothy and perennial rye grass and alfalfa also work well. But watch out: Clover, mint and chickweed covers actually stimulate nematodes.

● Rotate nematode-susceptible crops with repellent ones, or use an infested area as a chicken yard.

● Grow unappetizing (to nematodes) cole crops followed by corn for a year to starve them out.

● Fish emulsion fertilizers reduce nematode populations.

● Plant tomatoes near asparagus. Asparagus roots contain a juice that's toxic to tomato nematodes.

Favorite Victims: Many garden and orchard crops.

Range: Throughout North America.

Description: Soft-bodied, slimy mollusks, $^1/_2''$ to $3''$ long. Various colors, including gray, black, brown and yellow. Eyes located at the tips of two of the tentacles. Snails have a shell, slugs do not.

Mollusks live for several years, overwintering in plant litter or the soil.

Modus Operandi: Slugs and snails chew holes in foliage, fruits and stems, leaving behind a sticky telltale trail of slime. Most feed at night when it's cool and damp, seeking shelter during the day. Some snails prey on small insects.

Controls:

● Handpick. You may have to do this at night by flashlight. You can sprinkle salt once or twice on slugs to dissolve them, but watch out: Too much salt will harm your plants.

● Saucers of beer or a sweet yeasty concoction set at ground level will lure the pests to death by drowning.

● Set out objects for slugs and snails to hide under, then collect those that do. Lettuce and cabbage leaves, scooped out turnips and potatoes, boards and grapefruit rinds all work well.

● Lay down crushed eggshells, gravel or cedar or oak bark to irritate the soft-bodied invaders. Some gardeners have found that a seaweed mulch or border totally repels slugs.

● Use diatomaceous earth or wormwood tea.

● One gardener built an effective garden-surrounding barricade by setting boards on the ground so they stood at a 45° angle pointing away from the garden, then coating the undersides with petroleum jelly.

● Lightning bug larvae, ground beetles, rove beetles, turtles, salamanders, garter snakes and grass snakes all like the protein-rich pests. Chickens tend not to care for them, but ducks devour them. (Indeed, when a gardener once asked permaculture expert Bill Mollison what to do about her excess of slugs, he replied, "You don't have slug excess, you've got a duck deficit!")

● Grow plantain (the weed, not the banana) as a trap crop.

● Snail Barr is a commercially available copper strip that apparently emits a mild electric charge that deters snails and slugs.

| Spotted Cucumber Beetle
Diabrotica undecimpunctata howardi | Squash Bug
Anasa tristis | |

Alias: Southern corn rootworm.

Favorite Victims: Corn, cucumbers, melon, squash, peas, potatoes, tomatoes, eggplants and several tree fruits.

Range: Eastern U.S. (but a similar species is found in the West) and southern Canada.

Description: *Adult* is a greenish yellow, $1/4$"-long beetle with a small, black head and 11 or 12 black spots on its back. *Larva* is a $1/2$"-long, beige grub with a brown head on one end and a brown spot on the other. *Eggs* are yellow, oval, and laid in the soil near victim plants.

Modus Operandi: Adults chew holes in leaves, flowers and fruits. They transmit cucumber wilt bacteria and infect stone fruits with brown rot. The larvae feed on roots and stems, doing their worst damage early in the growing season.

Controls:
- Heavy mulching is an effective deterrent.
- Handpick the beetles. Look for them on the undersides of leaves.
- Rotate crops (especially corn) to control the larvae.
- Strew onion skins over each planting spot.
- Catnip, tansy, nasturtiums and goldenrod are repellent plants.
- Soldier beetles, tachinid flies, braconid wasps and certain nematodes are natural predators.
- Time plantings to avoid peak infestations.
- Grow resistant varieties.
- Spray a mix of equal parts of wood ashes and hydrated lime in water on the upper and lower surfaces of leaves.
- Hit the beetles with a home-brewed spray of hot pepper, garlic and water. As a last resort for serious invasions, use rotenone or pyrethrum.

Favorite Victims: Squash, melons, pumpkins and cucumbers.

Range: Throughout North America.

Description: *Adult* is a brown to black, $5/8$"-long, roach-shaped bug, with some orange or brown coloring around the edge of its abdomen. Gives off a nasty odor when crushed. *Nymph* is a yellowish green, tear-shaped crawler. Has a green body and reddish head and legs when newly hatched. *Eggs* are shiny and brown, laid on the undersides of plant leaves.

The squash bug goes through one cycle a year and hibernates as an adult, often in garden trash.

Modus Operandi: Both adults and nymphs pierce plants with their sharp mouths and suck the sap. Worse yet, they release a toxin as they feed that can make the plants wilt. Young plants are particularly susceptible and can be easily killed by squash bugs.

Controls:
- Handpick. You can drop the bugs or nymphs in a bucket of water topped with kerosene to kill them.
- Grow radishes, tansy, nasturtiums or marigolds near susceptible plants to repel the pests.
- Rotate crops, planting vulnerable crops far from their previous site.
- Clean up your garden at the end of the season to eliminate the bugs' overwintering home.
- Use black plastic, compost or other compact matter such as sawdust as a mulch. Squash bugs prefer loose mulches such as hay.
- Sprinkle a mixture of hydrated lime and wood ashes around vulnerable crops.
- Set thin boards in the garden for the bugs to congregate under so you can catch them.
- The tachinid fly is a natural predator.
- Grow resistant varieties of crops.
- Time plantings to avoid peak infestations.
- As a last resort, use sabadilla dust.

Spotted Cucumber Beetle	Squash Bug	
Diabrotica undecimpunctata howardi	*Anasa tristis*	

Larvae

Egg and newly hatched nymphs

Leaf damage

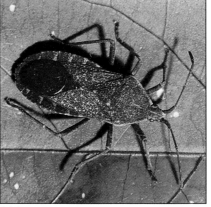

Adult

Adult

Adults

Squash Vine Borer *Melittia satyriniformis*	Striped Cucumber Beetle *Acalymma vittata*	Tarnished Plant Bug *Lygus lineolaris*

Larva

Adult with leaf damage and droppings

Nymph

Adult

Adult

Adult

Squash Vine Borer *Melittia satyriniformis*	**Striped Cucumber Beetle** *Acalymma vittata*	**Tarnished Plant Bug** *Lygus lineolaris*

Favorite Victims: Cucumbers, squash, melons, pumpkins and gourds.

Range: Eastern U.S. and southern Canada.

Description: *Larva* is a 1″-long, white caterpillar with a brown head. *Adult* is a 1½″-long, orange and black moth with clear or copper-colored wings. *Eggs* are brown and oval, laid along plant stems.

The squash vine borer goes through one generation a year (two in the South) and hibernates in the soil as a larva or pupa.

Modus Operandi: Bores into base of vine stem, wilting entire plant. Leaves telltale trail of yellow-green "squash dust" around entrance hole.

Controls:
- Slit stem just above entrance hole and remove borer. Cover the incision with soil.
- Inject *Bacillus thuringiensis* in borer holes with a syringe.
- Bury the plant stem at several places (particularly at junctions) to create extra root systems.
- Sprinkle wood ashes, crushed black pepper or real camphor around vine bases to deter invasion.
- Plant radishes around vine bases to repel borers.
- Wrap a foil collar, or piece of pantyhose, around plant base to keep moths from laying eggs there.
- Mound soil over vines up to the blossoms.
- The trichogramma wasp is a natural predator.
- Plant early or late to avoid peak midsummer infestation.
- Grow resistant varieties.

Favorite Victims: Cucumbers, squash, melons, pumpkins, peas, corn, beans.

Range: Eastern half of North America. (There is a similar species in the western U.S.)

Description: *Adult* is a ¼″-long, yellowish orange beetle with a black head and three black stripes running down its back. *Larva* is a slender, ⅓″-long, white grub with brown ends. *Eggs* are orange, laid in soil near victim plants.

Modus Operandi: Adults chew foliage and flowers. They love young seedlings, attacking when the shoots first emerge from the ground. Worst of all, they transmit the diseases bacterial wilt and cucumber mosaic. Larvae feed on roots and underground stems.

Controls:
- Heavy mulching is an effective deterrent.
- Handpick the beetles. Look for them on the undersides of leaves.
- Catnip, tansy, nasturtiums and goldenrod are repellent plants.
- Strew onion skins over each planting spot.
- Soldier beetles, tachinid flies, braconid wasps and certain nematodes are natural predators.
- Try sprinkling radish seeds around susceptible crop seeds. The quick-sprouting radishes are said to keep the female beetle from laying eggs.
- Plant victimized crops late in the season.
- Grow resistant varieties.
- Spray a mix of equal parts of wood ashes and hydrated lime in water on the upper and lower surfaces of leaves. If necessary, hit the beetles with a home-brewed spray of hot pepper and garlic.

Favorite Victims: These pests have the distinction of being the champion insect vegetarians—they'll eat more different plants (328 hosts have been recorded) than any other garden pest. On the good side, tarnished plant bugs do consume the eggs of Colorado potato beetles.

Range: Throughout North America.

Description: *Adult* is a ¼″-long, green to brown insect that is mottled with brown, black and yellow markings. Fairly nondescript-looking except for a black-tipped yellow triangle at the end of each forewing. *Nymph* is less than ¼″ long, pale or greenish yellow with black dots on abdomen and thorax. *Eggs* are curved and elongated, deposited on host plant.

The tarnished plant bug lives through three to five generations a year, overwintering in garden trash as either an adult or a nymph.

Modus Operandi: Both nymphs and adults suck juices from buds, fruits and stems. They inject a toxin that kills plant tissue and can cause deformed roots, disfigured flowers, defective fruit and blackened shoots or tips.

Tarnished plant bugs are hard to trace to their crimes because they're so active. They're easier to catch and treat in early morning when the coolness and dew slow them down.

Controls:
- Keep your garden clean to eliminate the bugs' winter home. In most instances, that is an effective preventive and can keep tarnished plant bugs from becoming serious pests in your garden.
- Cover plants with cheesecloth or a spunbond row cover such as Reemay.
- Use sabadilla dust for serious infestations. Remember to dust early in the morning when the bug is less active.

Thrips	**Whitefly**	**Wireworm**
Order Thysanoptera	Order Homoptera	Family Elateridae

Favorite Victims: White flowers. Also likes many garden vegetables and fruits (the citrus thrips give fruit a small, dark—harmless—ring).

Range: Throughout North America.

Description: *Adult* is a minute insect only 1/50″ long. Resembles a small, dark thread or gnat unless seen under a magnifying glass. If enlarged, you can see the distinctive feathery wings. *Nymph* also is minute, often green. Passes through many molts (instars), starting out pale and wingless. *Eggs* inserted into leaves and stems are too small to spot.

Modus Operandi: Thrips scrape holes in fruit and leaves and then suck plant juices. Leaves get scars, may turn pale and sometimes die. Thrips can carry the spotted wilt virus to tomatoes.

These are very active insects, and they flee when disturbed. Sometimes it's easier to find the black specks they leave behind than the pests themselves.

Thrips almost always operate in large groups—perhaps that's why their name is both singular and plural. Even so, they rarely inflict more than cosmetic damage, which can often be ignored. (There are also some beneficial species that prey on other mites and small insects—even other thrips.)

Controls:
- A spray of plain water knocks them off victim plants. Add a little dishwashing soap and you may suffocate them as well.
- Diatomaceous earth is quite effective.
- A spray made from field larkspur is a reported repellent.
- Sulfur and tobacco dusts were the standard treatment for years. They still work.
- Green lacewings prey on thrips.
- Remove and destroy infested plants.
- Keep plants well watered, and they'll be less susceptible to thrips damage.
- An aluminum foil mulch confuses thrips so much they often won't land on your crops.
- Some authorities recommend controlling weeds, since thrips like to eat many species.
- Rotenone or pyrethrum can be used when all else fails.

Favorite Victims: Most fruits and vegetables. Relish lots of indoor and greenhouse plants.

Range: Warm areas—southern U.S., both coasts, greenhouses.

Description: *Adult* is a tiny (1/16″ long), mothlike homopteran with two pairs of white powdery wings. Whiteflies may hide under leaves, but they fly up in a cloud when their host plant is disturbed. *Nymphs* go through various stages, are oval, generally white or green and have fine waxy hairs. *Eggs* are minute (1/100″) and pale yellow, laid on the undersides of leaves.

Whiteflies go through several generations a year, and hibernate as nymphs.

Modus Operandi: Both adults and nymphs suck plant juices, especially from tender young growth. Worse, whiteflies secrete a honeydew as they chew that's a haven for diseases such as sooty black fungus.

Controls:
- Knock the flies off plants with repeated strong water sprays.
- Spray plants with Safer's Insecticidal Soap or a homemade soapy or oily spray to suffocate the insect. Used properly, Safer's does not harm whitefly predators.
- Use a homemade nicotine-based spray.
- Ryania sprays are also effective.
- Commercial or homemade yellow sticky traps work well. Shake the plants so the whiteflies will take wing and notice—and land on—the traps.
- Marigold roots secrete a substance that is absorbed by nearby vegetables and repels whiteflies.
- The tiny wasp *Encarsia formosa* is a very effective predator. Ladybugs and lacewings also prey on whiteflies.

Favorite Victims: Potatoes, carrots, cabbage, lettuce, onions, corn, beets, beans, turnips.

Range: Throughout North America.

Description: *Larva* is a hard-shelled, jointed worm up to 1 1/2″ long. Usually reddish brown. They are sometimes confused with millipedes, but wireworms have only three pairs of legs—near the head—while millipedes have many legs. Also, wireworms do not have the millipede's habit of curling up when disturbed. *Adult* is a 1/2″-long, black, gray or brown beetle with dark head spots and wing bands. Commonly known as click beetles, because when put on their backs, they snap their bodies repeatedly, throwing themselves up into the air until they land upright. (Many a child has had fun playing with a click beetle.)

Life cycle may take several years to complete. Both adults and larvae overwinter in the soil.

Modus Operandi: Larvae chew underground parts of plants—seeds, roots, tubers. They can cause serious damage without ever being seen or suspected. Larvae are most numerous in poorly drained soil and new gardens that were previously sodded.

Controls:
- Cultivate the soil frequently in the fall and spring (as often as once a week) to expose and kill wireworms. This is a very important control practice.
- Bury potato pieces 1″ or 2″ deep in the soil as a trap crop. Pull them up once a week or so to remove the worms. (You may find a dozen or more on a single potato piece.) Some people attach sticks to the potatoes to make them easier to retrieve.
- Alfalfa and clover cover crops repel wireworms. White mustard and buckwheat are also said to repel wireworms, but timothy and other grass hays attract them.
- Milkweed juice repels wireworms. It can be used to treat the soil around victim crops.

| **Thrips**
Order Thysanoptera | **Whitefly**
Order Homoptera | **Wireworm**
Family Elateridae |

Adult

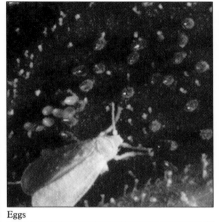

Eggs

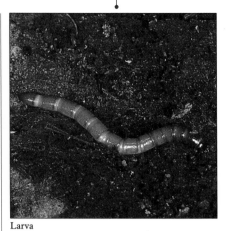

Larva

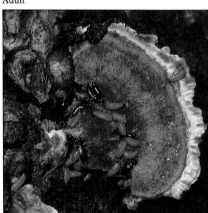

Nymphs and adults

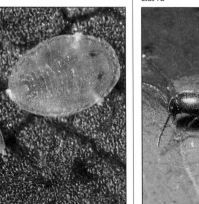

Nymphs

Adult

Leaf damage

Adult

Helpful Insects

| **Assassin Bug**
Family Reduviidae | **Braconid Wasp**
Family Braconidae | **Chalcid**
Superfamily Chalcididae |

Nymph

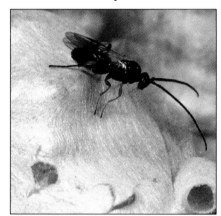
Adult getting ready to lay

Adult

Adult feeding on sulphur butterfly

Larvae spinning cocoons on tobacco hornworm

New adults emerging from moth cocoon

Adult laying eggs in an aphid

Adult laying eggs in an aphid

| Assassin Bug
Family Reduviidae | Braconid Wasp
Family Braconidae | Chalcid
Superfamily Chalcididae |

Alias: Kissing bug.

Likely Targets: Aphids, caterpillars, Colorado potato beetles, Japanese beetles, leafhoppers, Mexican bean beetles and many other garden pests.

Range: Throughout North America.

Description: *Adult* is a long-legged bug from $1/2''$ to $1^3/8''$ long. Different species can be quite varied in looks but, in general, assassin bugs are brown or black with a narrow head, large eyes and a strong, curved beak. The circular abdomen protrudes from under the folded wings. *Nymph* is similar to adult, but often brightly colored. *Eggs* are laid in the soil.

Various species have different life cycles, taking from one to several years to complete. They overwinter as adults, nymphs or eggs.

Modus Operandi: Assassin bugs hold their prey with their powerful front legs while they suck its body fluids. They feed mostly on larvae.

Don't pick up an assassin bug. Some species can bite humans. Their bite is painful and leaves an itchy spot. A few people are allergic to assassin bites.

Most assassins are great to have on garden pest patrol. The wheel bug (*Arilus cristatus*), for instance, loves Japanese beetle larvae and caterpillars—even very large ones. It's found east of the Rockies and has a series of raised, coglike protrusions near its head (hence its name). Still, there are a few species that prefer beneficial insects like honeybees. There are even a few assassins, like the Eastern blood-sucking conenose (*Triatoma sanguisuga*, also called the big bed bug or Mexican bed bug), that suck blood from vertebrates like us.

Assassin bugs are not commercially available.

Likely Targets: Aphids, hornworms, cutworms, imported cabbageworms, beetle larvae, gypsy moths, codling moths and tent caterpillars.

Range: Throughout North America.

Description: *Adult* is a very tiny ($1/16''$ to $5/8''$) wasp, usually black, but can be yellow or brilliant red. It has long antennae and often carries a long, bladelike stinger on its rear end. *Eggs* are tiny, laid within body of host. *Larva* is tiny, wormlike and white, and develops inside host. *Pupa* is a small cocoon, often seen on a victim's body or singly or in bunches on twigs.

Modus Operandi: The braconid parasitizes many insect pests. Landing on its victim, it swings its abdomen forward and stings. It may imbibe blood, sap or honeydew from its prey, or even lay eggs inside it. After the eggs hatch, the larvae (and, in some instances, the pupae) grow inside the host, weakening and often killing the victim eventually.

It's much easier to see clues of the wasp's presence than the little insect itself. For instance, take a hand magnifying lens to a cluster of aphids. Do you see any specimens with slightly enlarged, shiny bodies, often with a very neat circular exit hole on the back? A young braconid has developed inside that mummified aphid, leaving the dead shell when it became an adult ready to take wing.

Ever see a tomato hornworm with an adornment of white-to-beige "eggs" poking up on its back? Don't squash that caterpillar, thinking it's carrying around a future generation of hornworms. Leave it be. Those are braconid cocoons. That hornworm is rearing future hornworm destroyers.

Braconids do best in humid, warm (above 59°F) conditions, so they make good greenhouse predators.

They are not commercially available.

Likely Targets: Aphids, whiteflies, leafhoppers, caterpillars, beetles and scales.

Range: Throughout North America.

Description: *Adult* is a tiny, stocky ($1/16''$ to $3/8''$) wasp, practically unnoticeable. Mostly black, but sometimes metallic blue, green or golden yellow. The egg-laying organ (ovipositor) does not protrude. *Eggs* may be laid outside or inside the host. *Larva* parasitizes host.

Modus Operandi: In most species, the female stings a host, then lays her eggs inside. They develop into larvae, weakening and often killing the victim eventually. The chalcid leaves a small exit hole in the dead victim's shell, similar to that left by a braconid wasp. (It does not mummify the aphid with silk as the braconid does, however.)

Some adult chalcids also feed directly from a host. To do so, the wasp sometimes secretes a fluid that builds a hard shell around the stinger. Then it turns around and uses this feeding tube as a straw. (It won't feed from and parasitize the same host.)

A few chalcids cause harm (from the gardener's point of view) because they parasitize *other* insect parasites—a phenomenon called hyperparasitism. In fact, in one species, the male chalcid will parasitize the female of its own species. Almost all chalcids, though, are very beneficial. Given a warm, humid environment, they reproduce quickly enough to control many pest outbreaks. Indeed, some species lay eggs that can develop into from 10 to 1,000 larvae each, a process called polyembryony.

Chalcids are very susceptible to pesticides, another good reason to avoid broad-spectrum sprays (biological or not) whenever possible.

Two types, *Encarsia formosa* and trichogramma (both discussed separately), are commercially available.

Encarsia formosa Family Chalcididae		**Firefly** Family Lampyridae

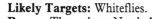

Likely Targets: Whiteflies.
Range: Throughout North America.
Description: *Adult* is a truly tiny wasp, a mere 1/40″ long. Requires a magnifying glass to examine. Female has a black and yellow thorax, shiny yellow abdomen and brown head. (The rarely seen male—they're literally one in a thousand—is larger and dark brown.) Wings are hairy edged and fold back flat over the abdomen. *Egg* and *larva* develop inside the host.

The average *Encarsia* lays about 30 eggs during its lifetime. Given the right conditions, it can complete its life cycle in 20 days.
Modus Operandi: The female deposits its egg inside a whitefly nymph where it develops into a larva. This process kills the nymph and leaves it blackened. If you see a smattering of what looks like black pepper among a cluster of whiteflies, you can be sure an *Encarsia* is at work. (It's often easier to see this telltale sign than to spot an adult wasp.)

Encarsia parasitize only the third or fourth instar (development phase) of the whitefly. If there are not enough of these around, they'll kill pupae and earlier instars for food. (They do this either with a feeding tube like other chalcids or by repeatedly stabbing and sipping from their victims.) While this will make a short-term dent in the whitefly population, it will sharply cut *Encarsia* breeding as well. If the wasps reduce their food supply drastically enough, they will even break their tradition of bearing only female offspring and (gasp!) start bearing males. This serves as a bizarre population control measure, because the males do not seem to mate —only to parasitize female *Encarsia* larvae.

The opposite problem—too many whiteflies—also occurs. To avoid this, introduce purchased *Encarsia* as soon as a whitefly problem becomes evident (or even beforehand if conditions seem right) so they can keep the pest's numbers from getting too large to control. A reputable breeder can be a big help by advising you when to release the parasites. *Encarsia* do best with high humidity, warm temperatures (in the 70s) and lots of light (14 to 16 hours a day). This makes it hard to keep them thriving in a winter greenhouse unless natural heat and light are supplemented. Also, be careful about throwing away dead leaves without examining their undersides for peppery wasp pupae. And if you have *Encarsia*, don't spray whiteflies with anything more than water unless a really serious infestation is at hand. Otherwise, the *Encarsia* wasp that was helping to keep the whiteflies in check might be wiped out, requiring restocking.

The moral? It's best to work for a balance between predator and prey: enough wasps to keep the whiteflies from getting out of hand, and enough whiteflies to supply the wasps with food.

Alias: Lightning bug, lampyrid beetle, glowworm.
Likely Targets: Snails, slugs, mites and insect larvae.
Range: Throughout U.S.
Description: *Adult* is that famous soft-bodied brown or black beetle (1/4″ to 3/4″ long) with the luminous abdomen that flashes on and off during summer nights. *Larva* is flat, with a toothed outline and strong jaws. Unlike most beetle larvae, which are soft grubs, the firefly larva looks like a beetle in its own right—hence its popular name, the lampyrid beetle. The larvae of many species can glow in the dark as well, earning an extra nickname: glowworms. *Eggs* are laid in the soil.

The firefly lives through one generation a year, overwintering as a larva.
Modus Operandi: Both adult and larva eat insects, but the larva is the more vicious killer. It likes to climb over the back of a snail, then clamp down with its jaws when the mollusk sticks its head out. It secretes an enzyme that paralyzes the victim and helps start digesting it. Like the adult, the larva is nocturnal, hunting at night for ground creatures to eat.

What is the adult's flashing all about? It's part of the mating game, of course. (No one knows why some larvae glow.) The male flies around signaling, hoping to find a perched or ground-level female of the same species. Watch the pattern of flashes—duration, timing, etc.—because different species use different signal patterns. (Apparently, the female of one species takes this lighting ploy one step further. After finding and mating with a male of her kind, she signals to males of other species. Then when they come close, she catches and eats them.)

Fireflies are not commercially available.

Encarsia formosa Family Chalcididae	**Firefly** Family Lampyridae	

Adult

Larva

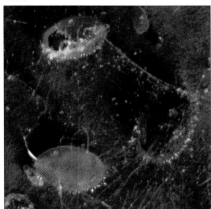
Whitefly parasitized by *Encarsia formosa*

Adult

Ground Beetle Family Carabidae	**Ichneumon Wasp** Family Ichneumonidae	**Lacewing** Family Chrysopidae

Larva with prey

Adult

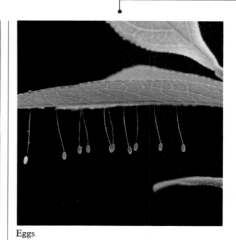

Eggs

Adult fiery searcher

Adult

Larva

Adult

Adult

Ground Beetle Family Carabidae	Ichneumon Wasp Family Ichneumonidae	Lacewing Family Chrysopidae

Likely Targets: Caterpillars, cutworms and other soft-bodied larvae. Some species are fond of snails and slugs.

Range: Throughout North America.

Description: *Adult* is a dark, shiny, heavily armored, 1"-long beetle. Some resemble June beetles, but are less rounded. *Larva* varies depending on species. Some have fearsome-looking pincer jaws. *Eggs* are laid singly in soil.

Both larvae and adults may live two years, hibernating in the soil or garden trash.

Modus Operandi: Both adults and larvae feed at night, and will run for cover if disturbed from their rock or log hiding place during the day. They are fierce predators with voracious appetites. Indeed, their fierce appearance may make a gardener want to squash them. Don't; you'll be losing one of a plant's best friends.

Avoid picking them up, however. One common species, the fiery searcher (*Calosoma scrutator*), gives off a stinging secretion. Another, the green pubescent ground beetle (*Chlaenius sericeus*), gives off a leathery smell when disturbed.

So when you spot a ground beetle, ignore its ugliness. Leave it alone, with respect and appreciation for the good work it does.

Ground beetles are not commercially available.

Alias: Ichneumon fly.

Likely Targets: Caterpillars, borers and wood-boring larvae. Enjoys various other insects and spiders.

Range: Throughout North America.

Description: *Adult* is a thin, delicate wasp with long antennae in front and, frequently, a very long ovipositor (egg-laying, stingerlike organ) behind. There are numerous species (Ichneumonidae is one of the largest insect families), varying from $^1/_8$" to 3" long. They resemble braconid wasps, except ichneumons are generally larger and slenderer. Most are yellow, brown or black. *Eggs* and *larvae* develop inside host.

Modus Operandi: The female uses her long ovipositor to inject eggs into hosts. Here the larvae almost always remain, roaming around internally. They may avoid the vital organs to let the weakened host survive as long as possible. Sometimes the host even pupates before it dies—with adult wasps, not the matured victim, emerging from the cocoon.

The value of this large family of insects in destroying crop pests is enormous. Silk moths, tussock moths, tent caterpillars and fall webworms all have their ichneumon counterparts—as do most garden-disturbing caterpillars, such as cutworms. Several ichneumon species have been deliberately used to control infestations of sawflies and European corn borers.

The most exotic ichneumon is *Megarhyssa macrurus*. This 2" to 3" wasp has an ovipositor that's an additional 2" to 4" long. It can work that ovipositor down through an inch of wood to lay an egg in its victim—a developing horntail larva. (Apparently, the wasp senses the vibrations of the larva's feeding.)

Most adults do not sting, but live on nectar, pollen and water. One wasp of the genus *Ophion* is often seen on window screens—it's 1" long, orange-black, long-antennaed and loves garden pests. For the most part, ichneumon damage is more visible than the wasp itself. A dry, brittle caterpillar or cocoon with small, hard, oval pupae cases inside is a sure sign that an ichneumon has been at work.

Ichneumons are not commercially available.

Alias: Aphid lion, aphis lion, aphid wolf, stink fly.

Likely Targets: Aphids, thrips, whiteflies, leafhopper nymphs, corn earworms, mites, scales and mealybugs.

Range: Throughout North America.

Description: *Adult* is a fairylike, green flying insect, $^3/_8$" to $^3/_4$", with iridescent eyes and delicate, almost transparent wings that fold over its back like a roof when at rest. Has a weak, fluttering way of flying. In many species, the adult gives off an odorous excretion when threatened. *Larva* is a $^3/_8$" long, grayish brown, grublike caterpillar with long jaws. *Eggs* are white, tiny and laid on threadlike stalks.

Lacewings go through three to four generations a year, overwintering as pupae in cocoons.

Modus Operandi: The larvae are nononsense predators: They seize their victims with their tusklike jaws, lift them high off the plant and suck them dry. They can consume up to 60 aphids an hour. (The adults will eat insects, but generally prefer pollen, nectar and honeydew.) In fact, the larvae's fierce eating habits may help explain why the adult lays each egg on top of a slender stalk made from secreted body fluids. That stalk guards the eggs from ants and other predators, but it also protects them from each other. Otherwise, the first larva to hatch might eat all its siblings.

Lacewing larvae tend to stay near the place they're born, assiduously hunting for the hundreds of prey they consume in the few weeks between hatching and pupating. This makes them good insects to import to an area—they're not as likely as, say, ladybugs to leave the garden. To encourage adults to stay, grow some flowers that provide nectar and pollen, and make sure they have a good supply of water.

The adults are attracted to light at night, so they can sometimes be found hanging on screen doors or smashed against cars. They are also quite vulnerable to insect sprays.

Green lacewings can be mail-ordered and imported to a garden, but they're also quite common naturally. Their cousin, the brown lacewing (Hemerobiidae family), is also widely found in nature and is a good predator. Slightly bigger than its green cousin, it attaches its eggs directly to plant foliage.

Ladybug Family Coccinellidae	Minute Pirate Bug *Orius* species	

Alias: Ladybird beetle, ladybird, aphid wolf.

Likely Targets: Aphids, rootworms, whiteflies, weevils, chinch bugs, Colorado potato beetles, mealybugs, scales and spider mites. Different species may prefer different pests.

Range: Throughout North America.

Description: *Adult* is an orange to red, 1/4″-long, spotted beetle (like a miniature speckled orange). That's the most typical ladybug, *Hippodamia convergens*. Other species may be black or tan, but almost all have the distinctive hemispherical shape. *Larva* is mean-looking, 1/16″ to 1/4″ and typically black with orange, red or white spots. *Eggs* are yellow-orange and laid in small clusters on stems, leaves, bark and ground debris.

Most ladybugs go through one generation a year (some species, several) and overwinter as adults in garden trash. Some species overwinter in the mountains of western U.S.

Modus Operandi: Both adults and larvae are serious predators. An adult may consume 300 aphids before it starts laying and then another three to 10 per egg, for a career total of 5,000 aphids. It chews its victims, hard parts and all. The larva can devour a good 400 aphids itself, but it likes to chew a hole in its victim, ingest digestive juices and then suck its meal out.

Ladybugs are some of the most beneficial of insects. In the late nineteenth century, the imported Australian, or vedalia, ladybug saved our nation's citrus industry from a destructive scale. Indeed, the beetle gets its common name from the Virgin Mary. It was named after our Lady by farmers in the Middle Ages who were grateful for its help in protecting their grapevines.

Of course, there are one or two members of the clan who aren't beneficial—notably that black sheep (actually, it's yellow), the Mexican bean beetle. Most good ladybugs stink as well. Perhaps that's why they're so brightly colored: to warn off predatory birds.

Ladybugs are commercially available, but if conditions aren't just right, purchased ones may fly away. Make sure purchased bugs have been "preconditioned" to reawaken their hibernating reproductive capacity. Otherwise they're likely to take wing and fly right back to those out-west mountains they were gathered from. Handle gently. Don't stock before there are enough pests for them to feed on. Release late in the evening in an area with a damp mulch for shelter.

Alias: Insidious flower bug.

Likely Targets: Aphids, thrips, whiteflies and spider mites.

Range: Throughout North America.

Description: *Adult* is a very small (1/20″-long), black or brownish bug with a pointy snout and large eyes. *Nymph* is similar to adult. *Eggs* are clear or white, laid inside the tissue of plants.

Modus Operandi: Well named, the minute pirate bug is a tiny raider of tiny pests. Both adults and nymphs prey on small insects—53 varieties of them, at latest count. The pirate earned its other name, the insidious flower bug, from the fact that it likes to attack thrips, which are often found on flowers. Indeed, the best chance of ever seeing a minute pirate bug is while it's gorging itself happily at the thrips' favorite eating place: white flowers.

Minute pirate bugs are not commercially available.

Ladybug Family Coccinellidae	**Minute Pirate Bug** *Orius* species	

Larva

Nymph

Adult

Adult

Adults

Praying Mantis Family Mantidae	**Robber Fly** Family Asilidae	

Nymphs hatching from egg case

Adult

Adult

Adult

Adult

Praying Mantis Family Mantidae		Robber Fly Family Asilidae

Likely Targets: Aphids, bees, beetles, bugs, butterflies, caterpillars, leafhoppers, flies, wasps—basically, anything it can get its forelegs on.

Range: Throughout North America.

Description: *Adult* is a slim, green or brown, 2″ to 4″ insect with large forelimbs for grabbing, large compound eyes and a unique ability to swivel its triangular head and look over its shoulder. Despite its size, the mantis blends in well on plants and can be hard to find. *Nymph* is similar to adult, but smaller, with undeveloped wings. *Eggs* are laid in a hard, light brown, cocoonlike sack of hardened froth.

Mantises go through one generation a year, overwintering as eggs.

Modus Operandi: The praying mantis (or mantid) gets its nickname from its habit of holding its front legs together as if in prayer while it waits for a victim to come near. When the unsuspecting prey strolls or flutters by, it reaches out those spiny limbs at lightning speed, snatches its meal and bites it in the back of the head. (This cuts the victim's main nerves, immobilizing it.)

The mantis will gladly wolf down beneficial as well as harmful insects—including other mantises. It may even tackle a salamander, shrew, small toad or hummingbird. That can make it something of a mixed blessing in a garden, but most people feel the mantids' good features outweigh their bad ones.

No one's sure if a male mantis would agree with this opinion, because, yes, it's true, the female does like to devour the male after mating (or even *during*). To mate at all, the smaller male must sneak up on his paramour from behind.

The easiest way to introduce mantises into the garden is to find egg cases and deposit them there. (These are widely available commercially.) Look for them attached to twigs or grass in open areas such as overgrown fields or the edges of fields or roads—wherever you can find a clump of plants a few feet high. Each 1″ to 2″ beige case holds from 100 to 300 eggs. Admire this handiwork. The female lays the entire case and eggs in one session, excreting a frothy substance that hardens with eggs inside and even includes one soft section (called the zone of issue) so the newly hatched nymphs have a way to get out.

Other than that, the case is quite durable and does a good job of protecting the eggs from hungry birds or other insects. But there is one small ichneumon wasp (there's an ichneumon for practically *everything*)—the Pidagrion mantis—that has a long ovipositor designed just for breaking into the mantis case and parasitizing those eggs.

Likely Targets: Leafhoppers, beetles, flies, bees, wasps, grasshoppers, grubs and grasshopper eggs.

Range: Throughout North America.

Description: *Adult* is a gray, $1/4$″ to $1^1/8$″ fly with long legs, a stout proboscis and a bearded mouth. Some species have slender, tapering abdomens; others are so stocky they look like bumblebees. *Larva* is white and resembles a tiny, flattened worm. *Eggs* are white and are laid in the soil.

The robber fly takes a year (or two) to complete its life cycle, overwintering in the soil as a larva.

Modus Operandi: Both the larva and adult are useful predators. The larva is less glamorous (but probably more important to gardeners). It crawls about underground eating grubs and grasshopper eggs. After pupating at the crust of the soil in early summer, the adult emerges, ready to attack other flying insects.

The mature robber is quite a hunter. It sits on a sunlit twig or some other perch, waiting for a potential victim to pass by. Then it darts out to intercept the meal ticket, grabbing it with its long legs, biting its back and injecting a paralyzing chemical. The robber then goes back to the perch with its meal.

This perch-and-pounce behavior is distinctive. A beelike or wasplike insect acting this way is likely to be a robber fly. Another giveaway is the loud buzzing sound all airborne robbers make.

The robber fly is quite widespread in nature. It is not commercially available.

Rove Beetle Family Staphylinidae	Soldier Beetle Family Cantharidae	

Likely Targets: Cabbage maggots, mites, beetle larvae, aphids and small worms.

Range: Throughout North America.

Description: *Adult* is a brown or black, $1/16$" to $3/4$" beetle. Its short wing covers lie over only a little of its abdomen. The rest sticks out and curls up—a bit like a scorpion's back end—when it runs. *Larva* resembles adult. *Eggs* are laid in soil or dead plant matter.

Rove beetles can go through several generations a year, overwintering as larvae, pupae or adults.

Modus Operandi: Both adult and larva are scavengers, dining on numerous small insects. The adult can run and fly swiftly, using its sharp mandibles to do the dirty work. (Don't pick one up—it may bite.) Some species can also defend themselves by spraying a stinky liquid wherever their tail points.

A few larvae are parasitic. One, in particular, likes to live off ants. But most are predators, and good ones. They can eat 20 aphids or grubs a day. One species, *Aleochara bimaculata*, is reportedly able to devour up to 80% of the cabbage maggots in an area.

Rove beetles are not commercially available, but they're widespread in nature, with almost 2,900 species.

Likely Targets: Aphids, spider mites, small caterpillars, grasshopper eggs, cucumber and other beetles.

Range: Throughout North America.

Description: *Adult* is a $1/2$" beetle that looks like a glowless firefly with long antennae. Color varies with species. *Larva* lives in the soil. Appearance varies with species. *Eggs* are laid in clusters in the soil.

The soldier beetle goes through one or two generations a year, and overwinters as a larva in the soil.

Modus Operandi: Adults are often found at flowers—particularly milkweed, hydrangea and goldenrod. There they feed on nectar and pollen as well as on small insects such as aphids. They may also dine on cucumber beetles, grasshopper eggs and caterpillars. The larvae like to devour insects in the soil or under bark.

All soldier beetles are closely related to fireflies. Two of the most common species are the downy leather-wing (*Podabrus tomentosus*) and the Pennsylvania leather-wing (*Chauliognathus pennsylvanicus*). The downy, gray-blue and covered with fine "hair," exists all over America. The Pennsylvania, yellow-orange with black blotches at the wingtips, is found east of the Mississippi.

While the larvae will do their good work underground and most likely go unnoticed by the gardener, the adults can often be spotted on their favorite flower, goldenrod. Here they can find "sweets as well as meats" and opportunities to mate as well. Another similar-looking beetle, the longhorned, often hangs out on the same flower. This vegetarian (indeed, it eats wood) is generally a bit bigger with zebra-striped wings.

Soldier beetles are not commercially available.

Rove Beetle Family Staphylinidae	**Soldier Beetle** Family Cantharidae	

Larva

Larva

Adult

Adult eating aphid

Adult

Web-spinning spider with cockroach

Crab spider

Larva eating aphid

Jumping spider eating butterfly

Adult

Wolf spider

Adult

Spider Order Araneae		Syrphid Fly Family Syrphidae

Likely Targets: Insects, any insects.

Range: Throughout North America.

Description: A spider is *not* an insect, but an arachnid. It has eight legs (not six) and two body segments (not three). Young spiders, called spiderlings, resemble adults. Most go through one generation a year, overwintering as eggs, frequently in beige sacs. Some spiders overwinter as adults.

Modus Operandi: After biting its victim with its two fangs, the spider injects a venom that paralyzes the prey. There are over 3,000 species of spiders in North America. They live almost anywhere—on plants, in webs, under debris, underground, etc. They are especially useful to gardeners because they are one of the first small predators to become active in spring.

All of which is to point out that the common human prejudice against spiders is badly misplaced—they are very helpful, and only a few species have venom that harms people. Instead, we should appreciate, even admire, this gardener's friend.

Spiders eat practically any moving insect and have two main styles of catching prey: trapping and hunting. When most of us think "spider," we picture the trapping spider that spins a sticky web and waits for an unsuspecting flying insect to get snared in the strands. An artist with silk, it is responsible for the class's name, arachnid. In Greek mythology, a Lydian princess named Arachne was the finest human spinner and weaver. When she challenged the goddess Athena to a weaving contest—and lost—Athena turned her into a spider, to spend her life spinning webs.

Spinning spiders snare a lot of garden insects, but hunting spiders are equally helpful because they often catch pests too immature to fly. The most common hunting spiders are the crab (family Thomisidae), wolf (family Lycosidae) and jumping (family Salticidae).

Crab spiders, named for their shell-like bodies and habit of running sideways, are numerous in gardens. They are likely to be seen perched on leaves and flowers, front legs spread and waiting for an unwary victim. Some so closely match the flowers where they lie that it is difficult to see them at all.

Most wolf spiders hunt at night and dig burrows, live under rocks or boards or have no home whatever. They have dark, mottled colors—the better to hide in wood, dead leaves and other debris, my dear—and the classic spider appearance.

Jumping spiders are anxious creatures, characterized by short, jerky movements and their skill at leaping on their prey. They are the big- and sharp-eyed members of the clan, with an ability to see victims all of several inches away.

Spinner, crab, wolf or jumper—cherish the spider you find in your plot.

Alias: Hover fly, flower fly.

Favorite Victims: Aphids, mealybugs, scales and leafhoppers.

Range: Throughout North America.

Description: *Adult* is a ½"-long fly mimic—it often resembles a honeybee, wasp, yellow jacket or bumblebee. Unlike these stinging insects, the syrphid has short antennae, one pair of wings and (the only distinguishing trait easy to spot) can hover motionless in the air. *Larva* is a ½" green or brown, sightless maggot with a cylindrical body that tapers toward the head. *Eggs* are glistening white, laid on foliage near victim species.

Syrphid flies go through several generations a year, overwintering as larvae.

Modus Operandi: Adult syrphid flies are not predators. These peace-loving flies spend their lives hovering near flowers (hence their nicknames) to feed on nectar and pollen. The larvae, though, are dedicated flesh eaters able to consume an aphid a minute. Like the lacewing larva, the syrphid lifts its prey off its feet with its fanglike hooks and then sucks the very life out of it. This blind, legless, sluglike hunter can consume over 400 aphids in its two weeks of larval life, making it an important natural predator of aphids and other small insect pests.

But while the larva does the dirty work, don't fail to appreciate the adult as well. Not only is its hovering ability remarkable to observe (and if you watch one very closely, you may notice that even when it's resting on a flower, its body continues to *buzz*), but it is a wonderful pollinator as well. In fact, they're second only to bees as flower pollinators.

So watch those "bees" and "yellow jackets" in the garden more closely this summer. Chances are some will do as much pest eating as flower fertilizing.

Syrphid flies are not commercially available.

Tachinid Fly Family Tachinidae	**Tiger Beetle** Family Cicindelidae	**Trichogramma Wasp** Family Trichogrammatidae

Likely Targets: Cutworms, sawflies, Japanese beetles, Mexican bean beetles, corn borers, gypsy moths, grasshoppers and many caterpillars.

Range: Throughout North America.

Description: *Adult* looks like a common housefly, about the same size ($1/8''$ to $1/2''$) and color (gray-brown). There is one significant distinction: Houseflies don't have the prominent abdominal bristles tachinids do. But those are hard to spot on a fly in flight, and tachinids are very active and quick fliers. *Larva* is gray to white, develops inside host. *Eggs* are tiny, white, deposited on foliage or host.

Tachinids go through several generations a year, overwintering as larvae.

Modus Operandi: Adult tachinids are fond of nectar and insect honeydew and are therefore often found on flowers or foliage. It's the tiny yellow larvae that parasitize garden pests.

Tachinid larvae feed mostly on muscle tissue and fat, allowing their host to remain alive, though sickly, for a good while. Sometimes a host caterpillar will even live long enough to spin a cocoon or chrysalis before it dies. No butterfly emerges from that tomb —just more tachinid flies.

Tachinid females mean business. They have three ways of assuring meal tickets for their offspring. First, a female may glue its eggs to the victim's skin, being careful to place them out of reach—right behind the victim's head. Second, she may lay on foliage near host insects. The hatched larvae will then find their hosts, or the eggs may even be *ingested* by unwitting victims. Third, some tachinids (there are over 1,300 species) can hatch the young within their own bodies and then attach the larvae to a host or leaf. This tactic can backfire, though. If the female doesn't find a good home for its offspring, they may devour her.

In all, tachinids make up the most important group of insect-eating flies. Small wonder—a single female may lay 6,000 eggs or 13,000 larvae, and the flies can go through their complete life cycle in as little as three weeks. So never swat a fly in the vegetable plot unless you know for sure what it is.

Tachinid flies are not commercially available but already live in most areas.

Likely Targets: Ants, bugs, caterpillars, flies, worms, aphids and spiders.

Range: Throughout North America.

Description: *Adult* is a $3/8''$ to $7/8''$ beetle, with big eyes, long antennae and long, thin legs for running swiftly. Metallic colors range from green, blue and purple to black and bronze, and are sometimes beautifully iridescent. *Larva* is an S-shaped, spiny grub that lives in ground burrows. *Eggs* are laid in the soil.

The tiger beetle takes from one to three years to go through its life cycle, overwintering in the soil as an adult or larva.

Modus Operandi: The lightning-quick adult runs or flies after its prey, grabs it with its strong, sickle-shaped jaws, bangs it against the ground until dead, then sucks and chews the carcass. It's an extremely wary insect and difficult to observe. It likes sunny, open areas. You may see it flying away about 15 feet in front of you as you walk along a dirt path or road.

The larva also lives in open, sunny areas, but it likes to hunt from a carefully dug burrow. Here it waits until prey comes by, then either grabs it tight while it stays anchored in its hole or rushes out, snags it and pulls it back into the burrow. The larva is even harder to spot than the adult, for it's very sensitive to vibrations in the earth and will hide if it feels someone approaching.

Not commercially available, this two-stage pest destroyer is widespread.

Likely Targets: Cutworms, armyworms, cabbage loopers, cabbageworms, hornworms, corn borers, codling moths, fruitworms, cotton bollworms, leafworms and 200 other destructive butterfly and moth species.

Range: Throughout North America.

Description: There's not much point in describing the distinctive features of a trichogramma wasp, since 45 of them, laid end to end, would equal only one inch. They are, therefore, exceedingly difficult to see.

Modus Operandi: Although trichogrammas are amazingly tiny, they are also amazingly effective parasites. For one thing, various trichogrammas attack hundreds of species. For another, while most insect parasites let their victim suffer a lingering death as a larva or adult (giving it more time to eat crops), trichogrammas nip pests in the bud: They parasitize eggs. The female lays one or more eggs in the host's eggs (depending on the size of the host's eggs). There the larvae feed and develop until they're ready to emerge as adult wasps, fly off, and lay eggs of their own. The victim never gets to hatch.

Trichogrammas are among the most popular commercially available beneficial insects. They've been used for over 20 years in Mexico to control that country's most destructive cotton pests, the bollworm and pink bollworm. The Soviet Union—the world's leader in trichogramma research and releases—has used the tiny wasps against the cabbage moth, corn borer and other pests. The wasps have reduced pest damage on some crops by over 80% and have led to substantial yield increases of wheat, corn, sugar beets, cabbage and apples.

One key to success with trichogramma releases is choosing the right species for particular pests. For instance, *Trichogramma minuium* is often used to protect orchards and ornamentals, and *Trichogramma platneri* guards avocado groves effectively. The best species for all-around garden use is the widely available *Trichogramma pretiosum*.

Although trichogrammas should be able to breed throughout the growing season in a good location, additional purchase and release may be required to deal with peak infestations. Flowers, including blooming weeds, provide the nectar-sipping adults with food.

Tachinid Fly Family Tachinidae	**Tiger Beetle** Family Cicindelidae	**Trichogramma Wasp** Family Trichogrammatidae

Adult

Larvae (head in tunnel) after a grasshopper

Adult parasitizing a host egg

Adult

Adult

Plant Allies

| **Feverfew**
 Chrysanthemum parthenium | **Four-O'Clock**
 Mirabilis jalapa | **Garlic**
 Allium sativum |

C. parthenium

M. jalapa

A. sativum

M. jalapa

M. jalapa

Feverfew	Four-O'Clock	Garlic
Chrysanthemum parthenium	*Mirabilis jalapa*	*Allium sativum*

Positive Effects: Insects in general don't like and avoid its pungent foliage.

Description: Cultivated as an annual in cool climates and as a perennial in warm ones, feverfew is easy to grow and is scented somewhat like chamomile. The 6"- to 3'-tall plant is upright and bushy, bearing much-divided leaves attached to short stalks. The 1" flowers either resemble typical mums and are all white, all yellow, or white tinted with yellow in the center, or they may look like daisies, with yellow disks and white ray petals. The flowers are borne in clusters and bloom from midsummer to late summer of the first year.

Culture: Feverfew is of the daisy family and will tolerate poor soils and dry conditions. Young plants are available from most herb nurseries but can also be easily started at home. Start seeds indoors eight weeks before setting out, or sow them directly in early spring as soon as the soil can be worked. Scatter seeds on the soil surface or cover *very* thinly, as they need light to germinate. Space plants a foot apart and grow in full sun.

Feverfew self-sows readily and is commonly used as a bordering plant.

Positive Effects: Japanese beetles willingly devour the foliage, but don't live to regret it. (Warning: The plants and seeds are poisonous to humans also—so beware if young children play freely in the garden.)

Description: Cultivated as a tender annual in all but frost-free areas, the four-o'clock bears clusters of 1" to 2" flowers that, as the common name suggests, open in the afternoon and close the next morning. (They also open on cloudy days.) The fragrant, trumpet-shaped blossoms bloom from midspring to midautumn. Common colors include white, pink, red, yellow and rose-purple. The blooms are often striped or mottled in more than one color. The 2"- to 6"-long leaves are smooth, shiny green and attached to soft, succulent stems. The plants are bushy and attain a height of 2' to 3'.

Culture: In frost-free areas, four-o'clocks grow as perennials. In frost-*prone* areas, they must be dug up in fall (and stored in a cool but not freezing room) or be simply treated as tender annuals.

Start seeds indoors four to six weeks before the last frost, or sow them outside after all danger of frost is past. (The seeds are large—about the size of peas.) Cover with 1/2" of good soil and keep moist, and they should germinate in about 12 to 14 days. Transplant them to the garden when spring frosts end, spacing plants approximately 2' apart.

Four-o'clocks are hardy plants that do well in poor soils, withstand heat and high humidity and are seldom bothered by pests. They do as well in partial shade as they do in full sun.

Positive Effects: Garlic is a potent deterrent to insect pests. The plant emits a strong scent that confuses a pest that's trying to sniff out a favorite crop. It's even more effective when the bulbs are blended into a liquid spray. Aphids, Japanese beetles, flea beetles and the Mexican bean beetle are merely a few of the better-known insects that are repelled by this wonderful herb. It can also rebuff mosquitoes, ticks and intestinal worms. Because of its antiseptic properties, it's effective against many human diseases as well.

Description: A member of the allium, or onion, family, garlic sends up a foot-long stalk that is topped by small white flowers. The plants are compact enough to be stuck into corners and odd spaces around vegetables, berries, fruit vines and trees.

Culture: In most areas, fall-planted cloves produce larger bulbs than those set out in spring. However, the cloves *can* be planted in spring as soon as the soil can be worked, or even started indoors eight weeks before the date of average last spring frost. Garlic roots can go 2' deep, so loose soil that's rich in humus is also a prime factor in producing bigger bulbs.

Separate cloves just before planting (small ones do just as well as larger ones) and push them into the soil, pointed end up, until they're just covered. In areas with strong frost heavings, plant 2" deep. Space cloves 4" to 6" apart.

Water thoroughly and deeply during the growing season, but slack off when the tops start to die back in midsummer to late summer. After most of the tops have browned, bend the remaining ones over at ground level so they, too, will give up the ghost. Now it's time to dig and dry the bulbs. If rain is coming or the ground is wet, get the bulbs under cover and let them dry indoors. Otherwise, let them lie on the soil surface for a day or so before taking them in to finish drying. (In hot climates, lay tops over bulbs to protect them from too much hot sun.) Once dry, the cloves may be ground to make an effective bug-chasing spray, or, needless to say, used in the cooking pot.

| Marigold
Genera *Calendula* and *Tagetes* | Mint
Genus *Mentha* | Nasturtium
Tropaeolum majus |

Positive Effects: All *aromatic* marigolds confuse insect pests that are trying to home in on vegetable crops. (Unscented varieties don't bother bugs a bit.) The roots of French marigolds excrete a substance that can actually kill nematodes in their vicinity. Studies show the effects can last years after the plants are pulled. (This works more effectively if the marigolds are planted thickly.) French marigolds are also used to deter whiteflies on tomatoes and in greenhouses. Mexican marigolds repel their compatriot, the Mexican bean beetle, as well as wild rabbits.

Description: Marigolds are vividly colored, tender annuals that are easy to grow. They range in height from about 8″ to 3′, with the most common colors being orange, yellow, red and cream. They can bloom all season long if kept dead-headed; that is, if fading blooms are removed before they set seed.

Culture: Start marigolds from seed sown indoors six to eight weeks before the last spring frost. Barely cover the seeds, since light improves their germination. Marigolds can also be purchased as transplants, or the seeds sown outdoors after all danger of frost has passed.

Marigolds like lots of light and warmth, so set transplants in a sunny spot. They do best in loose, well-drained soil, but struggle in clay. Space young plants 6″ apart for dwarf types and 12″ to 18″ apart for taller forms. Don't overwater, and go easy on the soil fertility, or lots of foliage will result at the expense of flowers.

Keep in mind, too, that slugs love marigolds almost as much as organic gardeners do, so be on the lookout if they're a problem in your area.

Positive Effects: Strong-scented mint repels fleas, ants, aphids and pests of the cabbage family. Rather than plant mint near crops, however, use a spray made from steeped leaves (whole or chopped) or scatter stems that have been dried with the roots removed. (Even then, don't be surprised if a piece takes hold—mint can root anywhere along a cutting.)

Description: Mints are aromatic, moisture-loving perennials that can be harder than stubborn goats to confine. They are shallow-rooted, with pointed, oval leaves, squarish stems and small, inconspicuous flowers. They tend to grow in ground-covering clusters.

Culture: Mints cross-pollinate readily and tend not to reproduce true to seed, so it's best to start with cuttings from a friend or an herb nursery. Remove the leaves from the bottom third of each cutting and set that section in a pot containing a light rooting medium. Moist sharp sand, vermiculite or perlite all work fine. Some peat moss or light, sandy soil can be mixed in as well. Press the medium around the cuttings and water well. Keep the stems well watered and in a partly shaded location for about two weeks. Then give them full sun (and less frequent waterings) until the plants look healthy enough to be put in the garden.

Since mints spread quickly by runners, set a metal barrier that extends at least 1′ underground around plantings. Mints love a somewhat damp soil; they always seem to do well next to a leaky faucet. They also appreciate fertile soil and some shade. As a bonus, earthworms love to congregate under a carpet of these pungent herbs.

A good mint patch will create enough foliage for strewing as a light mulch around brassicas, with plenty left over to spice up iced tea and that leg of lamb.

Positive Effects: Nasturtiums repel whiteflies, squash bugs, cucumber beetles and woolly aphids. They *attract* (and hence make a good trap crop for) most other aphids.

Description: The striking contrast of foliage and flower makes the nasturtium a popular garden flower. The leaves are bright green and shield-shaped. The 2″ to 2¹/₂″ flowers are funnel-shaped, with many brilliant colors, including creamy white, salmon, cerise, scarlet, deep red, orange, golden yellow and mahogany. The plants range from 1′ for dwarf specimens up to 6′ to 10′ for climbing varieties.

Nasturtiums do well in greenhouses, in beds or hanging baskets and as ground cover for fruit trees. Plants bloom continually in cool weather, emitting a tart fragrance. Add the fact that all parts of the plant are edible, and you have an all-around garden winner.

Culture: Nasturtiums are extremely hardy annuals; they seem to thrive on neglect. In fact, it's safe to follow an old garden saying, "Be nasty to nasturtiums," since too much care in the form of lavish fertilizing or frequent waterings will produce lush leaves and few flowers.

Start seeds indoors six weeks before midspring or plant 1″ deep outdoors when soil warms in early spring. Germination occurs in about two weeks. Plants like full sun and should be spaced at least 1′ apart. In regions with hot summers, try planting in partial shade for better blooms.

Marigold Genera *Calendula* and *Tagetes*	**Mint** Genus *Mentha*	**Nasturtium** *Tropaeolum majus*

T. erecta (African)

M. piperita (peppermint)

T. majus

C. officinalis (pot)

M. spicata (spearmint)

T. majus

T. patula (French)

M. pulegium (pennyroyal)

| **Pyrethrum** Genus *Chrysanthemum* | **Rue** *Ruta graveolens* | **Tansy** *Tanacetum vulgare* |

C. coccineum

R. graveolens

T. vulgare

Pyrethrum	Rue	Tansy
Genus *Chrysanthemum*	*Ruta graveolens*	*Tanacetum vulgare*

Positive Effects: This plant deters leafhoppers, aphids, corn earworms, cabbage loopers and thrips. Pyrethrum works better on adult pests than on larvae—it does not seem to harm honeybees and ladybug larvae. It *can* wipe out many beneficial insects (including adult ladybugs), however, and should be used with reserve for that reason. Pyrethrum paralyzes insects, but watch to see that they are truly killed, because they often recover. If that happens, try a stronger concentration or destroy the pest in another manner.

Pyrethrum does not work as a companion plant; use either dried or fresh blossoms in a spray. (A little soap added to the mix may increase its effectiveness.) Store the homegrown insecticide in closed containers in order to preserve its potency. The dust is nontoxic to humans, livestock and pets. It can even be used as a safe flea powder.

While pyrethrum is widely available commercially, beware of pyrethrum-*based* formulations that contain more serious toxins.

Description: Sometimes called painted daisy or painted lady, pyrethrum does have big, daisylike flowers in white, pink and red. It has fernlike foliage and grows to a height of 1′ or 2′.

Culture: The plant is a bit difficult to start from seed (a sterile medium is important) because it takes three to four weeks to germinate. It's easier to begin growing this perennial by buying starts from an herb nursery. Set them out 12″ to 18″ apart, and then increase the planting by root division (pulling clumps of roots apart) in the fall or in the next spring just as new growth starts. Pyrethrum prefers a sunny, well-drained spot and limy soil. Keep cultivated, as it is easily overpowered by weeds.

Positive Effects: Rue is used to repel Japanese beetles, fleas and flies. It's also said that rue repels cats. (And in ancient days, it was used to ward off disease.) Scatter clippings near pest-prone crops or spray a brewed rue tea on the plants. If you grow it around Japanese beetle territory, crush a few leaves to better release its fragrance.

Some people are allergic to rue's essential oil, so beware of a rash that looks much like poison ivy. Ironically, in the past, rue was considered an antidote to all kinds of poisons.

Description: Not one of the more common herbs, rue is a beautiful, evergreen perennial that is well suited to use in herbal knot gardens or as a border or backdrop. (A clump of rue resembles a little boxwood bush.) Its woody stems and hardy, blue-green foliage reach 2′ with greenish yellow flowers that appear from May until September.

Culture: Rue can be sown outdoors in midspring or started indoors in late February, but if started from seed, it may be a couple of years before a good stand develops. Quicker results come from buying your first plants from an herb nursery. Then, in July or August, take some cuttings by pulling off 3″ sections of new growth. (You'll get more rooting plant edge on the end of stems by tearing—not cutting—the sections.) Dip them in commercial hormone rooting powder, and plant them in pots filled with compost and sand or any good soil mix. New root growth should be evident by early fall. Overwinter the plants indoors and set them out in the garden the following spring.

Plants should be spaced 16″ apart. Rue tolerates poor soils (though it prefers better) and thrives in sunny locations. By the way, although rue is more than easy to obtain legally, an old Greek superstition held that plants stolen from a neighbor's garden flourished best of all.

Positive Effects: Japanese beetles, ants, squash bugs, borers and cucumber beetles are the well-known avoiders of tansy. This bitter herb also repels many other insects, including flies, fleas and ants. (Grow some near the doorstep to keep ants from entering the house.) The profuse foliage can be clipped, bruised and strewn about as a mulch, or an insect-chasing tea can be made from the leaves. A few leaves on growing plants can also be bruised from time to time to release the essential oils.

Description: This extremely pungent herb is 2′ to 6′ tall, has dark green foliage and, come July or August, sports clusters of yellow buttonlike flowers. (Some of its descriptive nicknames include parsley fern, bachelor's-button, bitter buttons and stinking Willie.) Tansy is commonly employed as a backdrop border to a flower bed, in berry patches, with grapes or with roses. The short ornamental variety *T. v. crispum* is considered excellent for gardens.

Culture: Tansy can be started from seed, but it's easier to buy young plants from herb nurseries and divide the roots the following autumn or spring. It's a hardy perennial (indeed, its Latin name is derived from *athanaton*, the Greek word for "immortal") that will tolerate many soils.

This vigorous plant needs to be put in a relatively long-term location so it can establish a good base and spread from there. Eventually, the main plant will become woody and spindly looking. Then it's time to dig it up and fill in the space with sections of the newer outer growth.

Historically, tansy has been used as a medicine, a meat preserver and as one of the bitter herbs in Passover rites. The oil has also been rubbed on the body as an insect repellent. Today it's used as an attractive, dried everlasting flower and in the kitchen. It makes an acceptable substitute for pepper—but be sure to sprinkle the pungent herb *sparingly* on your eggs.

Positive Effects: A weak wormwood tea repels a host of insects—including weevils in storerooms, aphids, black flea beetles and cabbage moths—as well as slugs and snails. It's not a good companion plant, however, since its roots secrete a substance that inhibits the growth of nearby crops.

Don't overdo this strong-smelling herb: Too potent or too frequent applications can actually stunt vegetable growth. And although history records several instances of human consumption, wormwood should be considered poisonous in concentrated form and kept away from children.

Description: Wormwood is a handsome perennial with gray-green foliage and tiny yellow or white flowers that bloom from midsummer through fall. Its silvery tint makes it a great-looking backdrop for flowers. The base of the plant is woody, and the entire "bush" reaches a height of 2' or over.

Culture: Wormwood is easily started from seeds sown in fall, from rooted cuttings or by root division in fall. (See "Mint" for information on how to root cuttings.) Plants are available from most herb nurseries.

Bitter wormwood does fine in poor soils and will even grow in clay soil, but it prefers sandy, well-drained ground. You can use the leaves fresh to make your repellent teas. Later in the season, gather the whole plant and let it dry. Then strip the foliage and flowers from the stems, rub them to a fine consistency and store this in sealed jars for future bug deterring.

Anise (*Pimpinella anisum*) repels aphids. An 18"- to 24"-tall, semihardy annual with finely serrated leaves and tiny, white, starlike flowers. Sow the seeds of this frost-tender plant 12" apart in midspring.

Borage (*Borago officinalis*) repels hornworms. An 18"- to 24"-tall annual with oval, grayish, hairy leaves and small, sky blue flowers. Direct-sow seeds in midspring or start indoors and transplant after all danger of frost. Will self-seed.

Coriander (*Coriandrum sativum*) repels aphids. A 1'- to 2'-tall annual with dark green leaves and bright or pale mauve flowers. Sow seeds 1" deep outdoors after last spring frost, and thin to 10" apart.

Costmary (*Chrysanthemum balsamita*) repels moths. A 2'- to 3'-tall perennial with dark green leaves and deep yellow flower heads. Propagate by root division in spring, or start seeds indoors and transplant outside in late summer.

Dahlia (*Dahlia rosea*) repels nematodes. A 3'- to 4'-tall annual with lobed green leaves and variously colored flowers. Propagate from winter-stored tubers put out after all danger of frost.

Flax (*Linum usitatissimum*) repels Colorado potato beetles when interplanted with potatoes. A 1' to 4' annual with short, narrow leaves, narrow stems and white or blue flowers. Plant seeds 1" deep (or less) after all danger of frost.

Larkspur (*Delphinium*, var. spp.) attracts and kills Japanese beetles (also toxic to humans). A 2' to 3' annual with light green, linear leaves and tall, variously colored flowers. Sow seeds indoors in late winter and transplant in early spring.

Lavender (*Lavandula officinalis*) repels moths. A shrubby 1'-tall perennial with small, downy, grayish, lance-shaped leaves but rather undistinguished flowers. Start from cuttings in winter and transplant outdoors in spring.

Opal basil (*Ocimum basilicum*) repels hornworms. A semihardy, 1'- to 2'-tall annual, with dark purple, lance-shaped leaves, small pink flowers and a bushy appearance. Sow seeds indoors and transplant after all danger of frost.

Petunia (*Petunia axillaris*) repels leafhoppers, Mexican bean beetles and some aphids. A 1'-tall annual with skimpy leaves and showy, trumpet-shaped, variously colored flowers. Plant seeds indoors and transplant after all danger of frost.

Rosemary (*Rosmarinus officinalis*) repels moths and Mexican bean beetles. A 1'- to 4'-tall perennial evergreen shrub with stalkless, linear leaves, woody stems and undistinguished flowers. Propagate from cuttings taken in late summer or from seeds sown in late spring.

Shoo-fly plant or Apple-of-Peru (*Nicandra physalodes*) poisons many pests, including whiteflies. A 1'- to 3'-tall annual, with succulent stems, deeply lacerated leaves and small blue flowers. Sow seeds outdoors after all danger of frost.

Summer savory (*Satureja hortensis*) repels Mexican bean beetles. An 18"-tall annual with hairy stems, downy, linear leaves and small white, pink or pale lilac flower clusters. Sow seeds 1/2" deep indoors in early spring and transplant outside—spaced 5" apart—after all danger of frost.

White geranium (*Pelargonium*, var. spp.) attracts and kills Japanese beetles. A 1'- to 2'-tall annual or perennial with heart- or ivy-shaped leaves and large, rounded flower clusters. Start from cuttings taken in late fall and transplant after all danger of frost in spring.

Wormwood	Other Flowers	
Artemisia absinthium	A Few More Beneficial Plants	

A. absinthium

Dahlia

Petunia

Blue Flax

Rosemary

Larkspur

Harmful Animals

Not all garden raiders have six legs.

Crows love to pluck corn sprouts.
Woodchucks go for the greens and
beans. Cats leave scat, and moles
dig holes. But they all can be
controlled.

Likely Targets: Corn seedlings, pea seeds, mature corn ears, blueberries, grapes, raspberries and strawberries.

Generally speaking, birds are a boon to the gardener because they prey on many small, destructive insects. Indeed, they are included in the "Helpful Animals" section as well as here. But certain crops are targets of certain species. When crows pull up corn starts to get the sprouted kernel beneath, blackbirds raid ripe corn ears, or some "innocent" songbird begins plucking ripe small fruits, it's time to take defensive measures.

Controls:

For young corn:
● Spread lime down sweet corn rows before and right after the seedlings are up to keep birds from digging up the seed.
● Run several taut strands of fishing line or black thread over rows of planted corn.
● Mulch heavily over corn seeds or plant them deeper than usual.
● Prestart corn plants and set them out as established seedlings.
● Make a feeding station of purchased feed corn next to the cornfield, so the birds will eat that instead of planted seeds.

For mature corn:
● Tie small rubber bands over the end of each ear when the silks turn brown.
● Build a scarecrow. This age-old method of putting the fear of humans into birds is only moderately effective. Don't be surprised if a crow perches on its shoulder.

For small fruits:
● The most effective tactic is to make some sort of physical barrier. Bird or mosquito netting is sold commercially and can be used to cover beds, berry patches, vines and small trees. In some cases, it may even be necessary to erect individual cages for certain crops and to cover them with netting.
● Plant elderberries or mulberries for the birds. They actually prefer these tart berries to sweet ones.
● Invite cats (or cat effigies) into the garden.
● Welcome snakes (or substitutes, such as inflatable snake decoys or even sections of garden hose).
● Some gardeners have painted strawberry-sized nuts red and put them in the strawberry patch right before the fruit ripened. The birds got tired of pecking at the "hard berries" and gave up before the real ones were ready.

Likely Targets: Leafy crops, fruit trees.

Deer nibble up garden greens. They'll also chew the tender growing tips of fruit trees in summer and the buds in winter. They can cause serious damage. And they're most likely to do it in the late evening or early morning when no one is around.

Controls:
● Hang bars of deodorant soap (Dial has the best record) around vulnerable crops or orchards. This has done a fine job of repelling deer, in both experiments and practice. One warning: Groundhogs love soap!
● Spread lion dung (available from some zoos and circuses) around vulnerable crops, or make it into a tea and spray it on plants. Some gardeners swear by this technique despite its exoticism.
● Scatter dog or human hair around or hang it in small cheesecloth sacks. (Check local barbers or dog groomers for supplies.) Another sworn-by method.
● Scatter dried blood, blood meal or fish heads around or hang in sacks. Yet another widely endorsed tactic.
● Blend an egg in a gallon of water and spray the solution on vulnerable plants.
● Get a good dog that sleeps outside and resents intruders.
● Hang tin or aluminum pie pans around so they blow in the wind. This technique seems to discourage *some* deer, but is ignored by others.
● Construct a blinking or rotating light to use at night. This works much better than a stationary light that's always on.
● To protect a few selected crops, a box cage can be made out of wood with chicken wire sides.
● Fencing, though expensive, is the permanent solution for an extensive deer problem. Deer can jump, though, so it needs to be at least 8′ high, or 4′ to 5′ high with a barrier of horizontal wires extending 5′ beyond the fence. A 6-strand electric fence, with the strands spaced 10″ apart and the bottom one 8″ off the ground, is also generally effective.

Deer

Tracks

2¾″

Scat

Trail

Dog

Tracks

32¼"

Scat

Cat

Tracks

Front

1½"

1⅜"

Hind

Scat

Gopher

Tracks

1"

Scat

Tunnel

Mole

Molehill

Mole ridge

Likely Targets: Garden soil (and whatever grows there).

Dogs can wreak havoc running over newly planted beds or digging up crops—often in search of something known only to themselves. And cats will wander at will through a garden plot, using it as a giant litter box.

In general, experienced gardeners are less frustrated by wild animals than by pets that are allowed to run loose. Nobody complains when a woodchuck is trapped and transported elsewhere. But should that befall someone's dog, a major ruckus will soon follow. Somehow, it always seems to be the neighbors' pets, not one's own, that do the damage. As a result, the problem becomes one of social relations.

Controls:
● Talk with neighbors about the problem. Such a conversation may well require a balance of tact, straightforwardness and a willingness to compromise.
● Spray the perimeter of the plot with a hot pepper solution.
● Fence the plot with barbed, woven or electric fencing. (Space the strands of an electric fence 10" apart, with the bottom strand 6" off the ground. And run wire loops into any dips the intruders might crawl through.) Fencing will work against dogs, but not cats.
● Plant a catnip patch away from the main garden to lure felines.
● Make sure compost piles are properly built so they don't have any exposed garbage, which will attract pets.
● Own a well-trained dog that chases off animal intruders.

Likely Targets: Gophers eat the underground parts of garden crops and some flowers. Their mounds sometimes smother small plants, and they can girdle and kill young trees. Moles eat insects but no garden crops.

While moles dig extensive tunnels that mar the looks of a manicured lawn or garden and can damage some plants, for the most part these animals are beneficial. Voracious insectivores, they eat their weight each day in cutworms, wireworms, sow bugs, grubs, centipedes, millipedes and Japanese beetle larvae. True, they do prey on earthworms, as well. And mice may move into their tunnels for an easy bit of crop nibbling. Rarely, however, do more than one or two moles occupy the same area, so their negative impact may be wholly inconsequential.

Gophers also tunnel around just below the surface, but these larger creatures (a gopher may weigh 12 ounces, a mole just 3) readily consume crop roots. They also live more communally, with as many as 16 to 20 animals per acre.

Controls:
● Castor beans or mole plant (*Euphorbia lathyris*) can be planted around or in a garden. The bean seeds can also be dropped in tunnels. However, both plants are highly poisonous and should not be used in any gardens visited by small children.
● Spray a solution of one tablespoon castor oil and one tablespoon liquid detergent per gallon of warm water on soil and plants.
● Scatter human or dog hair about.
● Set empty, narrow-mouthed bottles in tunnels. Winds will make a blowing vibration that is said to repel the pests.
● Place elderberry cuttings in the tunnels.
● Sprinkle chili powder and powdered garlic into tunnels weekly.
● Set baited live traps near gopher exits and in mole tunnels.
● For serious problems, erect a ¼" hardware cloth fence 2' below ground and 1' above.
● Scatter ground red pepper or tobacco dust to repel moles.
● Plant ornamental blooming scilla (or squill) bulbs as a garden border or around susceptible plants to repel gophers.
● Place rolled-up pieces of Juicy Fruit gum in mole tunnels. (Wear gloves to mask your scent when you unwrap the gum.) Moles love it, but it clogs their innards, fatally.

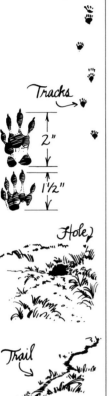

Likely Targets: Carrots, peas, beans, sweet corn, alfalfa, grass, weeds and more. The groundhog is a vegetarian, and a voracious one.

Often a garden won't be bothered at all until one day a mother woodchuck moves in with her young and clear-cuts it. They are serious plot spoilers.

Controls:

● Catch them in live traps and transport them far away. Set traps near their burrow (under a brush pile, beneath a tree root, near a fence or at some other concealed place) or along their main trails (look for lines of matted grass). Bait traps with apples, green beans, ripe bananas or carrots. (The National Park Service once trapped groundhogs that were chewing the rubber parts off car engines by baiting their traps with old radiator hoses.) To catch the entire family will probably require resetting the trap a few times. Afterward, plug the burrow to discourage another groundhog from moving in.

● A good dog will bark loudly and chase off any groundhogs it sees. A smart dog will carry its aggression no further; woodchucks are fierce fighters when cornered.

● Some people claim that planting garlic or onions around a groundhog burrow will send them packing.

● Sprinkle ground red pepper around their holes and throughout the garden.

● Alter their habitat. Remove brush piles, tall weeds and other shelter near the garden to deprive them of the cover they need.

● Fencing a groundhog out of the plot is difficult and unlikely to succeed, since the animals are good at both climbing and burrowing. If you want to try, however, build a sturdy fence at least 4′ high that extends at least 1′ underground.

● Plant alfalfa and clover away from the garden and hope they eat those favorites instead of your crops.

● Shoot them with a .22 rifle if you're willing to use the meat. To do so, bleed the fresh carcass, then skin and clean it. Be sure to remove the tear-shaped musk glands at the small of the back and directly behind the forelegs. Soak the meat in a marinade for a day or so, then roast, fry, bake or stew.

Likely Targets: Mice are known to move into mole tunnels and to use them to eat crop roots. They can gnaw the ground-level bark of fruit trees, sometimes girdling and killing the trees. They may overwinter in the mulch placed around strawberries or other perennials, chewing on the crop roots. They may also dig up every seed in a greenhouse overnight or nibble the young sprouts to the ground.

Controls:

● Encourage snakes and owls to stay near the garden to provide natural control. When a compost pile is turned in spring, it is not unusual to find some nests of baby mice. The likelihood is that a snake will also be there, enjoying a warm, cozy domicile—complete with mouse dinners.

● Scatter fresh or dried mint leaves as a repellent.

● Pull back any mulch around tree trunks. Keep the ground near the trunk closely mowed. Protect trunks by wrapping them with ¼″ hardware cloth or foil.

● Don't mulch perennials until after a few frosts. By then, the mice will have found other winter homes.

● Catch them with mousetraps. In a greenhouse, commercially available glue boards can also be used to capture them.

● Certain *mannerly* cats will help keep mice out of a greenhouse. (Turn back three entries for suggestions on unmannerly cats.)

● Store all garden seeds in mouseproof containers.

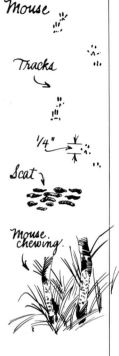

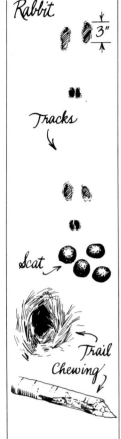

Rabbit
Tracks
Scat
Trail
Chewing

Likely Targets: Carrots, strawberries, peas, beans, lettuce, tulip shoots, grasses, weeds and the bark of fruit trees and raspberries.

Rabbits are famous garden raiders, but often don't live up to their reputation. Frequently they are present but cause little damage. Why is that? Because there are plenty of weeds around for them to dine on? Because an open and well-manicured garden offers little shelter for the nervous nibblers? Because humans are in and out of the garden every day, leaving their scent everywhere? Or because hawks circle in the sky above all season long? Probably all of these.

Controls:

● The long list of reputed rabbit repellents people sprinkle around a plot includes wood ashes, ground hot peppers, chili powder, garlic powder, crushed mint leaves, tobacco dust, tankage or blood meal, talcum powder and powdered rock phosphate. Most of these need to be replenished every so often or after rains. Fox urine (from hunting or trapping supply stores) and lion dung (from a zoo or circus) also have good reputations as rabbit deterrents.

● Set old leather shoes (say, from a local thrift shop) around the garden to give it that "humans are here" smell.

● Snake effigies, commercial or homemade from old garden hose, can be effective.

● Grow garlic, onions or Mexican marigolds (*Tagetes minuta*) in the garden.

● A well-mannered dog (one that doesn't itself damage your garden) can be a very effective deterrent.

● Share the harvest. Either plant extra for the rabbits, or sow extra crop seeds outside the main garden for the rabbits to enjoy.

● Wrap the bases of fruit trees with hardware cloth or other sturdy material to deter winter rabbit damage.

● Fence the garden. Wire fencing should be partially buried, extend at least 2' above ground and have holes smaller than 2". An electric fence should have two strands, set 4" and 10" from the ground.

● Live-trap them and release them somewhere else. Rabbits prefer covered to exposed traps. Apples and carrots make good bait.

● Alter the habitat to discourage rabbits and encourage predators such as owls and sparrow hawks by setting up nest boxes.

Likely Targets: Everybody knows what raccoons like most—sweet corn. And they have an uncanny knack of waiting until the night it's perfectly ripe before they harvest it. They're also fond of melons and fruit. A skunk's first love is insects—grasshoppers, beetles, crickets and grubs—so in general this animal should be left alone. But skunks often pull nocturnal corn raids, too, enjoying the treat but letting the raccoons take the blame. Prevention measures are the same for both.

Controls:

● Catch the raider in a live trap. Sardines, marshmallows and honey-soaked bread all make good baits. Start trapping a few days before the coveted crop is ripe. And if you catch a skunk, slowly walk up to the trap, cover it with a dark tarp and then *gently* transport the well-armed mammal far away.

● One ploy that's been used with some effectiveness is playing a radio in the corn patch all night long. Talk stations work best. One gardener vented his frustrations onto a continuous loop cassette tape. He played that speech (all about how angry he was and why the animals should leave his corn alone) at night in his garden and reported excellent results.

● An outdoor light that either blinks on and off or rotates will scare coons and skunks away. (One that remains stationary or constantly on doesn't work.)

● Several strands of low-strung electric fencing should work. Raccoons can climb over most noncharged barriers, but some growers report success with chicken wire fences that are not supported along their top foot of length. The fencing apparently bends so far backward when the animal climbs it that the creature can't make it over.

● Surround the corn or melon patch with a 3'-wide horizontal barrier that coons and skunks don't like to walk over—black plastic, newspaper or mesh fencing.

● Wrap individual ears in foil, plastic, stockings, etc. This method, however, is quite time-consuming and may damage the crop in hot weather.

● Plant a hairy vine crop like pumpkin, winter squash or Kentucky Wonder pole beans in among the corn to irritate and deter the animals.

● Electronic bug zappers set up in the corn patch are supposed to scare coons and skunks away.

Raccoon
Tracks
Scat
Skunk
Tracks
Scat

Helpful Animals

Bat	Bird

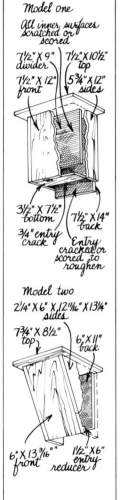

Two bat boxes
Model one
All inner surfaces scratched or scored
7½" X 9" divider
7½" X 10½" top
7½" X 12" front
5¾" X 12" sides
3½" X 7½" bottom
7½" X 14" back
¾" entry crack
Entry crack or scored to roughen
Model two
2¼" X 6" X 12¹¹⁄₁₆" X 13¼" sides
7¾" X 8½" top
6" X 11" back
6" X 13³⁄₁₆" front
1½" X 6" entry reducer

Effective Against: Mosquitoes, gnats, moths, beetles and other nocturnal flying insects.

This fur-bearing mammal flies through summer night skies, eating up to half its body weight in insects each evening. It finds its targets by echolocation, its own extremely sophisticated radar system based on high-pitched clicks or squeaks. The bat emits these ultrasonic sounds at the rate of four or five a second while patrolling and as many as 200 clicks a second when it's closing in on prey. Since such high-frequency sounds fade rapidly over distance, the bat has to "shout" its message, yet still be able to hear the faint echoes that return.

A bat frequently catches its prey in its mouth, but it can also use its wings as a fielding glove, or even catch a bug in its tail, then somersault in midair to bring the meal to its mouth.

In the Garden: So why do these remarkably efficient insectivores have such a bad reputation with most humans? It probably has something to do with visions of Count Dracula, fear of rabies and the notion that bats are likely to get caught in your hair. However, there are no vampire bats in the United States (and the ones in South America rarely prey on humans), a bat is no more likely to have rabies than any other wild mammal and these superb fliers have absolutely no trouble avoiding heads of hair.

We need to shed our unfounded prejudice against these amazing mammals and welcome them into our gardens as allies in natural insect control. (This will also help save the many endangered bat species from extinction.) The best ways to entice bats to your plot are to hang an outside light to attract moths or, better yet, to build birdhouse-type shelters for bats. Basic dimensions are shown in the accompanying drawings.

The most important feature of a good bat box is its ³⁄₄"-wide entrance. Keeping the opening that narrow helps exclude other creatures from taking up residence. Build the box tight to keep out drafts, and position it 12' to 15' off the ground on buildings or tree trunks in a spot that gets morning sun but afternoon shade.

It's time to take off our vampire-repelling garlic necklaces and invite these fine-tuned instruments of insect destruction to work the "graveyard shift" in our gardens.

Effective Against: While it would take any gardener hours to handpick 500 insects, a single wren can do that job in an afternoon, and use some of its harvest to feed a nestful of future bugnappers. Ants, moths, leafhoppers, grasshoppers, caterpillars, borers, aphids, cutworms—most all pesty insects are fare for some feathered friend. Hawks and owls, of course, dine on mice, moles, gophers and rabbits as well.

Many birds are full-time insect eaters. This group includes house wrens, barn swallows, flycatchers, swifts and some species of warblers and gnatcatchers. The great majority, though, enjoy a varied diet of seeds and other plant parts as well as insects. Bluebirds, catbirds, robins, nuthatches, hummingbirds, mockingbirds and certain sparrows and waxwings are omnivorous birds common to gardens.

In the Garden: To attract these winged exterminators to your plot, make them comfortable by providing an environment that satisfies their needs.

First, make sure they have a good source of water. A birdbath or shallow, water-filled pan set on a stump or similar pedestal works well. It lets them drink up off the ground, safe from cats and snakes. Birds are most attracted to slightly moving water, so drip a hose into the water or suspend a leaky can overhead and refill it from time to time.

Next, provide good habitat. The more plant diversity in a garden, the greater the variety of birds that will be attracted. For instance, shrubs and hedges harbor warblers and towhees, tall trees house orioles, and thick grasses invite meadowlarks. Evergreen shrubs, sugar maples, Russian olives, wild plums, sand cherries, hollies, Chinese chestnuts, flowering crabs and junipers are all good-looking landscape plants that provide prime nesting sites.

Birdhouses also encourage habitation. Avoid painting the interiors, though a light color on the exteriors will help prevent overheating inside. Also, face the entrance holes away from prevailing winds and clean out the dwellings after each nesting.

Last, supplement the omnivorous birds' insect diet by growing treats for them. Attractive food-bearing trees and shrubs include the elderberry, mulberry, virginia creeper, chokeberry, highbush cranberry, snowberry and *Rosa rugosa*.

Effective Against: Like their wild cousins, domestic fowl will devour most garden insects, taking them in their larval and pupal stages from the soil. They'll also pluck mature or larval pests off plants if allowed to forage along the rows.

Ducks and geese will eat slugs as well as insects. Chickens, however, don't seem to care much for those landlocked mollusks.

In the Garden: The problem with domestic fowl, of course, is not whether they'll devour insect pests, but whether they'll level the garden in the process. A chicken won't hesitate to scratch out newly planted seedlings to get to the grub it's after. Ducks and geese can't scratch, but they can dig holes with their beaks. (Actually, those waterfowl prefer grasses to broadleaf plants—geese are sometimes even used as weeders in farm operations—but they will happily munch Swiss chard to the ground.)

Can a garden and insect-eating fowl coexist? The number-one guideline is to control the birds' access. Good fencing around (and even in) a plot will determine when and where they'll go.

There is only one season when it is safe to let fowl roam through the garden: from late fall to early spring when nothing's growing. If the garden has been freshly tilled, they'll pick off the overwintering pupae and larvae brought up to the surface by tilling.

Fowl can also be employed during the growing season itself, provided that care and common sense are used. For example, they shouldn't be left alone in the garden. Additional factors should be considered as well:

The age and type of plants: Fowl should not be allowed to forage through new plantings, though well-established crops with definite pathways will tend to be less vulnerable to their attentions. They should also be kept away from leafy greens and ripe berries and fruits through such means as temporary fencing. Happily, fowl reduce the insect population even of nearby fenced-off crops. The very presence of the birds scares some pests away.

The type of garden: Traditional row gardens have the edge over bed and mulch gardens. The pathway room in a row garden makes it easier for the fowl to stay on the paths.

Keep fowl out of wet gardens of all types: The birds are too prone to uproot crops and help spread plant diseases.

Effective Against: Small mammals such as mice, gophers, voles, shrews and rabbits.

The fact that owls hunt at night and prey on small mammals rather than insects earns them a listing of their own in this field guide. You couldn't devise a nocturnal hunting machine more efficient than an owl for eliminating small nuisance animals from the garden. A pair of adult barn owls raising a family kill an average of 500 rodents a month. (Garden supply catalogues even sell inflatable replicas of owls in the belief that their shape alone will scare off pests.)

What makes an owl such a great hunter? For one thing, it possesses keen night-sensitive vision that sees in color and focuses sharply. It can hunt superbly even in pitch blackness, because its hearing is even finer than its sight. The dish-shaped face helps focus the sound waves that ultimately enter its funnel-shaped ears. (By the way, those distinctive "ear tufts" on many owls aren't ears at all. The real ones are on the sides of the bird's head, hidden under feathers.) Some species like the barn owl even have one ear higher than the other to help them better triangulate the location of their targets.

Then, too, an owl is a quiet flier; the sound of its large wings is muffled by a fine velvety fringe. It is also an excellent glider, so it can frequently approach prey without flapping its wings at all. Once on target, it quickly pulls its head back and its legs forward, seizing its victim with wide, sharp talons.

In the Garden: Many of the same measures that attract daytime insect-eating birds also entice owls. Providing a good water source and a variety of plant habitat are the most obvious examples. It's also possible to build nest boxes for owls. The accompanying drawings illustrate the designs of boxes for barn and screech owls. (As an added bonus, the screech owl nest attracts a beneficial day-flying bird of prey, the sparrow hawk.) Set the boxes 10 to 20 feet off the ground with direct access to an open area. Last, to encourage owls, don't poison rodents and other small garden invaders. The risk is that the bird that eats them will be poisoned as well.

You may never see the owls that help patrol your plot, but when you hear their night cry, cherish it. It's music to a gardener's ears.

Screech owl nest box

Barn owl box

Snake	Toad

Effective Against: All snakes feed on live prey (none eat plants), and a lot of creatures fit the bill of fare. Insect larvae, night-flying moths, caterpillars, mice, gophers, rats and small rabbits are frequently consumed by these generally helpful reptiles. True, snakes will swallow harmless—or beneficial—frogs, lizards, birds (and bird eggs), ground squirrels and other snakes as well. On the whole, however, they are more a plus than a minus in the garden despite their Biblical reputation. It's unfortunate that many people regard them with fear or, worse, with "kill first and ask questions later" behavior. If tolerated, snakes fill a useful role in any garden.

Considering that it's completely limbless and deaf, a snake is an amazingly efficient hunter. Agile and quick, snakes also have very sensitive skin, highly developed vision (which, however, is much better at distinguishing moving objects than still ones) and a thermo-receptor between eyes and nostrils that helps them locate prey. Their tongues, too, play an important role: Those organs can smell as well as feel. A snake can poke its tongue out even through a closed mouth and use it to track its prey.

When it catches a victim, the snake may strike but it won't chew. Instead, it swallows all prey whole, unhinging its jaws when necessary.

In the Garden: A good way to encourage snakes to come to the garden is to provide a variety of inviting habitats. Shrubs, trees, brush piles, stone walls and many other sheltered environments make safe homes for these slithering predators. If you're fortunate enough to find a garter, gopher or other nonpoisonous snake while on a walk or a drive, consider catching and transporting it home in a sack. Then release it for local garden duty.

Rest assured, however, that if there's live food worth eating in your garden, sooner or later a local snake will find its way there to partake. Indeed, to spot a serpent in a rat-infested potting shed, or under a mouse-filled compost pile or slithering across an insect-gnawed plot is cause to celebrate. It's also time to shed all those antireptilian prejudices we humans have and to leave the creature be. It's a nice arrangement: You give the snake room, it will take care of its board.

Effective Against: During the summer, a single garden toad can consume up to 3,000 cutworms, beetles, caterpillars, grasshoppers, snails and slugs a month. (Admittedly, spiders and earthworms are also on its diet.) Toads emerge from hibernation in the early spring, and, if the weather is moderate, they can remain active until Thanksgiving. That's a long season of free, safe insect control.

As much as it consumes, a toad will never eat anything that doesn't move. If a tempting insect freezes still, the toad will freeze as well and wait it out. When the bug finally tries to get away—ssssnnnnippp!—out flies the toad's sticky tongue to snag it. The amphibian's tongue moves faster than the human eye. Beyond that, however, a toad is slow, relying on its camouflage to fool prey into coming to it rather than engaging in pursuit of its own. It can't even escape quickly, limited to hops rather than the leaps of its cousin the frog. But, then, it doesn't have to leap, for though the toad does not cause warts as superstition states, it does secrete an irritating fluid to ward off enemies.

In the Garden: Toads can be caught and transplanted to the garden, but it may take a little doing. Look for them in wet areas early in the year, under rocks and logs later. Some gardeners have been known to drive around the countryside on rainy nights hoping to spot these insect-eaters on the road. Since toads are territorial, it may be necessary to keep them in a box or enclosure for a few days to squelch their homing instinct.

It's much easier to pamper whatever toads are local by providing a shallow pan of water in the garden and a cool, shady retreat. A small box turned on edge or an upside-down flowerpot with an entrance hole chipped out works well. So does an outside night light. By luring moths and beetles, it can keep a toad nicely contented.

Except when breeding, toads do not need to live near water, so they can thrive in a home garden. Moreover, since they live up to 30 years, good relations with them can lead to long-term insect control.

What about frogs? Most won't thrive in a garden unless there is a small pond nearby, for frogs are extremely dependent on water. Not so terrestrial tree or cricket frogs. Like toads, they don't need to swim a lot and will make a quick meal of almost any bug that moves, from mealworm to grasshopper.

Citrus peel yields an effective insecticide.

New Natural Controls

Research in organic pesticides is on the rise.

Spurred over the last couple of decades by increasing doubts about the safety of commercial pesticides, a new arsenal of sophisticated techniques for controlling garden pests without synthetic chemicals is gradually taking shape. Most of these techniques are still in the trial stages, but some are available for garden use right now. Clearly, back-yard growers will be able to choose from a greatly increased number of natural pest control methods in the near future.

Natural Anti-feedants

In several agricultural-school laboratories, the search is on for plant-derived "antifeedants"—chemicals that inhibit insect feeding on crops. At North Carolina State University, for example, experiments have shown that damage to young corn shoots caused by the larvae of the corn rootworm (*Diabrotica undecimpunctata*, also called the spotted cucumber beetle) can be significantly reduced by soaking corn seeds for two hours in liquid made from homogenized butterfly weed or English ivy. (The seeds were airdried before planting.)

The list of plants containing anti-feedant substances is growing rapidly, with most of these pest deterrents proving to be specific

for particular insect species. By experimenting with various plant extracts, home gardeners can themselves contribute to the overall research effort. (A good source for such extracts is Original Swiss Aromatics, P.O. Box 606, San Rafael, CA 94915.) To avoid damaging foliage, however, garden experimenters should be careful to limit the concentration sprayed on crops.

One currently available anti-feedant is Green Ban, made in Australia from kelp, English ivy, sage, garlic and eucalyptus. It is sold in the U.S. by Smith and Hawken (25 Corte Madera, Mill Valley, CA 94941).

Garlic Oil

Everyone knows that garlic makes a good insect repellent, but few people know that it can also be used as an insecticide. Not long ago, participants in a senior-citizen horticulture class in Reedley, California, experimented with a garlic-oil spray concocted approximately as follows. First, they packed lots of finely minced garlic in mineral oil and soaked it for 24 hours. After adding two teaspoons of the oil to a pint of water in which one-quarter ounce of Palmolive soap had been dissolved, they stirred the liquid and strained it into a glass container for storage. For spraying, they added one or two tablespoons of this oil mix per pint of water.

The results in the class were astonishing. Cabbage moths, cabbage loopers, earwigs, leafhoppers, mosquitoes (including larvae), whiteflies and some aphids were killed *on contact*. Houseflies, June bugs and squash bugs died within a minute after being sprayed. Cockroaches, lygus bugs, slugs and hornworms were also killed, though more slowly. Beneficial lady beetles were apparently unaffected by the spray, but neither were Colorado potato beetles, grasshoppers, grape leaf skeletonizers, red ants and sow bugs. Spider mites were "irritated": Some died after being sprayed, while others fell from the leaves but subsequently recovered.

Citrus Peel Insecticide

Limonene, a chemical found in the outer surface of citrus peel, has also been found to kill many insect-pest species. Unfortunately, it can damage plant leaves as well, unless it's applied at very low concentrations. Re-

search to develop a commercial limonene-based insecticide is well advanced and should result in an available product within a year or two. Meanwhile, limonene for home experimental use can be obtained simply by bending the outer surface of fresh citrus peel against a dish so that oil droplets collect in it.

Neem Insecticide

Extracts from the tropical neem tree (*Azadirachta indica*) are toxic to more than 80 pest-insect species, including Mexican bean beetles, Colorado potato beetles, grasshoppers, cucumber beetles, citrus mealybugs, cockroaches, leaf miners and Japanese beetles. When added to the soil, neem compounds enter plant roots and move into leaves, making them toxic to the insects. Thus, neem is a naturally derived *systemic* insecticide. It acts from *within* plants.

Are plants containing neem compounds safe for human consumption? The final verdict isn't in yet, but neem products have been used medicinally in Asia for centuries. In addition, neem cakes (left over from soapmaking) are regularly fed to livestock in India, evidently without ill effect.

The first neem-based insecticide to be registered by the Environmental Protection Agency for use in the U.S. is Margosan-O (Vikwood Botanicals, Inc., Box 1414, Sheboygan, WI 53082). However, it's approved for use only on certain *ornamental* plants for control of leaf miners.

Nematode Controls

Researchers in India report that, at least in pot experiments, chopped-up residues of certain weeds (notably those in the nightshade family, such as jimsonweed) added to the soil can greatly reduce populations of some kinds of harmful nematodes. The researchers added one- to two-tenths of a pound of residues to about two pounds of soil in each 6" pot. In Israel, chitin—a chemical produced by animals and some plants—has proved an effective nematode control when added to the soil in very small amounts (only 0.05% to 0.3% by weight). Unfortunately, chitin in the soil forms free ammonia, which can harm plants, so the treatment must be done before seeding or transplanting crops.

Shopping for Insects

Beneficial bugs by mail-order

Beneficial Insectary (245 Oak Run Rd., Oak Run, CA 96069): fly parasites *Muscidifurax raptor*, *Nasonia vitripennis* and *Spalangia endius*; grasshopper pathogen *Nosema locustae*.

Bio Insect Control (710 S. Columbia, Plainview, TX 79072): green lacewings; ladybugs; egg wasps; black scale parasite *Metaphycus helvolus*; fly parasites *Muscidifurax raptor* and *Spalangia endius*; grasshopper pathogen *Nosema locustae*; greenhouse whitefly parasite *Encarsia formosa*; greenbug parasite *Lysiphlebus testaceipes*; mealybug destroyer *Cryptolaemus montrouzieri*; nuclear polyhedrosis virus; predatory mites *Amblyseius californicus*, *Metaseiulus occidentalis* and *Phytoseiulus persimilis*; red scale parasite *Aphytis melinus*.

Burpee Seed Company (300 Park Ave., Warminster, PA 18974): ladybugs, praying mantises, egg wasps.

California Green Lacewings (P.O. Box 2495, Merced, CA 95341): green lacewings; egg wasps; fly parasites, various species; navel orangeworm parasites *Goniozus legneri* and *Pentalitomastix* spp.

Evans BioControl (P.O. Box 3266, Durango, CO 81302): fly parasites, various species for farm and dairy control; grasshopper pathogen *Nosema locustae*. BioControl's brand name for the latter is Nolo Bait.

Foothill Agricultural Research, Inc. (510 W. Chase Dr., Corona, CA 91720): ladybugs; egg wasps; black scale parasite *Metaphycus helvolus*; decollate snail *Rumina decollata*; fly parasites, various species; mealybug destroyer *Crytolaemus montrouzieri*; red scale parasite *Aphytis melinus*.

Gurney Seed & Nursery Co. (Yankton, SD 57079): green lacewings; ladybugs; praying mantises; egg wasps; fly parasites, various species; grasshopper pathogen *Nosema locustae*.

Mellinger's Nursery (2310 W. South Range Rd., North Lima, OH 44452): green lacewings; ladybugs; praying mantises; egg wasps; milky spore *Bacillus popilliae*; fly parasites *Spalangia endius* and *Muscidifurax zaraptor*; grasshopper pathogen *Nosema locustae*; greenhouse whitefly parasite *Encarsia formosa*; Mormon cricket pathogen; mealybug destroyer *Cryptolaemus montrouzieri*.

Natural Pest Controls (8864 Little Creek Dr., Orangevale, CA 95662): green lacewings; ladybugs; praying mantises; egg wasps; black scale parasite *Metaphycus helvolus*; fly parasites *Muscidifurax raptor*, *Nasonia vitripennis* and *Spalangia endius*; greenhouse whitefly parasite *Encarsia formosa*; mosquito bacterium *Bacillus thuringiensis israeliensis*; mealybug destroyer *Cryptolaemus montrouzieri*; mosquitofish *Gambusia* spp.; pink bollworm parasite *Microchelonus blackburni*; predatory mites, various species; red scale parasite *Aphytis melinus*.

Necessary Trading Company (653 Main St., New Castle, VA 24127): green lacewings; ladybugs; egg wasps; bean beetle parasite *Pediobius foveolatus*; milky spore *Bacillus popilliae*; Colorado potato beetle parasite *Edovum puttleri*; fly parasites, various species; grasshopper pathogen *Nosema locustae*; greenhouse whitefly parasite *Encarsia formosa*; mosquito bacterium *Bacillus thuringiensis israeliensis*; mealybug destroyer *Cryptolaemus montrouzieri*; nuclear polyhedrosis virus; predatory mites, various species; parasitic nematode *Neoaplectana carpocapsae*.

Peaceful Valley Farm Supply (11173 Peaceful Valley Rd., Nevada City, CA 95959): green lacewings; ladybugs, praying mantises; egg wasps; milky spore *Bacillus popilliae*; black scale parasite *Metaphycus helvolus*; decollate snail *Rumina decollata*; fly parasites *Muscidifurax raptor* and *Spalangia endius*; grasshopper pathogen *Nosema locustae*; greenhouse whitefly parasite *Encarsia formosa*; mealybug destroyer *Cryptolaemus montrouzieri*; mosquitofish *Gambusia* spp.; navel orangeworm parasite *Goniozus legneri*; nuclear polyhedrosis virus; predatory mites, various species; parasitic nematodes, various species; red scale parasites *Comperiella bifasciata* and *Aphytis melinus*.

Rincon-Vitova Insectaries, Inc. (P.O. Box 95, Oak View, CA 93022): green lacewings; ladybugs; fly parasites; greenhouse whitefly parasite *Encarsia formosa*; spider mite predator *Phytoseiulus persimilis*; mealybug destroyer *Cryptolaemus montrouzieri*; moth and butterfly parasite trichogramma wasp.

Organic Pesticides

Realizing that all bugs aren't bad, it naturally follows that pesticides, which often don't distinguish between the good and bad guys, should be used wisely. Your first line of defense should, of course, be those natural products considered to be less harmful to people and the environment than many of the dangerous but popular garden chemicals on the market today.

The previously listed **Peaceful Valley Farm Supply** is one of our favorites—not only for its wide array of organic pesticides, but also for its fine nursery stock, organic fertilizers, hand and power tools, propagation supplies, seed and bulbs, traps, advice and just about anything else a gardener might need. Its 180-page catalogue (from the above address) costs $2, refunded with the first order.

Necessary Trading Company, also mentioned, offers a Basic Garden Pest Control Kit ($19 plus $2.50 shipping and handling), which contains FoliaGro, Dipel, Safer's, rotenone/pyrethrins and a Bio Selector Chart for Insect Pest Control. Its Special Kit for Hard-to-Control Insects ($28 plus $2.50 shipping and handling) is made up of sabadilla/red devil dust, diatomaceous earth and milky spore powder. Order from the address given above.

Natural Gardening Research Center (Hwy. 48, P.O. Box 149, Sunman, IN 47041) sells ryania, pyrethrum/rotenone/ryania blend, rotenone/copper, sabadilla dust, 1% rotenone, 5% rotenone, Cucumber and Melon Dust, liquid rotenone/pyrethrin, copper dust, liquid copper, diatomaceous earth, nicotine sulfate (a natural product, but definitely not recommended), micronized sulphur, Bordeaux mixture, insecticidal soap and tree tanglefoot.

And from **Ecology Action** (5798 Ridgewood Rd., Willits, CA 95490) you can buy pyrethrum products, Safer's Insecticidal Soap, rotenone dust and tree tanglefoot.

PART THREE

Overcoming Plant Diseases

Diagnosis and treatment
for the main afflictions that
can strike the garden

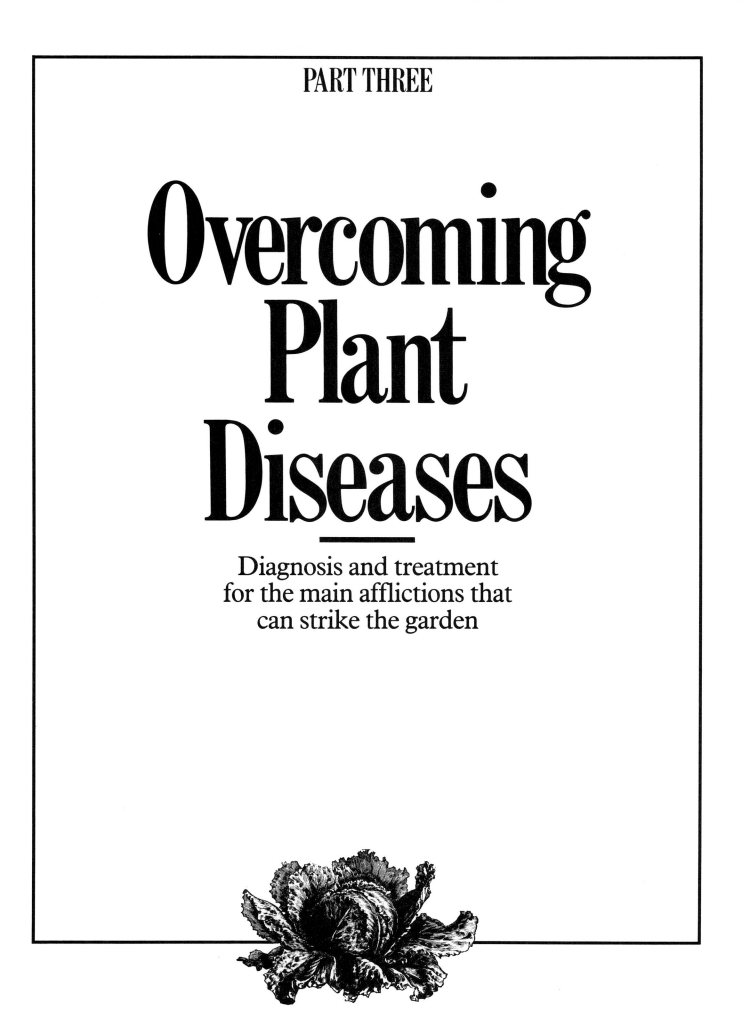

Rots, Smuts and Blights

The best control is prevention.

Plant maladies are generally caused by fungi, viruses or bacteria, though there are some diseases caused by substances toxic to the plants. The following chart describes common diseases and suggested controls. You will notice that the best control is prevention; diseases are difficult to cure once they get a good start. If all the preventive measures given in this chapter are followed and a crop still succumbs to disease, the gardener's only recourse may be to remove and destroy diseased plants immediately and to start again in uninfected soil.

Anthracnose
Dark red, dark brown or black lesions on stems, leaves and fruit. Pinkish mold spreads over fruit. Caused by fungi. Affects cucumber family, tomatoes, beans and other vegetables.
Controls: Plant disease-free, western-grown varieties. Avoid working around wet plants. Remove all infected plants. Practice crop rotation. Separate crops of beans and peppers.

Asochyta Blight
Purple specks on leaves and pods of peas, later turning to irregular brownish purple blotches. Elongated lesions on stems are common. Fungal disease.
Controls: Use western-grown seed. Clean up stubble and plant refuse. Rotate crops.

Asparagus Rust
Begins as a browning or reddening of smaller stalks. Discoloration spreads, covering entire plant with rusty spores. Plant tops die early in season. Finally affects rootstock. Fungal disease.
Controls: Plant recently developed resistant varieties. Cut off and burn affected stalks. After each cut, disinfect pruning shears with solution of one part bleach and one part water.

Bacterial Blight
Water-soaked spots on leaves, ranging from yellow to brownish and turning dark brown as leaf dies. Spots may have halos. Similar spots appear on fruit. Plant can be stunted or killed. Affects beans, peas, carrots and soybeans.
Controls: Plant western-grown seed. Avoid working around plants when foliage is wet. Remove and destroy affected plants. Rotate crops. Soak carrot seeds in 126°F water for 10 minutes.

Bacterial Canker
Open cankers form on stems of tomatoes. Fruits develop small, white, raised dots that turn brown with white halos. Plants are stunted, and leaves wilt and curl upward, turning brown. Fruits are distorted and may become yellow inside.
Controls: Use certified seed. Rotate crops. Remove diseased plants. Clean up crop refuse. Start seedlings in clean soil. Sanitize equipment.

Bacterial Pustule
Small, yellow-green spots with reddish brown centers appear on top of the leaf, and a raised pustule grows on the underside. Spots join to form brown areas. Disease generally appears in July. Most common in soybeans.
Controls: Plant resistant varieties. Practice crop rotation. Destroy diseased plants.

Bacterial Soft Rot
Rotting of the edges of lower leaves of lettuce is an early symptom. Head finally dissolves into a slimy ball.
Controls: Plant in hilled rows. Make sure soil is well drained. Remove affected plants.

Bacterial Spot
Yellow-green or dark, greasy spots on leaves. Leaves die and drop. Blossom drop can oc-

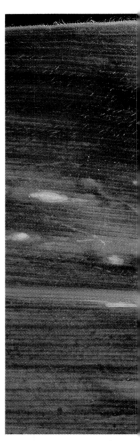

A plant disease sampler (clockwise from above): corn smut, leaf blight, fruit rot and leaf spot.

cur, and spots may develop on fruit.
Controls: Use certified plants of resistant varieties. Pasteurize potting soil for starting transplants. Rotate crops, especially peppers and tomatoes, on a three-year cycle.

Bacterial Wilt
Any of several vascular diseases caused by soil-harbored bacteria or carried by insects such as flea beetles or cucumber beetles. Affects beans, corn, cucumbers, squash and tomatoes. Leaves wilt, and plants die or are stunted. Corn tassels whiten early.
Controls: Plant resistant varieties. Control insect carriers. Practice long-term crop rotation; do not plant susceptible crops for four or five years.

Blackleg
In potatoes, a bacterial infection. Black spots appear on stem, which becomes soft and often slimy from the base upward for three or four inches. Lower leaves yellow; upper ones curl upward. Tubers are infected

through stem but may not rot till in storage. In other plants, particularly brassicas, blackleg is a seed-borne fungal disease. Shrunken area appears at base of stem, girdles it and turns black. Leaves and seed pods develop brown spots and sometimes turn purple.
Controls: Use certified, disease-free seed, or sterilize seed in 122°F water for 30 minutes. Sterilize seedbed soil and do not move plants from infected seedbed. Rotate crops on three-year basis. Foliage of infected plants is toxic to cattle.

Black Root
Roots blacken and decay until all are destroyed. Young plants are killed, and older ones are stunted in early stage.
Controls: Sterilize planting soils. Plant in well-drained sites. Rotate crops.

Black Rot
In sweet potatoes, a fungal disease that appears as round brown spots on tubers and possibly as decay in stem. In other plants, leaves yellow and vines become black and foul. Heads of cabbages and related vegetables rot or fail to develop properly.
Controls: For potatoes, use certified seed potatoes. For other vegetables, treat seeds in 122°F water for 20 minutes. Cultivate cleanly and water sparingly. Practice three- to four-year rotation.

Blight
Any of several fungal diseases causing spots or discoloration of leaves, resulting in their withering and in the rot and damage of the affected plant's fruit.
Controls: Plant resistant varieties. Practice crop rotation. Remove infected plants and damaged fruit.

Blossom-End Rot
A shrinking of the blossom end of the fruit. Causes a dark, sunken or flattened, tough spot that may include half the fruit.
Controls: Water if drought follows excess of rain early in season. Treat soil for calcium deficiency and cut back on nitrogen. Prepare soil deeply. Mulch to conserve moisture.

Celery Mosaic
Young leaflets mottled green and yellow. Stalks narrow and twisted, later cupped. Central stalks are stunted; outer ones lie horizontal to ground and develop rusty spots.
Controls: Remove diseased plants. Control aphids, as many species carry the virus.

Club Root
First sign is a daytime wilting followed by nighttime partial recovery. Plant may be stunted but alive. Outer leaves may yellow and fall. Roots become mass of large and small swellings or can lump together into a single large gall with scabbed and fissured lateral roots. Often affects members of the cabbage family.
Controls: Maintain neutral (pH7) soil alkalinity. Provide good drainage. Rotate crops on

long-term basis. Check seedlings for signs of infection. Remove and destroy affected plants.

Corn Smut
A fungal disease that begins as grayish white galls on any part of the plant. These burst, releasing black spores that have an oily appearance.
Controls: Rotate crops. Plant resistant varieties. Turn under garden trash and remove stalks in the fall. Follow good soil-enrichment program. Remove and destroy galls and severely affected plants.

Damping Off
A fungal disease that affects newly sprouted seeds of many plants—in the ground or, more commonly, after the plant has broken through the ground. Succulent stems take on water-soaked appearance, and the plants fall over. Woody seedlings wilt but remain upright. Root decay follows. Fungus forms a weblike growth on soil's surface.
Controls: Start seedlings in sterile medium. Avoid overwatering. Use abundant compost.

Downy Mildew
Called false mildew, the sporangia make white, gray or yellow patches on the leaves, which eventually turn brown and die. Affects a large number of vegetables, including cucumbers, melons, lettuce, onions, soybeans and spinach.
Controls: Plant resistant varieties. Rotate crops. Plant in well-drained sites. Avoid overwatering.

Early Blight
Brown spots on leaves enlarge, forming concentric rings, which kill the leaves and reduce yield. Fungus spreads to tubers or fruit, forming lesions that allow mold or rot to occur. Affects potatoes in particular.
Controls: Select disease-resistant varieties and certified seeds. Use plenty of compost in preparing soil. Clear away plant debris. Remove and destroy afflicted plants. Practice crop rotation.

Fruit Rot
This seed-borne fungus affects all aboveground parts of plants, especially eggplants and cucumbers. Seedlings rot at ground level, circular gray-to-brown spots appear on leaves, leaves yellow and die, stems develop gray lesions or constrictions, and fruits develop lesions that are pale brown, sunken and marked by black pycnidia, or growths, arranged more or less concentrically. Fruit eventually rots.
Controls: Plant resistant varieties. Rotate crops, not planting the same family of plants in the same spot for three years.

Fusarium Wilt
In some plants, there's a yellowing and wilting of leaves of at least part of the plant. Celery displays a reddening of the ribs. Some variations of the fungus are harbored in the soil and enter plants through the roots; others are carried by the black-striped cucumber beetle. In addition to celery, the disease also affects peas, cabbage, lettuce and tomatoes.
Controls: Plant in clean, well-drained soil. Rotate crops. Control cucumber beetles. Pull and destroy affected plants. Plant resistant varieties.

Internal Black Spot
Tissue under the skin on tubers breaks down and turns black.
Controls: Avoid adding too much nitrogen to the soil. Handle harvest carefully.

Late Blight
On potatoes and tomatoes, fungal growth begins on leaves as dark, watery spots and spreads to stems and fruits, where it causes rot. On celery, yellow spots turn gray with black speckles.
Controls: Remove and destroy affected plants. Destroy culled fruit. Plant resistant varieties. Do not plant potatoes, tomatoes and celery in succession.

Leaf Blight
Appears first as yellow or white spots on leaves. Spots later turn brown. Spots girdle roots, which die below the ring. Roots also develop lesions, dark spots, craters or pustules.
Controls: Treat seeds in water for 10 minutes at 126°F before planting. Till the soil thoroughly. Rotate crops on a four-year basis. Remove and destroy afflicted plants.

Leaf Spot
Various diseases that cause small gray or brown spots on some plants and water spots that turn brown or purplish gray on others. Leaves yellow and die.
Controls: Use disease-free seed. Treat seed in 122°F water for 30 minutes before planting. Rotate crops. Till deeply.

Lettuce Drop
Fungal disease that develops quickly in cool weather. Seedlings grow only a few leaves, then wilt and die. Older plants may wilt quickly, looking like an old green rag, or they may develop water-soaked translucent leaves. The entire head eventually decays into a watery brown mass.
Controls: Assure good drainage and ventilation around the plants. Clean up refuse after harvest. Remove diseased plants.

Mosaic
There are many plant-specific mosaics, most of which can infect any other vegetable. For disease symptoms and controls of tomato mosaic, cucumber mosaic and mosaics of potatoes, squash, peppers and other vegetables, see the heading "tobacco mosaic."

Pink Rot
Water-soaked white to light pink spots develop on stalks. Stems become bitter-tasting and later rot. Fungus may cause damping off in seedbeds. Affects cabbage, celery and lettuce.
Controls: Plant resistant varieties. Rotate crops. Avoid successive plantings of lettuce, cabbage or celery in the same soil. Destroy affected plants.

Powdery Mildew
White, powdery mold covers leaves, stems and fruit. Infected plants are often stunted and produce small, poor fruit. Often attacks peas.
Controls: Avoid watering, especially in the afternoon, unless absolutely needed. Dust with sulfur, except cucurbits, most of which are sensitive to this element. Practice clean cultivation. Turn remnants of plants under or remove plant refuse. Do not use overhead sprinkling when watering.

Psyllid Yellows
A toxin-induced disease that causes older leaves to thicken and roll upward and younger leaves to turn yellow with purple veins.

Plant becomes spindly and dwarfed. If plant is infected early, few or no fruits develop; if attacked late, fruit will be soft and poor.
Controls: Keep area free of host weeds such as ground cherries. Garlic spray may control the disease-spreading insects, psylla.

Rhizoctonia

Chiefly attacks tissue. Causes damping off in seedlings, bottom rot in midseason, head rot during formation and development stages, and root rot toward the plant's maturity. Stems of seedlings have water-soaked appearance.
Controls: Practice long-period crop rotation, and water plants only as necessary.

Ring Rot

Highly infectious bacterial disease of potatoes. Symptoms evident late in season and often none visible aboveground. A few stems may wilt and become stunted. Decay of tuber starts with a ring $1/8''$ under the skin. Interior decays, leaving a shell of firm tissue.
Controls: Use disease-free seed potatoes. Disinfect tools used around infected plants.

Rust

Reddish discoloration of leaves from damage, sprays or weather are often mistaken for rust. True rust has powdery pustules or gelatinous wormlike accumulations on leaves. Leaves yellow before drying up and dropping.
Controls: Plant resistant varieties. Remove diseased stems, leaves and stalks. Clean up plant refuse at end of season. Dust leaves with lime. Avoid working around wet plants. Use new stakes each year for climbing plants.

Scab

Generally appears in tubers or fruits when they are small and forms brown or gray cankers over sunken spots. Stems and leaves may display watery cankers or lesions. Fruits ooze gummy substance. Widespread fungal disease of potatoes, also affects cucumbers and squash.
Controls: Plant resistant varieties. Rotate crops. Avoid low, soggy ground and overly alkaline soil for tubers. Plant soybeans in infested soil and plow under.

Scurf

Circular brown or black spots form on belowground parts of potatoes. Pits develop on tubers, which are often uniformly covered.
Controls: Maintain soil acidity at low end of acceptable pH range. Plant resistant varieties. Set only healthy slips. Keep storage facilities sanitary.

Seed Rot

Soil-inhibiting fungi cause either a semidry or a moist rot soon after seeds sprout. Young plant is killed. Prevalent in beans, cabbage and corn.
Controls: Cultivate soil rich in humus. Avoid planting in soil that's too moist or too cool. Rotate crops. Do not sow too thickly. Avoid overwatering.

Smut

Black areas appear on leaves and between segments of the bulb. Young plants have twisted and curled leaves and may die outright. On corn, white growths form on stalks. When they burst, masses of black spores are released.
Controls: Plant healthy sets and resistant varieties. Start seeds in clean soil. Destroy infected plants.

Stem Rot

Stems of sweet potatoes split near ground, and vines become brown or black. Sprouts yellow and die about two weeks after planting. New roots sometimes develop above decayed section, and plant survives. Tubers become small and decayed at stem end, and harvest is poor.
Controls: Use seed potatoes certified as disease-free. Practice clean cultivation. Rotate crops. Use resistant varieties.

Tip Burn

Very prevalent disease of lettuce in which small yellowish spots develop on the edges of leaves, turning brown and leading to rot.
Controls: Plant resistant varieties. Maintain a uniform supply of moisture.

Tobacco Mosaic

Various symptoms range from malformed leaves on young plants to mottled appearance on older leaves. Plants wilt more severely than is normal on sunny days that follow cloudy periods. Highly contagious virus is harbored in the soil and is spread by touch or by aphids.
Controls: Tobacco users should wash hands thoroughly before working around plants. Spray infected seedlings with a weak milk solution. Clear away perennial weeds. Control aphids. In removing a diseased plant, also take out one to either side.

Verticillium Wilt

Fungal disease that causes yellowing and curling of leaves with an eventual browning of the leaves and stems. Seldom kills plant outright, but plant may bloom and then peter out, producing pitiful fruit. Rhubarb, tomatoes and potatoes are particularly susceptible.
Controls: Use resistant varieties. Pull and destroy affected plants. Rotate crops, leaving the ground free of any wilt-affected plants—either verticillium or fusarium wilt—for three years of a four-year cycle.

Yellows

Also called fusarium wilt (see page 142).

Editor's Note: Gardeners can minimize the threat of many diseases by researching and selecting resistant varieties: strains that are bred to oppose the attack of various diseases or to withstand the damage if attack does occur. New disease-resistant varieties are continually being marketed as the diseases change, evolving into new strains. Because any list of resistant varieties can quickly become dated, you would be wise to check with your state agricultural experiment station for the most recent listings.

PART FOUR

Remedies for Common Garden Problems

A vegetable-by-vegetable
guide for identifying and reversing
crop failure

Curatives

Into each garden must come a few failures. Sometimes a June hailstorm or July drought is to blame. Other times, a lapse in weeding or bug picking is the culprit.

But, somehow, worse than losses due to

weather or laziness are the ones with unknown causes.

The best answers we know to common and mysterious garden headaches are contained in this section. Study our choices and your plants, then experiment with solutions. And don't be discouraged—be stimulated. Solving such garden puzzles and watching plants bear productively in gratitude are two of the secret pleasures of gardening.

Asparagus

Shoots don't come up in newly planted bed:
- The soil may be too heavy. Lighten it with applications of compost and sand.
- The crowns may have been buried too deeply. Plant crowns 8" deep in trenches, but cover them with only about 2" of dirt. As they grow, continue covering, with an additional 2" of dirt at a time, until the soil is at ground level.

Plants turn yellow:
- The pH of the soil may be below 6.5. Test for pH, and apply lime if needed.
- The plants may be underwatered. Water deeply, then not again until the soil is dry from 4" to 8" down.
- The plants may also be over watered. If the soil's constantly wet, oxygen and nutrient uptake will be restricted.
- Note that plants naturally turn yellow, then brown, when they die at the end of the season.

Twisted, crooked spears:
- This damage may be caused by careless weeding, cultivating or harvesting of other spears. Tend the plants more carefully.
- The spears may have been injured by wind-blown sand. Use barriers of burlap, cheesecloth, etc., to protect the plants.

Second- and third-year beds still not producing well:
- They may not have had enough initial fertilizer. Perennials stay in one place for a long time, so they need large doses of humus and amendments incorporated into their soil.
- Production can be boosted if the plants are fertilized each year with side-dressings or garden teas in the fall or spring.
- You may have been harvesting too early. Don't cut any spears until their third spring (counting the spring they were planted as spring number one). And harvest only spears as big around as your finger. Leave skinny spears to develop into ferns.

Frozen spears:
- Early shoots were caught in a late cold snap. Cut and discard them, and cover the rest with protective devices (milk jugs, hot caps, etc.) if another cold snap threatens.

Spears are tough:
- They may not have been harvested early

enough. Cut the spears when the tops are tightly closed and the stalks are not too tall.
- Lack of soil fertility can affect quality. Side-dress the plants with compost and soil amendments, or water them with a garden tea.
- The soil may be too acid. Test for pH, and lime if it's below 6.5.

Plants are generally declining in health:
- They may be overharvested. Cutting for too long a period each year does not allow the plants to grow big enough to store the root food necessary for next spring's growth. So cut for no longer than four weeks on a three- or four-year-old bed, or eight weeks on established beds.
- The plants weren't mulched. Almost all gardening authorities agree that mulch is important for asparagus. It keeps down weeds, adds soil moisture, provides nutrients as it breaks down and helps regulate soil temperatures.
- They may have been damaged by garden centipedes (see below).
- Deep cultivation may have damaged the crowns. Plant crowns eventually work their way near to the surface, so cultivate asparagus shallowly if at all.
- In some areas, winters are too warm to give plants a dormant season. If you live in such a region, raise your asparagus in the shade and mulch heavily.

Common pests:
- Asparagus aphid (p. 78).
- Asparagus beetle (p. 78).
- Cutworm (p. 84).
- Garden centipede (also called garden symphilid). This subterranean pest eats holes in the underground parts of asparagus. The best currently known controls are moderate cultivation to disturb its home and growing your asparagus in full sun—the garden centipede abhors light. Commercial growers sometimes flood their fields with water to drown the pest.
- Spotted cucumber beetle (p. 96).

Common diseases:
- Asparagus rust (p. 140) is characterized by dark, reddish brown spots or blisters. Foliage tops also turn yellow and die. This is by far the most common and serious asparagus disease.
- Anthracnose (p. 140) symptoms are rust-colored spots with gray or tan centers.
- Root rot and crown rot also occur from time to time. Root rot stunts plants and may produce reddish streaks at roots and bases. Crown rot creates soft, mushy spots on shoots and tips. Prevent them both by planting resistant varieties (like the well-known Mary Washington) and using only treated seed. If rot does afflict your plot, you will have to destroy the infected plants and start a new bed in a new location.

Beans

Poor germination:
- The seeds may have been planted too early, so they rotted in the cold, wet soil. Purple-pod varieties fare better in such conditions.
- Heavy soils (like clay) can become crusted over when dry, so the seeds have trouble sprouting. Keep the soil surface moist.
- The seeds may have been planted too shallowly. This is most often a problem late in the summer when the surface of the soil dries out readily. Plant about 1″ deep.

Flowers drop:
- A sudden change to hot, dry or windy weather (or a combination of the three) can ruin the flowers—and your chances for a crop.

Low production:
- Beans must be picked frequently or the pods will mature and send signals to the plants to stop production.
- Poor soil nutrition will affect productivity.
- Low moisture will cut output (and frequently causes stunted pod ends).
- The bean seed may need to be inoculated to have nitrogen-fixing bacteria on its root nodules.

Beans do not mature:
- The warm-weather growing season wasn't long enough. This is a particular problem for lima beans, which need 65 to 75 warm days for bush varieties and 90 to 120 days for pole varieties.

Beans taste tough:
- They were harvested too late. Pick them regularly once they start producing.

Spots or streaks on bean pods:
- This problem may be sunscald created when hot sunlight followed watering or previously cloudy conditions. It may also be created by one of the diseases described below.

No true leaves emerge:
- The plants have baldhead, a condition in which only the seed leaves (cotyledons) germinate but no true bean leaves follow. It's a problem of poor-quality seed. Buy new seed from a reputable seed house.

Bean vines turn yellow:
- They may have been affected by the onset of cold weather.
- They may not have sufficient fertilizer.

Common pests:
- Aphid (p. 78).
- Blister beetle (p. 80).
- Corn earworm (p. 82).
- Cucumber beetle (pp. 96, 98).
- Cutworm (p. 84).
- Grasshopper (p. 86).
- Japanese bean beetle (p. 90).
- Leafhopper (p. 90).
- Mexican bean beetle (p. 92).
- Root-knot nematode (p. 94).
- Tarnished plant bug (p. 98).
- Wireworm (p. 100).
- Deer (p. 128).
- Groundhog (p. 130).
- Rabbit (p. 131).

Common diseases:
- Anthracnose (p. 140) is characterized by dark brown sunken spots (with, perhaps, a pink mold) on pods or seeds.
- Bacterial blight (p. 140) produces leaf spots (often with yellow rings) and watery- or greasy-looking pods.
- Blight (p. 141) creates dark, watery-looking spots (which eventually become covered with a cottony mold) on leaves, stems and pods.
- Curly top virus symptoms are puckered leaves or stunted young plants. Curly top usually kills young plants, but older ones may hold their own. Prevent by planting resistant varieties.
- Downy mildew (p. 141) affects only the limas of the bean family. It produces white, cottony patches (sometimes with a purple halo) on pods.
- Mosaic (p. 142) deforms pods and mottles leaves, changing their color to pale or dark green and making them wrinkle and turn under.
- Powdery mildew (p. 142) looks as if a fine white powder was randomly dusted on stems and pods.
- Rust (p. 142) creates many orange-brown blisters, mostly on the undersides of leaves.

Beets

Poor germination:
- The soil may be too hard and crusty. Incorporate organic matter before planting, and keep the ground well watered until germination. An old sheet, boards, plastic or similar cover can be put over the beds to keep in moisture until the seeds sprout. (Then be sure to take it right off.)
- Heavy rains can wash the seed down the sides of raised beds. Prevent that by covering the bed to protect it until the seeds sprout.
- The temperature may be too high for the seed to germinate. Plant beet seed in spring or late summer (or fall for a winter crop in extreme southern locations). If the weather turns hot unexpectedly, erect a temporary shade cloth or add a 1″-deep layer of sifted compost or leaf mold over the soil. Keep the soil well watered.

Germination too thick:
- Beets are frequently planted too thickly, since many people don't know that each beet "seed" is actually a cluster containing several seeds.

White rings inside beet root:
- These are often due to uneven soil moisture during the beets' growing cycle, especially if that's combined with a period of high temperatures. So keep beets watered in times of drought, and try to plant them in cooler months. Of course, some varieties, such as Chioggia, naturally have concentric circles of red and white.

Roots are tough and flavorless:
- Beets become tough and woody if they're harvested beyond their prime.
- High temperatures (over 85°F) reduce beet quality. Avoid this by planting in cooler months.
- A lack of water will help make them tough. Remember to water as needed to maintain even soil moisture.
- Overcrowded growing conditions will also hurt quality. Thin young beets as needed.
- Too much weed competition will reduce the flavor and texture of beets.

Beet roots too little:
- A lack of water will limit growth.
- Beets not thinned properly won't grow properly.

- A lack of potash will stunt growth. Add greensand, crushed granite or kelp meal, if needed, to bring K levels up.
- A lack of phosphorus will also hurt growth. Add bone meal, colloidal phosphate or cottonseed meal to raise P levels.

Misshapen beets:
- Fresh manure in the soil damages beets. Use only well-rotted manure in beet soil.
- Rocky soil forces beets to grow in odd shapes.

Leaves slowly turn red:
- You'll first notice that leaf margins or tips turn red. Then the whole leaf changes color. Older and middle leaves may wrinkle, and leaf tips may die. This is due to a boron deficiency in the plants—which, in turn, may be because overly acid soil makes boron less available to the plants. Check soil pH. If it's at or below 6.5, add lime. If that's not the problem, you have a real boron deficiency. Mix 1½ teaspoons of common borax into 15 gallons of water, and apply the solution over 100 square feet of garden space.

Common pests:
- Aphid (p. 78).
- Beet or garden webworm. This caterpillar may be a variety of colors from yellow or green to gray-black. It has a stripe down its back and three spots on each segment. It feeds on leaves and causes rolled-up leaves that are held together with what looks like spider silk. Control the pests by handpicking, by picking off and destroying rolled leaves or with sabadilla or pyrethrum.
- Blister beetle (p. 80).
- Cutworm (p. 84).
- Flea beetle (p. 86).
- Grasshopper (p. 86).
- Leaf miner (p. 92).
- Deer (p. 128).
- Groundhog (p. 130).
- Rabbit (p. 131).

Common diseases:
- Curly top virus symptoms are puckered leaves or stunted young plants. Curly top usually kills young plants, but older ones may hold their own. Prevent by planting resistant varieties.
- Leaf spot (p. 141) is characterized by small brown spots with dark purple borders. The centers may turn gray and fall out.
- Mosaic (p. 142) mottles the leaves, which usually wrinkle and curl up.
- Yellows (p. 143) makes the margins and veins of leaves turn yellow. It's frequently transmitted by aphids.

Broccoli

Poor germination:
- Broccoli won't germinate if the soil's too warm or too cold. Generally, it's best started indoors under controlled conditions and transplanted out after a few weeks of growth.

No heads form:
- The plants were probably grown out of season. Broccoli does best if it matures in late spring or fall. (You can still eat the leaves, which are more nutritious than the heads, anyway.)

Heads are small or premature:
- Broccoli needs loose soil, lots of nitrogen and adequate water to produce heads of good size.
- The young seedlings were exposed to low temperatures (40°F or below).
- The plants were stressed at an early age, so they're rushing to complete their life cycle. (Don't buy any nursery six-packs that are already heading.)

Heads flower:
- The heads weren't harvested when they were ready.
- The planting is maturing during hot weather. High temperatures—say, above 85°F—encourage rapid flowering.

Plants wilt and turn yellow:
- They may have been stricken by yellows, root-knot nematodes or club root (see below).
- Cabbage maggots may be attacking your plants (see below).
- Lack of water or proper fertilizer will affect the plants.

Common pests:
- Aphid (p. 78).
- Blister beetle (p. 80).
- Cabbage looper (p. 80).
- Cabbage maggot. These 1/3"-long, white grubs chew on young plants just below the soil surface. (You can find them or their white eggs if you pull a little dirt away from the plants.) Control maggots by using tar-paper collars around your plants, practicing clean soil cultivation, covering the plants with a protective row cover to deter the adult flies or interplanting with mint.
- Cutworm (p. 84).
- Flea beetle (p. 86).
- Harlequin bug. This black, 3/8"-long bug has distinctive orange and red markings, an

unappealing odor and a penchant for cabbage-family plants. It can blotch, drain and eventually destroy plants. To control, handpick the bugs and squash their eggs (two rows of small white pegs), plant a trap crop of another brassica, keep weeds down or use pyrethrum or sabadilla dust.
- Imported cabbageworm (p. 88).
- Root-knot nematodes (p. 94) create swollen galls on the roots. The whole plant becomes stunted, yellow and sickly.
- Slug (p. 94).
- Deer (p. 128).
- Groundhog (p. 130).
- Rabbit (p. 131).

Common diseases:
- Blackleg (p. 140) starts as light brown or gray spots that turn to dark patches. It may affect leaves or stems.
- Black rot (p. 140) produces yellow, wedge-shaped leaf areas with black veins and a foul odor.
- Club root (p. 141) creates large, knotty, rotting roots and yellow, wilting leaves.
- Downy mildew (p. 141) usually affects only seedlings. It starts with small gray or purple downy spots that enlarge and turn yellow.
- Rhizoctonia (p. 142) causes damping off in seedlings (which have a water-soaked appearance). It also can lead to root, bottom and head rot of the maturing plant.
- Watery soft rot makes the plants or heads turn soft and collapse. It's encouraged by cool, damp weather. The rot is hard to control organically. The best measures are to destroy infected plants and practice general good-gardening health measures.
- Yellows (p. 143) starts when lower leaves turn dull and yellow and their veins turn brown. Eventually the leaves turn brown and drop off.

Brussels Sprouts

No heads form:
- You probably didn't plant them at the right time of year. Brussels sprouts won't mature well in hot weather, yet have a long growing season (as long as 100 days). Most people do not grow them in spring, but plant them in early summer or midsummer for a fall crop.

Sprouts taste unusually bitter:
- Don't pick them in hot weather; their flavor improves considerably after frost.
- Do pick before they turn yellow and toughen.

Sprouts stay small:
- The plants may have too much foliage. Remove the lower leaves around forming sprouts to encourage them to grow bigger, sooner. Continue up the stalk as new sprouts form.
- The weather may be too hot. Time your plantings to mature in fall.
- The plants may not have enough water.
- The plants may not have enough fertilizer, especially nitrogen. Try side-dressing them with liquid manure, blood meal, fishmeal or compost.

Loose-headed sprouts:
- The first sprouts starting from the bottom usually do have loose heads. Be patient; subsequent ones should be tighter.
- Temperatures are too high. The temperature must be below 75°F for the plants to form compact sprouts.
- Lack of fertilizer (use liquid manure or green leaf teas when sprouts start to form).

Hard little bumps or scars on leaves and stems
- These are most often scars from wind-blown soil particles that hit the plants. They are harmless marks. To prevent them, if desired, protect the plants with barriers like burlap, spunbond row covers, old sheets, etc.

Plants fall over:
- If this is a problem, the plants can be staked when they're 1' high for support. (However, they'll probably still grow and produce just fine even if they have fall-

en over.)

Common pests:
- Aphid (p. 78).
- Blister beetle (p. 80).
- Cabbage looper (p. 80).
- Cabbage maggot. These $1/3$"-long, white grubs chew on young plants just below the soil surface. (You can find them or their white eggs if you pull a little dirt away from the plants.) Control maggots by using tar-paper collars around your plants, practicing clean soil cultivation, covering the plants with a protective row cover to deter the adult flies or interplanting with mint.
- Fall armyworm (p. 86).
- Flea beetle (p. 86).
- Grub (p. 88).
- Harlequin bug. This black, $3/8$"-long bug has distinctive orange and red markings, an unappealing odor and a penchant for cabbage-family plants. It can blotch, drain and eventually destroy plants. To control, handpick bugs and squash their eggs (two rows of small white pegs), plant a trap crop of another brassica, keep weeds down or use pyrethrum or sabadilla dust.
- Imported cabbageworm (p. 88).
- Slug and snail (p. 94).
- Stinkbug. This $1/2$"-long, bright green, round, shield-shaped bug pierces plants and sucks their sap, leaving distorted or discolored areas. The control measures are the same as those for the harlequin bug.
- Vegetable weevil. Problems primarily in the South, the adult (a $1/2$"-long, grayish brown weevil) and the larva (a $1/4$"-long, greenish, wormlike caterpillar) eat foliage. Control by cultivating the soil well in the fall and spring, rotating brassica plantings, practicing good garden sanitation or using diatomaceous earth.

Common diseases:
- Bacterial soft rot (p. 140) creates slimy, foul-smelling top foliage that easily falls off.
- Blackleg (p. 140) starts as light brown or gray spots that turn to dark patches. It may affect leaves or stems.
- Black rot (p. 140) produces yellow, wedge-shaped leaf areas with black veins and a foul odor.
- Club root (p. 141) creates large, knotty, rotting roots and yellow, wilting leaves.
- Downy mildew (p. 141) usually affects only seedlings. Small gray or purple downy spots enlarge and turn yellow.

- Rhizoctonia (p. 142) causes damping off in seedlings (which have a water-soaked appearance). It also can lead to root, bottom and head rot of the maturing plant.
- Watery soft rot makes the plants or heads turn soft and collapse. It's encouraged by cool, damp weather. The rot is hard to control organically. The best measures are to destroy infected plants and practice general good-gardening health measures.
- Yellows (p. 143) starts when lower leaves turn dull and yellow and their veins turn brown. Eventually the leaves turn brown and drop off.

Cabbage

Heads crack or split:
- Early varieties that are exposed to warm weather will start to form a seed stalk and thus split. Get them in the ground sooner next time.
- The soil may have dried out and then been watered or rained on heavily. Do what you can to moderate the plant's water supply. Once a head has begun to split, you can twist or pull it a few inches to break and loosen some roots. This will slow the growth for a few days and stave off further splitting.

Some heads large, some small:
- Seeds may have been poor in quality. Purchase more reliable seeds.
- Fertilization may have been uneven. Distribute compost and amendments more uniformly.

Pinhead-size bumps on leaves and stems:
- This cosmetic damage was probably caused by wind-blown soil particles. You can protect the plants with a spunbond row cover, cheesecloth or something similar.

Good foliage but no heads:
- There is probably too little lime or fertilizer. Test your soil and correct any deficiencies. Bone meal or soft phosphate rock will boost phosphorus levels. Greensand, kelp meal or crushed granite will add potash.

Long stems but no heads:
- You may have set out root-bound seedlings or not transplanted them deeply or firmly enough.
- The plants may have come from poor-quality seeds.
- The soil may be lacking in potash or phosphorus.

Heads generally poor in quality:
- The plants may not be getting enough nitrogen during their growth period. Side-dress them with chicken or rabbit manure, blood meal, bone meal or cottonseed meal. However, don't add a lot of nitrogen just before a fall harvest—it makes the heads too succulent and susceptible to frost damage.
- The bed may not have been kept weeded.
- The soil may not have been firmed well around transplanted seedlings.
- Too much warm weather will reduce head quality.

● The plants may not have had sufficient water.

Cabbage heart dies:

● This problem—along with tough, bitter heart leaves and browned margins on older leaves—is probably due to a boron deficiency in the plants, which, in turn, may be because overly acid soil makes boron less available to the plants. Check soil pH. If it's at or below 6.5, add lime. If that's not the problem, your soil is deficient in boron. Mix 1 1/2 teaspoons of common borax into 15 gallons of water and apply to 100 square feet of garden space.

Goes to seed early:

● The plants were probably set out too early and exposed to cool temperatures (40° to 50°F) for several weeks.
● The seedlings may have been exposed to prolonged cool temperatures before they were planted out.

Multiple heads:

● The main growing tip may have been injured—usually by frost.
● Seedlings may have been planted out too early or may not have been properly hardened off.
● Seedlings grown in a southern climate were sold and transplanted out in a northern one. Plant locally grown seedlings or start your own.

Common pests:

● Aphid (p. 78).
● Blister beetle (p. 80).
● Cabbage looper (p. 80).
● Cabbage maggot. These 1/3"-long, white grubs chew on young plants just below the soil surface. (You can find them or their white eggs if you pull a little dirt away from the plants.) Control maggots by using tar-

paper collars around your plants, practicing clean soil cultivation, covering the plants with a protective row cover to deter the adult flies or interplanting with mint.
● Fall armyworm (p. 86).
● Flea beetle (p. 86).
● Grub (p. 88).
● Harlequin bug. This black, 3/8"-long bug has distinctive orange and red markings, an unappealing odor and a penchant for cabbage-family plants. It can blotch, drain and eventually destroy plants. To control, hand-pick bugs and squash their eggs (two rows of small white pegs), plant a trap crop of another brassica, keep weeds down or use pyrethrum or sabadilla dust.
● Imported cabbageworm (p. 88).
● Slug and snail (p. 94).
● Stinkbug. This 1/2"-long, bright green, round, shield-shaped bug pierces plants and sucks their sap, leaving distorted or discolored areas. The control measures are the same as those for the harlequin bug.
● Vegetable weevil. Problems primarily in the South, the adult (a 1/2"-long, grayish brown weevil) and the larva (a 1/4"-long, greenish, wormlike caterpillar) eat foliage. Control by cultivating the soil well in the fall and spring, rotating brassica plantings, practicing good garden sanitation or using diatomaceous earth.

Common diseases:

● Bacterial soft rot (p. 140) creates slimy, foul-smelling top foliage that easily falls off.
● Blackleg (p. 140) starts as light brown or gray spots that turn to dark patches. It may affect leaves or stems.
● Downy mildew (p. 141) usually affects only seedlings. It starts with small gray or purple downy spots that enlarge and turn yellow.
● Rhizoctonia (p. 142) causes damping off in seedlings (which have a water-soaked appearance). It also can lead to root, bottom and head rot of the maturing plant.
● Watery soft rot makes the plants or heads turn soft and collapse. It's encouraged by cool, damp weather. The rot is hard to control organically. The best measures are to destroy infected plants and practice general good-gardening health measures.
● Yellows (p. 143) starts when lower leaves turn dull and yellow and their veins turn brown. Eventually the leaves turn brown and drop off.

Carrots

Poor germination:

● The soil probably dried out and formed a hard crust. Add organic matter to the soil; cover it with boards, plastic, sheets, etc., to hold in moisture until germination occurs; or cover seeds with sifted leaf mold, sifted compost or vermiculite.
● Heavy rains may have scattered the seeds or washed them away. Protect them with a spunbond row cover, old sheets, boards or the like.
● The seeds may have accicentally gotten weeded out of the growing bed. This is easier to avoid if you plant carrots in rows rather than broadcast the seeds.
● The seeds may have been planted too deeply. Carrots should be sown very shallowly.

Carrot roots fork:

● Fresh manure in the soil will create this problem.
● Rocks or other large soil obstructions will make carrots split.
● The carrots may have been sown too thickly, so that they twist around each other.
● The soil may need more lime.

Many small roots instead of one straight one:

● Soil nematodes may create multiple carrot roots.
● The soil may need more lime.

Stunted carrots:

● The soil may be too heavy for good root formation. Carrots need light soil with good tilth (add sand if necessary).
● They may not have been thinned properly.
● They may have suffered from a lack of water or fertilizer.
● The soil may be too warm. Carrots prefer ground temperatures between 60° and 70°F.
● They may have been planted too late in the season to get good growth before winter.
● Leaf blight can stunt roots.
● You may simply have planted a short, stubby variety.

Carrots long and thin:

● The soil temperature was probably too low (below 50°F).

Poor taste:

● There may have been too much nitrogen

in the soil.
- Hot or dry weather can affect flavor.
- The soil may not have enough potash (add greensand, crushed granite or kelp meal) or phosphorus (add soft phosphate, bone meal or phosphate rock).
- The soil may need lime. Carrots prefer a soil with a pH of 6.5.

Green shoulders:
- The shoulders have been exposed to sunlight and formed chlorophyll. Hill them over with soil.

Core turns black:
- The soil probably has a manganese or boron deficiency. Correct for manganese unavailability by lowering the pH of your soil. Boron availability can often be boosted by adding lime. If that doesn't work, mix 1 1/2 teaspoons of common borax into 15 gallons of water and apply to 100 square feet of garden space.

Carrots crack or split open:
- Dry weather followed by heavy rain or heavy watering often causes cracking. Moderate moisture conditions by using more humus in the soil, mulching the plants and watering before the soil becomes totally dry.
- The soil may have a boron deficiency.

Carrots lack color:
- There may be too much nitrogen in the soil.
- The carrots may have been grown in cool weather for an extended period.
- The soil may not have enough lime.

Hearts tough:
- Growing conditions were probably dry.

Plants go to seed the first season:
- Carrots are biennials. They shouldn't go to seed until the second year. If they produce flowers the first year that look like Queen Anne's lace, they were probably planted too early and exposed to too much cold.

Common pests:
- Aphid (p. 78).
- Carrot rust fly (p. 80).
- Carrot worm. This green caterpillar has black stripes and white dots and sticks out little orange horns when threatened. (It's the larva of the black swallowtail butterfly). Morning handpicking, *Bacillus thuringiensis* or rotenone should control it.
- Leafhopper (p. 90).
- Nematode (p. 94).
- Wireworm (p. 100).
- Deer (p. 128).
- Gopher (p. 129).
- Groundhog (p. 130).
- Rabbit (p. 131).

Common diseases:
- Aster yellows symptoms are yellow leaves

that then turn reddish rust. Eventually the shoulders turn black. To control, keep weeds down. Destroy infected plants. Do not plant carrots near asters or lettuce. The disease is transmitted by leafhoppers, so controlling them should help control the disease.

● Leaf blight (p. 141) produces white to yellowish spots on leaves that eventually turn brown and fatal. The root crown may develop dark pits and eventually die.

● Mosaic (p. 142) mottles leaves with light to dark shades of green. It's spread by aphids.

● Vegetable soft rot is a bacterial disease that discolors the foliage and causes the roots to become soft and slimy. Hot, humid weather encourages the development of this disease. (It can also strike carrots in storage, so cull stored, bruised roots and allow for aeration.) To avoid it, practice crop rotation, and provide loose, well-drained soil for your carrots.

Cauliflower

Poor germination:

● Cauliflower won't germinate if the soil's too warm or too cold. Generally, it's best started indoors under controlled conditions and transplanted out after a few weeks of growth.

● Mice love to eat cauliflower seeds. If they're a problem, screen or otherwise protect your seeds.

Heads turn brown:

● There is probably a boron deficiency in the plants—which, in turn, may be because overly acid soil makes boron less available to the plants. Check soil pH. If it's at or below 6.5, then add lime. If that's not the problem, you have a real boron deficiency. Mix $1\frac{1}{2}$

teaspoons of common borax into 15 gallons of water and apply to 100 square feet of garden space.

Heads turn yellow or purplish and then bitter:

● The heads may not have been "blanched." When cauliflower heads are about 3″ across, they should be covered in some manner to keep out the sun. This is usually done by tying or breaking over the plants' own leaves. (Purple-headed and self-blanching varieties do not need this treatment.)

● The plants may have matured in hot weather. Cauliflower is a cool-weather crop that should be grown for spring or fall harvest.

Heads are small:

● The seedlings probably suffered stressful setbacks that made them bolt prematurely.

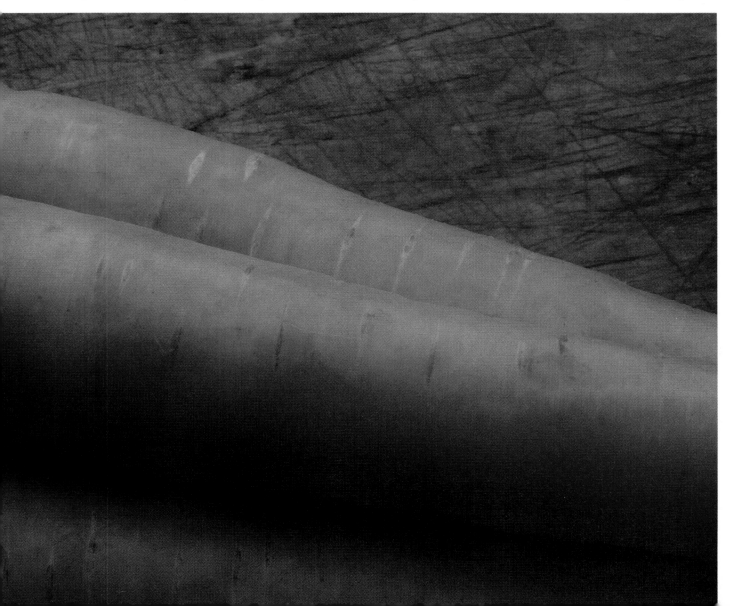

Care must be taken that seedlings do not go through drastic temperature or watering changes. You might want to mulch your cauliflower plants with black plastic to help keep their soil warm. (And do not buy nursery seedlings that are already heading.)

Some plants form heads, others don't:
● Seeds may have been inferior. Purchase from a quality seed house.
● Some of the plant's growing tips may have been eaten by rabbits or insects, so heads cannot form. Take appropriate protective action.

Heads start to rot:
● You may have covered the heads too tightly for blanching so that water is puddling and there is little aeration.

Parts or all of head turns dark and mushy:
● The plant may have suffered frost damage. Cauliflower is not as cold-hardy as broccoli or cabbage.

Leaves long and thin, may have no heads:
● This malady, called whiptail, is caused by a molybdenum shortage, which is often due to very acid soils. Test for pH and, if needed, correct to a more neutral number. If that doesn't help, apply about $1/2$ ounce of ammonium molybdate for every 500 square feet of ground space.

Heads turn gray or brown when cooked:
● They may have been cooked in water that has too much iron or in cast-iron pots. Try steaming, not boiling. Or use other water or cookware.

Common pests:
● Aphid (p. 78).
● Blister beetle (p. 80).
● Cabbage looper (p. 80).
● Cabbage maggot. These $1/3$″-long, white grubs chew on young plants just below the soil surface. (You can find them or their white eggs if you pull a little dirt away from the plants.) Control maggots by using tar-paper collars around your plants, practicing clean soil cultivation, covering the plants with a protective row cover to deter the adult flies or interplanting with mint.
● Fall armyworm (p. 86).
● Flea beetle (p. 86).
● Grub (p. 88).
● Harlequin bug. This black, $3/8$″-long bug has distinctive orange and red markings, an unappealing odor and a penchant for cabbage-family plants. It can blotch, drain and

eventually destroy plants. To control, handpick the bugs and squash their eggs (two rows of small white pegs), plant a trap crop of another brassica, keep weeds down or use pyrethrum or sabadilla dust.
● Imported cabbageworm (p. 88).
● Slug and snail (p. 94).
● Stinkbug. This $1/2$″-long, bright green, round, shield-shaped bug pierces plants and sucks their sap, leaving distorted or discolored areas. The control measures are the same as those for the harlequin bug.
● Vegetable weevil. Problems primarily in the South, the adult (a $1/2$″-long, grayish brown weevil) and the larva (a $1/4$″-long, greenish, wormlike caterpillar) eat foliage. Control by cultivating the soil well in the fall and spring, rotating brassica plantings, practicing good garden sanitation or using diatomaceous earth.

Common diseases:
● Bacterial soft rot (p. 140) creates slimy, foul-smelling top foliage that easily falls off.
● Blackleg (p. 140) starts as light brown or gray spots that turn to dark patches. It may affect leaves or stems.
● Black rot (p. 140) produces yellow, wedge-shaped leaf areas with black veins and a foul odor.
● Club root (p. 141) creates large, knotty, rotting roots and yellow, wilting leaves.
● Downy mildew (p. 141) usually affects only seedlings. It starts with small gray or purple downy spots that enlarge and turn yellow.
● Rhizoctonia (p. 142) causes damping off in seedlings (which have a water-soaked appearance). It also can lead to root, bottom and head rot of the maturing plant.
● Watery soft rot makes the plants or heads turn soft and collapse. It's encouraged by cool, damp weather. The rot is hard to control organically. The best measures are to destroy infected plants and practice general good-gardening health measures.
● Yellows (p. 143) starts when lower leaves turn dull and yellow and their veins turn brown. Eventually the leaves turn brown and drop off.

Celery

Stalks hollow, tough or tasteless:
● The weather was probably hot and dry. Start celery early and give it lots of water (it's actually a marsh plant).
● The soil may not have sufficient fertilizer. Shallow-rooted celery needs copious amounts of fertility in the top 12″ of the soil.
● You may have planted poor-quality seeds. Buy from a reputable seed house.

Stalks taste bitter or too strong:
● The stalks weren't blanched. There are various ways of shielding the plants to improve their flavor: hilling up soil, covering the stalks with paper collars or milk cartons, etc.
● Some varieties have a stronger taste than others.
● Dry, hot weather can hurt the flavor.

Leaf margins and tips look burned:
● Your soil is probably deficient in magnesium. Have it tested, and correct it, if necessary, by adding dolomitic limestone.

Stems brittle or cracked, leaves turn brown:
● The plants probably have a boron deficiency—which, in turn, may exist because overly acid soil makes boron less available to the plants. Check soil pH. If it's at or below 6.5, add lime. If that's not the problem, you have a real boron deficiency. Mix $1^1/2$ teaspoons of common borax into 15 gallons of water and apply to 100 square feet of garden space. You can also plant resistant varieties such as Golden Self-Blanching, Dwarf Golden Self-Blanching and Giant Pascal.

Leaves but no stalks:
● There were probably sudden changes in temperature when the plants were seedlings. Maintain constant temperature if starting celery indoors, and use hot caps or other protectors if the weather turns cold after the plants are set out.

Inner leaves turn dark and die:
● This problem, called blackheart, is associated with a deficiency in calcium. Do a soil test and add calcium as needed. Certain varieties, such as Golden Pascal, Emerald and Emerson, are less susceptible to this problem.

Common pests:

- Aphid (p. 78).
- Blister beetle (p. 80).
- Cabbage looper (p. 80).
- Celery leaf tier. This 3/4"-long, white-striped, yellow caterpillar actually looks green when it's young. (The adult is a small, nocturnal moth with dark, wavy lines on its brown wings.) Control this pest by handpicking, spraying with *Bacillus thuringiensis* or rotenone, or using predatory insects such as lacewings, ladybugs and praying mantises.
- Celery worm (also called carrot worm). This green caterpillar has black stripes and white dots and sticks out little orange horns when threatened. (It's the larva of the black swallowtail butterfly). Morning handpicking, *Bacillus thuringiensis* or rotenone should control it.
- Grub (p. 88).
- Nematode (p. 94).
- Slug and snail (p. 94).
- Tarnished plant bug (pg. 98).
- Deer (p. 128).
- Dog and cat (p. 129). These pets may be attracted to fish emulsion or manure used to fertilize the celery.
- Groundhog (p. 130).
- Rabbit (p. 131).

Common diseases:
- Aster yellows turns leaves yellow, stunting them and making them curl. To control, keep weeds down. Destroy infected plants. Do not plant carrots near asters or lettuce. The disease is transmitted by leafhoppers, so controlling them should help control the disease.
- Blight (p. 141), both early and late, begins as small dots on the leaves that can spread and cripple the plants.
- Fusarium wilt (p. 141) makes the plants pale and sickly-looking. They turn light green or yellow and may develop streaks of dark rust color on the stalks.
- Mosaic (p. 142) mottles leaves with marks or stripes of off-green or yellow.
- Pink rot (p. 142) produces white or pink cottony growth at the plant base. The stems may have water-soaked spots.
- Stem rot (p. 142) makes the stems turn so soft they wilt or collapse.

Corn

Poor germination:
- You may have planted too early, so the seed rotted in the cold ground.
- Corn generally has only a 75% germination rate. To compensate, plant it closely and thin it later.

Young plants lying on ground:
- Crows or other birds may have pulled up the just-sprouted seedlings.
- Cutworms may have felled the seedlings.

Corn falls over (lodges):
- You may need to hill up dirt around the corn's roots to brace it against strong winds and rain.
- Runner beans or other climbing crops will sometimes pull corn over.
- Root or stalk rot (see below) can fell your plants.

Ears not filled out:
- The plants were probably poorly pollinated. Corn should be planted in blocks instead of in a few long, thin rows so the plants can wind-pollinate more easily.
- The cornstalks may have been planted too close together.
- The soil may have too much nitrogen and not enough phosphorus (add soft phosphate, bone meal or phosphate rock) or potash (add greensand, crushed granite or kelp meal).
- Rains could have washed away pollen at tasseling time.
- The corn borer may have hurt your plants' productivity.

Ears never mature:
- The weather may have gotten too dry. Water as needed.
- Cold weather hit before the corn finished growing. Plant earlier or use a short-season variety.

Doesn't produce well:
- The plants may be too close together. They should be from 6" to 1 1/2' apart, depending on variety and soil condition.
- The problem may be underfertilized soil. Corn is a heavy feeder.
- You may have let weeds get too big, so they interfered with productivity.

Streaks of purple on foliage:
- There is probably a phosphorus deficiency. Add soft phosphate, bone meal or phosphate rock.

Leaves roll:
- There is probably insufficient moisture. Keep your corn well watered.

Common pests:
- Corn earworm (p. 82).
- Cutworm (p. 84).
- European corn borer (p. 84).
- Flea beetle (p. 86).
- Grasshopper (p. 86).
- Wireworm (p. 100).
- Bird (p. 128).
- Deer (p. 128).
- Raccoon and skunk (p. 131).

Common diseases:
- Bacterial wilt (p. 140), or Stewart's disease, creates long, white or pale yellow-green streaks on leaves that eventually turn brown. The stalks may exude a sticky, yellow sap when cut. Wilt is spread by flea beetles and most often strikes early sweet corn.
- Corn smut (p. 141) produces large, silver-white galls all over the plant. These eventually turn dark and burst.
- Ear rot symptoms are dried and bleached-looking husks. The husks may also be stuck together, and the kernels may become pinkish or moldy-looking. Control by using resistant seed and practicing clean cultivation. Remove old stalks.
- Leaf blight (p. 141) makes brown to gray-green spots appear on lower leaves. It may stunt ear development.
- Root and stalk rot may corrode and fell cornstalks. The only known control is to grow your corn on well-drained soil and use good crop rotation.

Cucumber

Poor germination:
- The seeds may have been planted too early. They won't sprout in cold ground.
- The seeds may be poor-quality. Buy from a reputable seed house.

Bitter cukes:
- The problem is probably a lack of consistent water supply. Incorporate humus or add mulch to regulate the soil's water-holding capacity, and water deeply once a week if needed.

Low production:
- The problem may simply be lack of water. Cucumbers are 95% water. They must have ample water to produce well.
- The plants may be spaced too close together.
- You may not have kept the ripe cukes picked. If they mature fully, they signal the plant to stop producing.
- There may be a lack of bees to pollinate flowers. You can hand-pollinate cucumbers, if need be, by picking male flowers (the ones without the little swelling underneath) and rubbing their pollen on the female flowers.
- Initial low production may be due to the fact that only male flowers have formed and the females are soon to follow.
- Some varieties, listed as all-female hybrids, come with only a few seeds that produce male flowers. If these male plants happen not to germinate, you won't get a cucumber crop.
- Seeds planted late in the summer may not have enough time to mature before cool weather sets in.

Yellow or shriveled fruits:
- The plants may not be getting enough water. Incorporate more organic matter to retain moisture, and water as needed.
- They may have been poorly pollinated. Plant bee-attracting plants like buckwheat or borage nearby, or hand-pollinate the cucumber flowers.

Plants generally don't do well:
- Cucumbers started indoors may have suffered transplant shock. They are quite sensitive to transplanting; make sure to harden them off and handle their roots gently.
- The plants may lack water, fertilizer or

warm weather.

Young plants turn yellow and break off:
- This common problem is caused by the chewing of the larvae of the spotted cucumber beetle (see below). It's also called the southern corn rootworm.

Common pests:
- Aphid (p. 78).
- Cutworm (p. 84).
- Pickleworm. This $3/4''$-long, green or copper-colored pest chews holes in leaves, blossoms and fruits. It is a big problem in the South and Gulf states, but can move up as far as Michigan later in the season. Control by cleaning up plant refuse, applying *Bacillus thuringiensis* or rotenone, using squash as a trap crop or practicing good crop rotation and fall cultivation.
- Spotted cucumber beetle (p. 96).
- Squash bug (p. 96).
- Squash vine borer (p. 98).
- Striped cucumber beetle (p. 98).

Common diseases:
- Anthracnose (p. 140) starts as dark, red-black spots on the leaves. Early cucumbers may turn black and fall off. Later ones may get sunken craters filled with salmon-colored growth.
- Bacterial wilt (p. 140). At first, only a few leaves wilt, then the entire plant. A cut stem reveals a white, sticky substance. It's spread by cucumber beetles.
- Blight (p. 141) creates angular splotches on the leaves and roundish, watery spots on fruits.
- Downy mildew (p. 141) produces yellow to brown spots on upper leaf surfaces and a cottony, purple to gray mold underneath.
- Fusarium wilt (p. 141) makes the leaves and stems turn yellowish. It also stunts growth, as the vines start dying back from the tips.
- Mosaic (p. 142) mottles leaves with yellow to dark green splotches. The leaves eventually crinkle and curl up.
- Scab (p. 142) creates dark, oozing spots on fruits. These eventually dry up and leave holes with a gray-green fungus inside.

Garlic

Poor germination:
- The cloves may have been planted too deeply ($1''$ to $2''$ deep, plump-side-down, is recommended).
- They may have been fall-planted in too cold a climate (or without sufficient mulch protection).

Bulbs too small:
- They may have been planted too late. Plant as early as possible in the spring. Or, in areas where winters are not severe, you can plant them the prior fall, and mulch them if the ground is likely to freeze some.
- Weed competition may have hurt your crop. Keep garlic well weeded or mulched. A good mulch for the job is shredded leaves covered with straw.
- The weather may have been too cool. Garlic needs cool weather to start, but long, warm days to mature properly.
- The location may be too shady. Garlic needs full sun for best growth.
- The seed heads weren't kept picked off. Pinch off those seed heads so the plants will direct their energy into the bulbs.
- The plants may have been short on water. Add humus (to retain water) and water as needed.
- The soil may have lacked fertility. Incorporate compost or other organic matter into the soil before you plant.

Leaves turn yellow and fall over:
- The garlic is mature and almost ready to harvest.

Bulbs rot in the ground:
- There may be too much moisture in the ground. Stop overwatering and be sure to incorporate compost in your garlic plot to absorb rainfall.
- You may have left the bulbs in the ground too long. Harvest after the tops have fallen over and yellowed but before they have dried up.

Tops won't die back:
- This happens occasionally to super-strong or well-fertilized strains. If after 90 to 110 days the plants are still going strong, bend the tops over manually.

Garlic cloves small and poorly formed:
- You probably harvested it too early while it was still young. (You can still eat it at

this stage, but it won't keep well.)

No papery skin around bulb and cloves:
- That skin won't be there when the plants are just harvested. It forms after the bulbs have cured in a dry, shady place for a week or so.

Common pests and diseases:
- None. In fact, garlic is often used as an all-around insect and disease deterrent.

Lettuce

Poor germination:
- The seed may be poor in quality. Lettuce seed has a limited storage life, so old seed (such as may be on a store rack late in the season) may not grow well.
- The soil temperature may be too high. Lettuce prefers germination temperatures of 70° to 75°F. If you're starting lettuce seed in warm areas or in summer, put it in the refrigerator a day or two before sowing to fool its biological clock. Also, try planting heat-resistant varieties like Black Seeded Simpson, Great Lakes and Waldmann's Grand Rapids.
- You may have planted the seed too deeply. It should be barely covered by soil.
- Germination is enhanced by exposing the seed to light for a day before planting. If you're starting your seed indoors, you can simply press it into the soil and leave it uncovered. This requires a watchful eye, though, to make sure the top 1/4″ of soil stays moist.

Leaf tips turn brown:
- This is probably "tip burn," caused by the intense heat of direct midsummer sun, especially if the heat follows cloudy weather or hits plants raised under pampered conditions. Protect your plants by using a shade cloth, growing them in a shady area of the garden or raising them in the shadow of tall crops.

Lettuce bolts:
- Lettuce naturally goes to seed when warm summer weather hits. To stave that off, use a shade cloth, grow the greens in a shady area or in the shadow of taller crops, or plant varieties that resist bolting (such as Salad Bowl, Oak Leaf, Ruby, Slowbolt and many of the lesser-known European varieties).
- The crop may be stressed by lack of water and thus rushing to go to seed.

Small heads:
- They were probably planted too close together. You must thin or plant out lettuce at the proper spacing. Loose leaf varieties are usually grown from 6″ to 10″ apart, heading varieties from 12″ to 14″.

Tastes bitter or has white milky sap:
- The lettuce was allowed to grow past its prime. Pick it earlier, when the taste is good and the plant juices are clear.

Common pests:
- Aphid (p. 78).
- Cabbage looper (p. 80).
- Cutworm (p. 84).
- Fall armyworm (p. 86).
- Grub (p. 88).
- Leafhopper (p. 90).
- Tarnished plant bug (p. 98).
- Slug (p. 94).
- Wireworm (p. 100).
- Deer (p. 128).
- Groundhog (p. 130).
- Rabbit (p. 131).

Common diseases:
- Aster yellows turns leaves yellow, stunting and curling them. To control, keep weeds down and destroy infected plants. Do not plant lettuce near asters, carrots or celery. The disease is transmitted by leafhoppers, so controlling them should help control the disease.
- Bacterial soft rot (p. 140) starts when the lower leaves near the ground get a slimy, wet, brownish rot. It can spread and affect the whole plant.
- Big vein symptoms are brittle leaves and yellow and swollen veins. To treat, destroy infected plants, do not plant lettuce on the same site for three to four years, and keep its soil on the dry side.
- Pink rot (p. 142) creates water-soaked white to light pink spots on stalks. Stems become bitter-tasting and later rot.
- Downy mildew (p. 141) produces light green to yellow patches on the upper surfaces of leaves and a purple-gray mold on the undersides. The spots next get an off-white mold that eventually turns brown and invites rot.
- Fusarium wilt (p. 141) causes dark brown streaks in stems and veins. Plants may grow one-sided.
- Mosaic (p. 142) gives the leaves a characteristic mottling of light to dark green. It also makes the whole plant more yellowish, stunts growth and often keeps heads from forming.

Melons

Poor germination:
- The soil temperature may have been too low. Plant after the last spring frost when the soil has warmed, or start indoors in individual pots.
- The soil may be too heavy. Melons like light soil, so incorporate humus and sand if necessary.

Small melons:
- They may have had too little water. Melons need a lot of water to produce well.
- The problem may be generally poor soil fertility (add compost) or a lack of potash (correct by adding greensand, crushed granite or kelp meal) or phosphorus (add soft phosphate, bone meal or phosphate rock).
- Melons may have been planted too late in the season to have enough time to mature.
- Your season may be too short for the variety you planted. Grow a variety with a shorter growing season.
- There may have been too many fruits. Thin next time so that there are only a few per vine.
- If insects heavily damage leaf growth, fruit production will be reduced.

Melons taste bland or bitter:
- There may have been fluctuations in soil moisture. Incorporate more humus into the soil to retain water, water the soil deeply whenever it dries out, and mulch the melons unless that encourages slugs or squash vine borers in your area.
- The fruits may have never fully matured, because of insect leaf damage; cool, cloudy weather; planting too late; or growing a variety not suited to your growing season.
- You may have grown a variety that doesn't have a lot of sweetness.
- You may have picked the fruits before they were ripe. When cantaloupes are ripe, they turn a yellowish hue, and the stem ends start drying up and separate easily from the vine. Watermelons are ripe when they produce a hollow thud when thumped (instead of a high, quick sound), the rinds turn yellow on the side that rests on the ground, and the tendrils nearest the fruit dry up.
- The problem is *not* crossbreeding between your melons and cucumbers. That's impossible.

Melons rot on the bottom:
- The ground is too wet, so the fruits need to be set up on clean mulch, boards, coffee cans, etc.

Cantaloupes have green, smooth skin with no netting:
- The fruits are still immature.

Common pests:
- Aphid (p. 78).
- Cutworm (p. 84).
- Pickleworm. This ³/₄″-long, green or copper-colored pest chews holes in the fruits, leaving melon-colored frass (excreta) behind. It is mostly a problem in the South and the Gulf states, but can move up as far as Michigan later in the season. Control by cleaning up plant refuse, applying *Bacillus thuringiensis* or rotenone, using squash as a trap crop, or practicing good crop rotation and fall cultivation.
- Squash vine borer (p. 98).
- Spotted cucumber beetle (p. 96).
- Striped cucumber beetle (p. 98).

Common diseases:
- Anthracnose (p. 140) produces dark, redblack spots on the leaves that sometimes run together. The centers of the spots may dry up and fall out.
- Bacterial wilt (p. 140) may start with just a few leaves, but the whole plant may then rapidly wilt. It's spread by the cucumber beetle.
- Blight (p. 141) produces small, dark splotches on the leaves and round, watery spots on the fruits.
- Curly top virus symptoms are puckered leaves or stunted young plants. Curly top usually kills young plants, but older ones may hold their own. Prevent by planting resistant varieties.
- Fusarium wilt (p. 141) will rapidly wilt the vines—sometimes overnight.
- Leaf spot (p. 141) covers the leaves with brown spots. The leaves eventually die.
- Mosaic (p. 142) produces a characteristic mottling of yellow to green on wrinkled, irregular leaves. Sometimes, leaves die while the vine continues to grow, a strange condition known as rat-tail.
- Powdery mildew (p. 142) looks like a fine white powder sprinkled over the leaves. They may subsequently turn brown and die.
- Scab (p. 142) creates light green or watery-looking spots on the leaves. They turn white, then gray, then brown. The melons may crack.

Onions

Poor germination:
- The temperature may be too warm. Onions germinate best in cool soil (55° to 65°F).
- Conversely, you may have set your onions out too early, so that they rotted in the cold, heavy soil.
- You may have accidentally weeded out the onions (the young shoots do look a bit like grass).

Onions form seed heads early:
- They could have been planted too early or could be suffering from uneven watering. Pick off any flower heads as soon as you see them forming. If the seed stalk gets too big and tall, the onions will not dry or store well.

Tops turn brown and fall over:
- Your onions are probably mature and ready to harvest (spread them out to dry in a shady place with good aeration, and cut off the tops when the plants have dried thoroughly). If this happens too early in the season, when the bulbs are not mature, it could be a sign of dry soil conditions or thrips damage.

Onion shoulders are green:
- White onions will sometimes get "sunburned" and turn green at the tops. Hill dirt over the tops if need be, and harvest as soon as the tops start falling over.

Bulbs split into two sections:
- Uneven watering can cause bulbs to look like they're trying to make two halves. Incorporate more humus into the soil to retain moisture, and water as needed throughout the growing season.
- There may be too much nitrogen in the soil, particularly late in the season.
- The sets may have been poorly stored before planting. Keep onion sets in a cool, dry place.

Small bulbs, poor production:
- The soil may be poor. Onions develop best in a highly nutritive soil that's moist but well drained. Sandy loam is ideal. If your soil is hard or nutrient-poor, work in lots of compost or well-rotted manure.
- The problem may be weed competition. Onions are easily overwhelmed by plant competitors. The easiest way to keep weeds down is to mulch the onions with organic matter or black plastic.

Common pests:
- Onion maggot. This legless, $^{1}/_{3}''$-long, pearly white maggot (usually found in northern or coastal areas) tunnels into the bulb. The leaves also fade and lose rigidity. White onion varieties are most susceptible, red are least. To control, cover your plants with a spunbond row cover or other protective material, incorporate wood ashes into the top inch or two of soil, destroy infected onions, or sow a trap crop of radishes. Best of all, plant your onions individually, tucked into places all around the garden. The maggot will starve if it can't find more than one onion at a time.
- Onion thrips. This is probably the most serious onion pest. The adult thrips is practically invisible (only $^{1}/_{25}''$ long), and the larva is smaller still. Thrips feed in groups by puncturing cells. They can cause leaves to become bleached brown at the tips, the neck to become thick, and bulbs to be disfigured and stunted. See thrips (p. 100) for controls. Spanish varieties are fairly resistant.
- Wireworm (p. 100).

Common diseases:
- Bacterial soft rot (p. 140) makes bulbs and leaves appear mushy and watery. Afflicted plants usually have a bad odor.
- Downy mildew (p. 141) starts with sunken, watery spots that are yellow, green or gray. This is followed by a downy, purple-gray mold and perhaps a black fungus as well.
- Neck rot (or *Botrytis* rot) makes the neck spongy, soft and sunken. A gray or brown mold may form on the bulb and between the leaves. To control, keep weeds down, destroy infected plants, and use lots of organic matter in the soil.
- Pink rot (p. 142) creates stunted leaves that die back from their tips. The bulbs turn pink and shrivel up with rot.
- Smut (p. 142) causes black patches on leaves and in the layers of white bulbs. It looks like someone sprinkled chimney soot or very fine black pepper on the onions.

Peas

Poor germination:

● You may have planted the peas in hot or dry weather. Peas like cool, moist conditions. Indeed, peas are the first spring crop many gardeners plant.

● You may have poor seed. Buy from a reputable seed house.

● You may have planted the seeds too deeply. Plant the seed shallowly in a heavy, clay soil, a bit deeper in a light one.

● Cabbage maggots (see below) may have devoured your germinating seeds.

Pods tough or peas flavorless:

● You probably harvested too late. Peas must be picked when they're young, tender and sweet. So keep sampling your crop until the day the taste and texture are just right.

Blossoms don't produce pods:

● Pea flowers are self-pollinating; still, they may occasionally need a little jostling to help the pollen move from the male part of the flower to the female one. If your area has had little wind, you might lightly brush the vines with a soft cloth to help them pollinate.

Vines don't latch onto their support:

● The trellis or fence probably is too high off the ground. Pea vines cannot reach very high to start grabbing their support, so the bottom of your fencing should be no more than 2″ off the ground.

Good vine growth but few blossoms:

● There may be too much nitrogen in the soil. Do not add manure or nitrogen amendments to the soil before planting peas. The legumes fix their own nitrogen.

● Sometimes this happens for no known reason. In such a case, pinching back the vine tips may help send more energy into flowering.

Peas generally doing poorly:

● The weather may be too hot and dry, especially at night.

● The soil may be too acid. Peas like a pH between 6.0 and 7.5.

● The vines may be growing in partial shade. Peas need full sun and particularly appreciate morning sun.

● The soil may be too heavy and have poor aeration. Incorporate organic matter.

● The soil may be short on potash (add greensand, kelp meal or crushed granite) or

phosphorus (add bone meal, soft phosphate or phosphate rock).

● The vines may need water.

The pods don't fill out:

● They may need more water.

● Hot weather may be stunting their growth.

● You may be growing an edible-pod pea. These don't fill out with big round seeds the way ordinary garden or English peas do.

Common pests:

● Aphid (p. 78).

● Cabbage maggot. This ¹/₃″-long, white grub chews on young plants just below the soil surface. (You can find them or their white eggs if you pull a little dirt away from the plants.) Control maggots by using tarpaper collars around your plants, practicing clean soil cultivation, covering the plants with a protective row cover to deter the adult flies or interplanting with mint.

● Pea weevil. This ¹/₅″-long, brownish beetle has black, gray and white flecked markings and feeds on pea blossoms. To control it, do not monocrop peas in large numbers (the beetles are attracted to the blossoms' scent), practice general garden cleanliness, deeply cultivate the soil in fall and/or spring, and plant as early as possible (warm weather stimulates the weevils' mating cycle).

● Slug (p. 94).

● Bird (p. 128).

● Deer (p. 128).

● Groundhog (p. 130).

● Mouse (p. 130).

● Rabbit (p. 131).

Common diseases:

● Anthracnose (p. 140) produces white spots on the leaves and brown leaf margins.

● *Ascochyta* blight (p. 140) begins as tiny purple flecks on the leaves and pods. As these enlarge, they cut off nutrient flow, killing leaves. Roots and lower stems may turn dark purple and rotten.

● Downy mildew (p. 141) creates watery-looking, yellow to brown splotches on upper leaf surfaces. The undersides will be stricken with various-colored molds.

● Fusarium wilt (p. 141) makes plants turn yellow and pale. They will wilt if temperatures are warm.

● Powdery mildew (p. 142) looks like a fine, white powder sprinkled randomly on stems and pods.

● Black root (p. 140) makes the roots and ground-level stems turn dark and rotten. Foliage and upper stems turn yellow and sickly.

Peppers

Poor germination:
- The soil may be too cold (below 60°F); the seed rotted instead of sprouted.
- You may not have given it enough time. Germination takes three to four weeks. Since peppers are slow-starting and need warm soil, most gardeners start their seed indoors.

Lots of foliage but little fruit:
- There may be too much nitrogen in the soil. Do not add manure or any nitrogen fertilizer to pepper's soil.
- The temperature may be too high. Though peppers like hot weather, you may have to plant them in a season of less intense heat if your summers are scorching.
- The temperature may be too low (probably the more common temperature problem). Use black plastic mulch to help warm the soil, and be sure to grow your peppers in the warmest part of the season.
- The plants may be suffering from poor pollination. You can jostle the plants lightly to promote pollen transfer.
- The soil may be short on phosphorus (add bone meal, soft phosphate or phosphate rock) or potash (add greensand, kelp meal or crushed granite). A magnesium deficiency will also hurt production. You can correct this with dolomite lime, talc or Epsom salts, or by dropping a few unused matches in each pepper plant's hole.
- You may have purchased seedlings that were flowering and fruiting while they were still small. Such stressed plants won't produce well.

Blossoms drop:
- The weather could be too cool (below 60°F).
- Of course, it could also be very hot.

Fruit drops:
- Temperatures may have been too high when the blossoms were setting fruit.
- There may be a boron deficiency in the plants—which, in turn, may be because overly acid soil makes boron less available. Check soil pH. If it's at or below 6.5, add lime. If that's not the problem, your soil is deficient in boron. Mix 1½ teaspoons of common borax into 15 gallons of water and apply to 100 square feet of garden space.
- The soil may have too much nitrogen.

Lots of small peppers:
- You may have planted too late for the peppers to mature.
- The soil may have too much nitrogen. Do not pinch the plants back to force them to develop fruits—this will, instead, only further delay pepper development.

Plants develop light, gushy areas that turn dry and concave:
- Sunscald is caused by direct exposure to hot sun. Either the sun in your area is too scorching or the leaves were damaged in some way and cannot shade the fruit. Use a shade cloth or similar material to shade the crop, or grow your peppers in the shadow of other, taller plants.

Peppers won't turn red:
- You probably haven't let them grow long enough.
- You may not have a long enough growing season for them to mature.
- You may be growing an off-color pepper (such as yellow or chocolate) that does not turn red.

Peppers taste bitter:
- There may be a lack of water, a lack of fertility (incorporate compost and soil amendments as needed) or a boron deficiency (see above).

Common pests:
- Aphid (p. 78).
- Blister beetle (p. 80).
- Colorado potato beetle (p. 82).
- Cutworm (p. 84).
- Flea beetle (p. 86).
- Hornworm (p. 88).
- Leafhopper (p. 90).
- Nematode (p. 94).
- Pepper weevil. This ⅛"-long, brass-colored beetle with a brown or black snout and its ¼"-long larva (a white worm with a beige head) chew holes in blossoms and buds. They can cause misshapen and discolored fruits. You can control weevils by handpicking (but that's tedious because they're so small), by practicing general garden cleanliness, by cultivating the soil deeply in the fall or spring, or by using rotenone.
- Pepper maggot. This ⅓-inch long, yellow fly has brown stripes on its wings. Its larva is small, peg-shaped and white or yellow. The pepper maggot is a problem mostly in the eastern and southwestern U.S. It feeds on the insides of peppers, causing them to rot and drop off. To control, sprinkle diatomaceous earth, talc or rock phosphate on fruits. Also, destroy infected fruits and practice general garden cleanliness.
- Thrips (p. 100).

Common diseases:
- Anthracnose (p. 140) inflicts fruits with dark, sunken spots that are soft and watery. Eventually the whole fruit becomes limp and soggy and falls off.
- Bacterial spot (p. 140) makes small, yellow-green, raised spots appear on younger leaves. Older leaves get larger spots that have dark halos and dead, light-colored centers.
- Blossom-end rot (p. 141) produces tan-colored, sunken, watery spots on the blossom end of fruits. These spread, become larger and darker, and host fungal growth.
- Early blight (p. 141) creates dark spots on leaves and lower stem parts. Eventually the leaves turn yellow or brown and die.
- Mosaic (p. 142) mottles the leaves of young plants with dark and light splotches. The leaves then wrinkle and curl. Fruits on older plants may be bumpy and bitter.
- Verticillium wilt (p. 142) starts at the lower leaves, turning them yellow and wilted. Stems and leaf margins may turn dark.

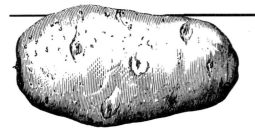

Potatoes

Poor germination:
• The eye pieces may have rotted in the ground. In damp areas, cut your potatoes up a few days or weeks before planting to let the cuts heal over. Some people also dust the pieces with sulfur to deter rotting.
• You may have planted supermarket potatoes that were treated with a chemical sprout inhibitor.
• You may have planted too early. Potatoes can stand light frost, but not a heavy freeze.

Potatoes turn green:
• They were exposed to the sun while growing or while curing after they were dug. Be sure to hill your potatoes as they grow (until they start blooming) and cure and store spuds in shaded areas. And don't eat green parts of potatoes; they contain solanine, which is mildly toxic.

Dead tuber tissue:
• This condition develops in warmer areas of the country if you leave the potatoes in the ground after the tops have died down. In cooler regions, you can leave potatoes in the ground for a month or two (just as long as they don't freeze).

Foliage turns yellow, dies and falls over:
• Most likely the plants are simply maturing. Normally, when the tops die, the potatoes are ready to harvest. (You can, of course, harvest some tasty early potatoes not long after the plants bloom.)
• The weather may be too dry. If that's a problem, mulch to conserve moisture, and water as needed.

Potatoes too small:
• They may have been planted too late in the season to reach maturity.
• They may have suffered from a lack of water.
• The soil may be too alkaline. Potatoes like acid soil.
• The soil may be short on phosphorus (add bone meal, soft rock or phosphate rock) or potash (add greensand, kelp meal or crushed granite).
• Weed competition may have stunted production. Many gardeners hill their potatoes until the plants flower, then they mulch them well to keep weeds down.

• You may have harvested early potatoes too early. Wait a couple of weeks and try again.
• The seed potatoes may have been of poor quality or stored at high temperatures and in light. Buy from a reputable dealer, and properly store any seed potatoes you're saving.
• The plants may have been grown in too much shade.
• There may have been too much nitrogen in the soil. That promotes foliage over tuber growth.
• The plants may have been afflicted with speckle leaf. This phenomenon (symptoms are foliage with dark splotches above and sunken areas below) is apparently caused by too much ozone in the atmosphere. Keep plants as healthy as possible to deter the stress of this modern malady. Resistant varieties are now being developed.

Transparent spots on tubers:
• Tubers were probably injured by freezing temperatures. Harvest before a hard freeze hits the soil.

Lush foliage but no potatoes:
• There is probably too much nitrogen in the soil. Avoid using fresh manure or nitrogenous amendments in your potato plot.
• The nights may be too warm for good tuber production. Potatoes do best if nighttime temperatures are around 55°F.

Hollow heart:
• Hollow areas in the center of tubers are caused by rapid and uneven growth. Plant your seed potatoes closer together, hold up on the watering and heavy fertilizer, and avoid susceptible varieties like Sequoia, Irish Cobbler and Russet Rural.

Common pests:
• Aphid (p. 78).
• Blister beetle (p. 80).
• Colorado potato beetle (p. 82).
• Cutworm (p. 84).
• European corn borer (p. 84).
• Flea beetle (p. 86).
• Grasshopper (p. 86).
• Grub (p. 88).
• Nematode (p. 94).
• Potato leafhopper (see Leafhopper, p. 90).
• Wireworm (p. 100).
• Mouse (p. 130).

Common diseases:
• Bacterial wilt (p. 140), or brown rot, makes leaves turn brown and rot from the inside out. The plants eventually wilt and die.
• Blackleg (p. 140) turns foliage yellow (beginning with top leaves). A black, slimy rot at ground level destroys the main stalk and tubers.
• Black scurf gives lower stems a purple-gray fungus and makes leaves curl and turn pinkish or yellow. To control, rotate crops, destroy infected plants, and plant certified disease-free potatoes.
• Early blight (p. 141), also called leaf spot or target spot, begins with small brown leaf spots that develop concentric rings as they grow. Tubers may develop puckered skin and discolored spots.
• Late blight (p. 141) hits plants, after they have blossomed, with dark purplish patches that have thin, watery outer borders and pale rings.
• Leak creates gray or brown spots on tubers, which become gushy, yellowish brown, liquid-filled craters that leak when punctured. The organism enters through nicks or cuts and is more prevalent in hot weather and sunburned and sunscalded tubers. To control, time your potatoes to mature in cool weather, handle spuds carefully to avoid injury to skin, and keep the tubers as dry as possible.
• Mosaic (p. 142) produces characteristic mottled and curled leaves. Plants eventually die, and tubers may have brown specks.
• Rhizoctonia (p. 142), or black scurf, can cause dark brown cankers on terminal growth; large, dead pits on the main stalk; stunted leaves and tubers; and hard, black flecks on tubers.
• Ring rot (p. 142), or bacterial rot, may be hard to spot. It produces rot in the vascular layer (just under the plant's skin), evidenced by a yellow goo when a stem is cut in half and squeezed. Growth may be stunted, and tubers rot from the inside.
• Scab (p. 142) produces tough, corky, scab-like lesions on tubers. Scab is more likely under dry or alkaline conditions.
• Verticillium wilt (p. 142) starts by yellowing and then killing older leaves. Leaf tips may also look burned.

Radishes

Poor germination:
- The soil may have developed a hard crust. Incorporate more organic matter before planting.
- The soil surface may have dried out. Cover it with boards, sheets, plastic, etc. (just until germination), if necessary to keep the surface moist.
- The temperature may be too high. Don't plant radishes in the heat of summer (unless they have a cool and semishady place).

Radishes are woody or pithy:
- The soil may have been too dry. Water as needed.
- The radishes may have been harvested beyond their prime. You should make succession plantings of quick-maturing crops like radishes in order to have an ongoing supply.

Radishes are cracked:
- They had too much moisture. Try not to overwater your crop.

All tops, no radishes:
- The plants weren't thinned properly or soon enough. Most varieties should be thinned to about 2″ apart as soon as the first true leaves appear.

Plants grew a little, then stopped:
- They were probably planted when the weather was too hot. In most areas, radishes need to be grown as a spring or fall crop.

Radishes taste hot:
- You may have grown a fiery-flavored variety; some cultivars are hotter than others.
- Hot weather (above 90°F) can produce hot flavor.
- Dry weather can also spice up radishes. If that's the problem, incorporate organic matter into soil to retain moisture and water as needed.

Many fuzzy roots:
- The soil may be too heavy. If so, add organic matter to lighten the soil.
- The plants could be overcrowded. Thin radishes to 2″ or 3″ apart.

Common pests:
- Aphid (p. 78).
- Flea beetle (p. 86).
- Root maggot. This ¼″- to ½″-long, legless, yellowish white maggot tunnels into the roots. To control, do not follow cabbage with radishes, and incorporate a goodly amount

of hardwood ashes into the soil before planting radishes.

Common diseases:
- Black root (p. 140) creates dark areas where smaller roots meet the main root.
- Fusarium wilt (p. 141) afflicts leaves and stems. They turn yellow and die.
- Downy mildew (p. 141) produces yellow to brown spots on upper leaf surfaces and a cottony purple to gray mold underneath.
- Blackleg (p. 140) starts with gray to light brown spots on leaves and stems. Then the stems turn black and rot. It's spread by cutworms (p. 84) and root maggots.
- Yellows (p. 143) makes leaves turn pale, dull yellow and then die.

Rhubarb

Quality of stalks declines:
- The plants may have been allowed to get too old without being divided. Divide the roots every four to five years. Replant or give away the parts you dig up.
- You may have let the seedpods grow, which saps the plant's energy. Remove seedpods as soon as you notice them.
- The plants may need some fertilizer. Although rhubarb is a perennial, you can't just plant it and forget it. It needs continuous feeding. So mulch it with plant residue mixed with manure in fall, side-dress with well-balanced amendments, or feed occasionally with garden teas.
- The plants may need water. Don't stop watering rhubarb after you've finished the season's harvesting. The plants need moisture the rest of the growing season to grow well and to produce next spring's harvest.

Generally poor plants:
- You may have harvested some stalks the first year after planting. Don't harvest any stems the first year (and cut only a few the second). Let your transplants grow and build up their strength.
- The plants may be suffering from lack of fertilizer or water, or you may have left seed stalks growing.
- The plants may have been grown from seed. Rhubarb doesn't always mature well from seed. It's much more reliable when started from crown divisions.
- The chief pest of rhubarb, the curculio (see below), may be weakening your plants.

The stalks are mostly green instead of red:
- Your rhubarb is probably suffering from too much warm weather. It needs temperatures below 50°F during its winter dormancy to thrive and produce red stems. For this reason, rhubarb does not grow well in the Deep South.

Eating the plant makes you sick:
- Only the leaf stems of rhubarb are edible. The roots and leaves contain toxic amounts of oxalic acid.

Common pests:
- European corn borer (p. 84).
- Imported cabbageworm (p. 88).

● Rhubarb curculio. This ³/₄″-long beetle is brown with yellow powdery flecks (some people describe it as rusty-looking). It bores into the crowns, stalks and roots of the plant and also preys on wild dock. It's easily controlled by handpicking. You can head off next year's curculio infestation by pulling and burning nearby wild dock in July, after the beetle has laid its eggs there.

● Stalk borer. This thin, 1¼″-long borer is creamy white with a dark purple band around its body. (It also has several brown or purple stripes down its length when young.) It bores into the stem of the plant, weakening and even killing the part above. To control, slit the stem above the entrance hole and remove the borer. Then pamper the plant with extra water for a few days.

Common diseases:

● Verticillium wilt (p. 142) yellows leaves early in the season. Late attacks kill veins and margins of leaves, causing the whole plant to wilt.

● Leaf spot (p. 141) produces small, round, brown spots on the leaves. This fungous disease causes mostly cosmetic damage.

● Anthracnose (p. 140), also called stalk rot, makes parts of the stalks soft and mushy. The leaves then wilt and die.

● Crown rot makes crowns and roots water-soaked and rotten. Leaves turn yellow, and eventually the whole plant collapses. To control, dig and burn infected plants. Start over with new, disease-free plants in a new location.

Spinach

Poor germination:

● Spinach can be hard to start. It definitely won't germinate well in hot weather. Many gardeners help it along by sprinkling the seeds over a damp blotter or paper towel, then covering them with another layer of the same material and storing this in the refrigerator for about five days. By that time, the seeds should show small breaks, indicating that they're ready to be sown.

● You may have planted your seed too deeply. Sow it from ¼″ to ½″ deep.

● Your seed may be too old or of poor quality. Buy current seed from a reputable seed house or use home-saved seed the season after harvesting.

Leaves turn yellow or don't produce well:

● The soil may be short on nitrogen. Spinach is a heavy nitrogen feeder, so plant it in well-fertilized soil or side-dress it with a nitrogen-rich amendment like manure, blood meal or fish meal. A leaf spray of fish emulsion or other N-rich tea may give a quick boost to your ailing spinach patch.

● A manganese deficiency can cause yellow, pointed leaves. Soil that's too alkaline can limit manganese availability, so test for pH and acidify your soil if necessary by omitting lime amendments and incorporating oak leaves or other acidic materials. If that doesn't help, add manganese by using a well-balanced organic fertilizer or a trace mineral supplement such as seaweed.

● Spinach leaves naturally yellow as they age and the plant begins to bolt. Remove old plants from the garden unless you're saving seed.

● Weed competition will limit yields.

Stems and leaves elongate, leaves become tough and bitter:

● The crop is probably past its prime and on its way to seed. Harvest spinach leaves when young and compact for best texture and flavor.

Plants bolt quickly:

● You probably planted too late in the spring. Spinach bolts quickly in hot, dry weather. Start spinach very early in the spring and make succession plantings. In many areas, fall-planted spinach will survive

winter and produce luxuriously early the following spring. Bloomsdale spinach resists bolting better than most other varieties.

Common pests:

● Aphid (p. 78).
● Flea beetle (p. 86).
● Leaf miner (p. 92).
● Bird (p. 128).
● Deer (p. 128).
● Groundhog (p. 130).
● Rabbit (p. 131).

Common diseases:

● Downy mildew (p. 141) produces yellow to brown spots on upper leaf surfaces and a cottony, purple to gray mold underneath.

● Yellows (p. 143) starts when lower leaves turn dull and yellow and their veins turn brown. Eventually the leaves turn brown and drop off.

● Fusarium wilt (p. 141) makes the whole plant turn yellow and bottom leaves become limp.

● Anthracnose (p. 140) creates dark, reddish brown or black splotches on foliage.

Squash

Note: This section includes summer squash, winter squash and pumpkins.

Poor germination:
- The soil is probably too cold. Squash like soil that's around 75°F, so wait until the ground warms to plant, or start your squash indoors in individual pots and transplant it (carefully) when warm weather arrives.
- The seeds may need more water. They have tough outer coats that require a good bit of moisture to soften. Some gardeners presoak their squash seeds by wrapping them in dampened paper towels a few days before planting.

Many flowers but not much fruit:
- You may simply need to wait a little longer. Female flowers appear before any male blooms. Those not-fertilized flowers don't bear fruit. If that's your problem, be patient. Once the male blooms appear, you'll probably have all the squash you can handle.
- If, because of bad weather, lack of pollinating insects, or chemical pesticides on your plants, the female flowers don't get well pollinated by the males, you won't get many fruits. If necessary, you can pollinate squash blossoms yourself. Simply use a soft brush to gather some pollen from the stamen of a male flower and transfer it gently to the pistil of a female one. (A male flower has a single fat stamen in the middle of its blossom, while each female bloom contains a four-part curved pistil and an ovary swelling that later becomes a squash.)
- Some gardeners pick off the pretty yellow squash flowers to use in bouquets or cooking. Obviously, though, if you pick all the flowers, you won't get any fruits.

Summer squash too tough or bland:
- You probably let the fruit grow too large before harvesting. Pick summer squash when it's young and tender. Do this even if you don't eat the fruits as fast as the plants produce them, so the plant will keep on producing more young squash (rather than having big ones go to seed and signal the plant to stop production).
- The plant may be too dry. Water squash as needed if there is no rain.

Winter squash does not store well:
- You probably harvested it before it was

fully mature. Harvest winter squash as late as possible in the season—but before the fall frost comes. Leave some stem on and cure it in a warm place in the house for several weeks. Then store it in a dry place, about 45° to 60°F, where it can't touch any other squash.

Strange-looking fruit:
- You had poor-quality seed. The problem was *not* caused by two varieties cross-pollinating in your plot this season. Such crossing affects the next year's crop. So either you used home-saved seed that crossed the previous year or you need to buy your seed from a more reliable company.

Leathery, dark areas form on blossom ends:
- This condition, called blossom-end rot, is caused by harsh fluctuations between wet and dry soil. To prevent it, incorporate organic matter in your soil to retain moisture, and water as needed. Be sure to water deeply.

Pumpkins taste bitter:
- They may have needed more water while they were growing.
- They may have needed more nitrogen. Add manure, blood meal, cottonseed meal or leather meal to your pumpkin plot.
- You might have planted them too early or too late. Pumpkins do best if they do most of their growing during a long warm weather season.

Common pests:
- Aphid (p. 78).
- Cutworm (p. 84).
- Pickleworm. This ³/₄"-long, green- or copper-colored pest chews holes in the fruits, leaving squash-colored frass (excreta) behind. It is mostly a problem in the South and Gulf

states, but can move up as far as Michigan later in the season. Control by cleaning up plant refuse, applying *Bacillus thuringiensis* or rotenone, using squash as a trap crop, or practicing good crop rotation and fall cultivation.
- Spotted cucumber beetle (p. 96).
- Squash bug (p. 96).
- Squash vine borer (p. 98).
- Striped cucumber beetle (p. 98). Several squash diseases, including bacterial wilt, mosaic and powdery mildew, are spread by cucumber beetles.

Common diseases:
- Fusarium wilt (p. 141) stunts plants and yellows leaves. The vines may also turn yellow and slowly begin to die back.
- Anthracnose (p. 140) creates rusty to black splotches on the leaves. They may eventually dry up in the center and fall out.
- Bacterial wilt (p. 140) may begin with the wilting of only a single leaf. This leaf dies, followed by a few more. Eventually, vine by vine, the whole plant wilts and dies. When cut across the stem and squeezed, an afflicted vine oozes a sticky fluid.
- Mosaic (p. 142) starts with mottling and wrinkling of leaves. Plants are usually stunted and fruit may have spots.
- Powdery mildew (p. 142) produces a white dusting on leaves that looks like fine powder.
- Scab (p. 142) creates yellowish green spots on leaves that may appear water-soaked. Eventually they become pitted and contain a brown or olive-gray mold.

Strawberries

Blossoms die, no fruit:
- The blossoms were probably killed by a late frost. Keep mulch over the plants if frost threatens. Pull it away after all threat of frost is past.
- The variety you're growing may be unable to make fruit without being pollinated by another variety. This condition, called being pistillate, is not as common as it used to be.

Bland taste:
- You may be growing a variety that produces large but less tasty fruit. Hybrid-strawberry breeders have, to an extent, sacrificed taste for size.
- You may have overfertilized your plants, resulting in large but less flavorful fruits.

Fruit production low:
- The plants may be too crowded. You must have a system for thinning the runners that develop, or the plants will become a tangled mat. (You may simply let your patch "migrate" along its leading edge, digging up the trailing edge. Another system is to alternate the bed and pathway, each year tilling up the used bed and letting new runners fill the former pathway.)
- They may lack water. Strawberries have shallow roots and need water. Water often and deeply when the berries are filling out. A good layer of mulch also helps conserve moisture.
- The plants may simply be getting too old. Though considered perennials, strawberries must be culled when they're two or three years old and replaced with the new runner plants.
- Weeds may be crowding out your crop. Keep the bed weeded. Again, mulch is a big help.
- The plants may have "wet feet" from growing in a heavy soil. Incorporate organic matter and possibly sand to lighten up their ground.
- They may lack fertilizer. Plants grown in a semipermanent bed need occasional side-dressing with compost, manure, soil amendments or garden teas to keep fertility up. If you let your strawberries migrate, incorporate these as you till up the new areas.
- You may not have picked the blossoms

the first year after planting. Doing this helps the plants build energy for the second and subsequent years' production.

Everbearing varieties not bearing well:
- Although everbearing strawberries do fruit over a longer time period than standard varieties, they often give smaller overall yields. (Some growers say the taste is inferior, as well.) You can try pinching off the early blossoms, along with watering and side-dressing well to boost production of the late-season crop.

Established plants don't take off well in spring:
- They probably weren't covered by a good mulch. In areas where temperatures go down to 20°F and below (and there's not much snow for insulation), the plants should be mulched thickly every fall.
- The plants may be getting old. Remem-

ber to let new runners replace older plants every two or three years.

Plants generally not doing well:
- The soil may be too heavy. Lighten with organic matter and possibly sand.
- The soil may be too alkaline. Strawberries need slightly acid soil with a pH from 5.5 to 6.5. Test and correct if needed. Acid mulches like peat moss and pine needles also help.

Common pests:
- Aphid (p. 78).
- Japanese beetle (p. 90).
- Mite. This little arachnid has four pairs of legs, looks like a tiny tick and comes in different sizes and shapes. Mites begin laying eggs on plant leaves when warm weather comes. Leaves turn yellow or purplish and may become curled and covered with the fine webs the mites spin. A slurry of buttermilk, wheat flour and water sprayed on plants once

or twice will dry and suffocate the mites without harming the plants. Also, encourage ladybugs, lacewings, damsel bugs, dance flies and other predacious mites. Also helpful are good crop rotation, garden cleanliness and not handling clean plants after you touch infected ones.

- Nematode (p. 94).
- Slug (p. 94).
- Strawberry crown borer. This small, $^1/_5$"-long, brown beetle has reddish patches on its wings. The adult eats stems and leaves of strawberry plants. The eggs are laid in the crown of the plants, and hatch out white grubs that are actually the most destructive stage of the pest. If they become a serious problem, you can start a new bed at least 300' from the old one. The beetles can't fly, so they won't be able to migrate well to the new location. If you use your own plants for

this, dig them up before mid-March (when the eggs are laid).

- Strawberry leaf roller. This small, reddish brown moth lays eggs on the undersides of leaves. These hatch into $^1/_2$"-long, yellow-green or greenish brown caterpillars that roll up in the leaves and feed on them. Plants may turn brown and die if an infestation is severe. Control by handpicking, spraying with *Bacillus thuringiensis* or dusting with rotenone. Be sure to spray inside rolled-up leaves, or the caterpillars may be safe in their little hideaways.

- Bird (p. 128).
- Mouse (p. 130).

Common diseases:

Note: Strawberries are susceptible to a variety of hard-to-treat diseases. It is more important to use *certified* disease-free and disease-resistant stock when growing strawberries than it is for any other fruit or vegetable in your garden.

- Leaf blight, leaf scorch and leaf spot look similar, seldom hurt production seriously and are controlled with the same techniques. Leaf blight produces large red-brown spots surrounded by purple borders. Leaf scorch creates small, purplish spots on leaves and stalks. It's most prevalent during moist springs. And leaf spot gives leaves and stalks dark purplish spots with white or gray centers. It sometimes gives fruit a few black spots. To control all three, use resistant varieties (like Fairfax, Midland, Catskill and Blakemore for leaf scorch). Plant your strawberries in a sunny location. Keep weeds down, especially cinquefoils (they get the same three diseases). Cull out old plants and put in young ones. Grow in well-drained soil, and practice garden cleanliness.

- Powdery mildew (p. 142) makes plants look like they were dusted with fine, white powder. Leaf margins may curl upward, as well.

- Verticillium wilt (p. 142) makes leaves wilt and dry up when berries are ripening. Some plants may die completely.

- Leaf variegation (also known as June or spring yellows) causes a yellow mottling of leaves in cool spring weather. It is hereditary, not infectious, so avoid planting susceptible varieties like Blakemore, Premier and many everbearing varieties if it is a problem in your area.

- Fruit rot produces gray, fuzzy growth on

blossoms and fruit or brown or leathery spots on fruit. It's most rampant in damp weather and spread by handling. So stay out of the patch when it's wet and destroy infected fruits (don't just toss them to the side). A good mulch helps protect the crop from damage.

- Red stele is a destructive, extremely infectious fungal root disease that stunts plants and causes them to wilt, usually just before fruit ripens. Plants will become dull, bluish green. You'll need to look at the root system to identify red stele for sure. Infected plants have long "rattail roots" that do not have side-branching feeder roots. These will often be discolored at the tip and may have interior red discoloration at the tip or along the whole length. There is no organic control for red stele. If it is prevalent in your area, you may not be able to grow strawberries.

- Black root rot turns roots from their normal white (when young) or yellowish tan (when older) to black. Poor drainage, winter injury and overly acid or alkaline soil will encourage this problem. To control, be sure new plants have healthy white roots. Plant in soil that is well drained (or incorporate organic matter and sand to a depth of at least 2'). Adjust pH to around 5.5 to 6.5.

Sunflowers

Poor germination:
- Assuming your seed was good and the soil moist, the most likely problem is that mice dug up and ate the seed before it germinated.

Plants fall over:
- They were probably overcrowded.
- Varieties with very large heads may need some kind of staking or other support to withstand strong winds.

Heads droop over:
- As the heavy heads develop, they usually droop. This causes no harm.

Poor production:
- Too much weed competition can hurt yields.
- The soil may have been too dry during the three weeks between flowering and head maturity. Sunflowers are generally quite drought-tolerant but do need water during the seed-growing stage.

No, or small, heads:
- You probably didn't plant early enough. Sunflowers may need from 80 to 110 days to mature. (The seedlings are hardy, so they can be planted two weeks before your last spring frost.)

Multiple small heads instead of one big one:
- You could be raising a wild volunteer sunflower instead of a cultivated variety.
- The seed you planted could have crossed the previous year with a wild sunflower. This is more likely with home-saved than with purchased seed.

Seed pods empty (no meat in the shells):
- They were most likely poorly pollinated. Too much rain during pollination might have washed the pollen away, a surprise early frost may have nipped the flowers before pollination was complete, or your garden may not have been visited by enough fertilizing insects.
- Although it's not likely, the variety you grew might not have been very attractive to bees and other pollinators.
- Even less likely, you may have purchased poor-quality seed that did not have good fertility.

Common pests and diseases:
- Sunflowers have almost no common pest or disease problems. Birds are the exception.

They like to eat maturing seeds right off the plants. Protect developing seed heads with mesh bags, cheesecloth or perforated plastic bags. Or leave about 2' of the stems attached and hang harvested heads upside down in a dry, well-ventilated place (such as an attic or garage) until they're fully dry.

Sweet Potatoes

Transplanted slips die:
- The slips may have been too succulent and thin. Use thick-stemmed slips that have more food resources to tide them over until their roots take hold.
- The slips may not have been kept watered.
- They may have been allowed to dry out too much before planting.

Note: Sweet potato slips are tougher than this description makes them sound. They may look dead when you get them, yet they most often survive.

Small potatoes:
- Too much nitrogen encourages lush foliage growth, but thin potatoes.
- The soil may be too heavy and clayey. Incorporate as much organic matter as you can into the soil. Adding sand may also help.
- The soil may have been kept too wet. Water deeply as needed, but not again until the ground is dry a full 8" down.
- Your growing season may have been too short. Most sweet potatoes need an average of five frost-free months. A few short-season varieties, such as Centennial, can mature in 90 or 100 days.

Roots rot in storage:
- They may have gotten scarred and bruised when they were dug up. Dig sweet potatoes carefully and from the side of the row.
- The skins may not have been cured properly. Let harvested potatoes lie on top of the soil for an hour or two after digging. Then keep the unwashed tubers in a "nest"—a warm, dark place about 70° to 80°F for about two weeks. After that, wrap each one in newspaper and store in a well-ventilated 55° to 60°F room.

Parts of the potatoes are still hard after cooking:
- The tubers may have been stored at temperatures that were too cold. Do not store sweet potatoes in a refrigerator or cold root cellar.
- They may have been left in the ground too long. Harvest before cold weather sets in.
- They may have internal cork, a disease (described below) transmitted by aphids.

Poor flavor:

- The soil may have been left too dry for too long.
- The tubers may have been left in the ground during cold weather.
- The soil may have had too much nitrogen.

Common pests:
- Aphid (p.78).
- Root-knot nematode (p. 94).
- Sweet potato weevil. This ¼"-long weevil has blue wings, head and snout along with a reddish orange prothorax and legs. The larva is ⅜" long, legless and white. The adults feed on all parts of the plant and lay eggs in the stems. The developing larvae then tunnel through and feed on the tubers. To control, use state-certified slips, practice good crop rotation, handpick, apply rotenone, cultivate the soil in fall and spring, or grow radishes, summer savory and tansy as repellent companion plants. If necessary, eliminate all sweet potatoes and plant residue from the garden (and from the surrounding half-mile if possible) for a year or more. This should starve the weevils out.
- Groundhog (p. 130).

Common diseases:
- Fusarium wilt (p. 141) kills seedlings and makes the leaves of older plants turn yellow, wilt and possibly die. Stems may rot and be streaked with dark lines.

- Black rot (p. 140) produces sunken black spots on underground stems and tuber skins. These spots enlarge and cause surrounding flesh to turn green and corky. The tubers may develop a bitter taste.
- Scurf (p. 142) creates hard brown to black spots on the skin. Damage is mostly cosmetic.
- Foot rot causes a brown or black rot on the stems near the soil line and on the potatoes, starting at the end closest to the vine. It's spread by the sweet potato weevil.
- Internal cork makes the potatoes hard and corklike. The leaves may become mottled and yellow along the veins. To control, keep aphid infestations down and plant certified virus-free slips.

Tomatoes

Poor germination:
- The seeds were probably planted in soil that was too cold. They grow best when the air temperature's around 80°F. To achieve that, most gardeners have to start their tomato plants indoors five to seven weeks before the last frost date in spring and plant out three weeks after the last frost.

Blossoms drop off, so there are no fruits:
- Too much nitrogen encourages foliage, not fruit. Use more phosphorus and less nitrogen in your plot.
- The temperature may be too low for fruit to set. If the mercury drops below 55°F, cover and protect your plants.
- The temperature might be too high. If so, try to shade your plants temporarily.
- Hot, dry winds may be damaging blossoms. Shelter your plants.
- Continued heavy rains may be having the same effect. Again, try to protect your plants.
- Sometimes flowers don't get pollinated for one of the above reasons—or for an unknown one. If so, around midday, shake the plants or lightly bang on their stakes to help pollination occur.

Yellow patches, green shoulders or uneven ripening of individual fruits:
- The problem is sunscald, caused by direct exposure to the sun and high temperatures. Don't prune heavily; look for and correct any insect or disease problems that are causing leaves to fall; don't stake plants in a way that exposes too many fruits to sun, or grow varieties that have heavy leaf cover (such as Early Girl and Marglobe). Sometimes, only the first fruits have this problem, because they don't have as much protective foliage as later ones.

Fruit cracks:
- The cause may be heavy watering or rain after a dry spell. Keep the soil watered during dry spells to even out moisture.
- The problem may be sunscald.

Fruits are misshapen:
- The blossoms may have been damaged by low temperatures or other harmful weather. Protect blooming plants as needed. If you have a short growing season, grow early-maturing varieties that are conditioned to

lower temperatures.
- Several of the insects and diseases discussed earlier can cause misshapen fruit.
- The fruit may have catfacing, an ugly deformity and scarring caused by abnormal development of the flower pistils or by blossoms that stick to young fruit and later tear, creating scars. You can remove any attached blossoms from small fruits if you want to deter this largely cosmetic problem.

- You may have planted a paste tomato, which naturally produces pear-shaped fruits, or some other uncommonly shaped variety.

Brown scar down the side of fruits:
- This cosmetic problem, called zipper streak, occurs when the blossoms stick to tiny fruits in cold, damp weather. You can remedy it by removing any attached blossoms from small fruits.

Fruit has puffy air spaces inside:

- The plants were pollinated when temperatures were too low (below 55°F) or too high (above 85°). Time your planting to avoid extreme weather or take crop-protecting measures.

Fruits taste too mild or too acid:
- Try growing a different variety. The range of taste in tomato varieties is very wide.

Thick skins but little taste:
- The fruits probably ripened in too-hot

weather. Start your plants earlier indoors, so they'll mature in average temperatures. Mulch the tomatoes and keep them well watered.

Lower leaves roll up:

• Leaf roll seems to follow heavy pruning of plants, wet weather or overly heavy waterings, and deep cultivation. Most times, it does not hurt production. Try to keep watering even, practice shallow cultivation, re-strict your pruning, and, if need be, incorporate humus into the soil for better drainage.

Dark splotches on green fruit:

• These could be due to low temperatures. Try to time your plantings so they mature in warm weather, and protect plants from sudden cold spells.

• The fruits may not be getting enough light. Prune foliage if necessary and avoid heavy chemical fertilization, which can cause overly thick foliage.

• The soil may be too heavy and wet. Incorporate more organic matter.

• Some tomato diseases (see below) cause splotching.

Plants wilt:

• They may need water. Wilting sometimes occurs if you practice the gardening trick of planting much of the tomato vine horizon-

tally just under the soil. While this may encourage the development of a good root system, many of those roots will be in the top 6″ of soil, where they're more prone to dry out. Either set your tomatoes in the ground vertically or be sure to keep them watered.
● Some tomato diseases cause wilting.

Plants stop growing:
● The most probable cause is you're growing a determinate variety which bears all its fruit at once. These reach a certain height and then stop growing. Indeterminate plants keep growing and producing indefinitely.
● Cool temperatures or lack of water or nutrients may have stopped growth.

Branches tear and/or stems develop scars:
● You probably staked the plants on the wrong side of the prevailing winds, so strong winds made your ties cut into the vines. To avoid such damage, set your stakes on the downwind side so that wind pushes plants onto—not away from—your stakes.

Plants generally unhealthy:
● The seedlings may well have been stressed. Raise tomato seedlings carefully, and don't buy ones that are pot-bound, already flowering or tall and spindly.
● Hot, dry winds can weaken tomato plants.
● They may be growing in too much shade.
● Tomatoes generally don't do well when planted near walnut trees. The trees' roots give off a toxin.
● They don't do well planted in soil that recently grew tobacco.

Dark, leathery, sunken patches on ends of fruits:
● This condition, blossom-end rot, is often the result of a lack of the trace element calcium or a surplus of nitrogen that's blocking the plants' uptake of calcium. Test and correct if needed. Limestone, wood ashes, bone meal and oyster shells are good calcium sources.
● Blossom-end rot can also be caused by water problems. Damaged feeder roots (caused by careless transplanting) and irregular watering (including too much water as well as too little) can restrict calcium uptake.

Leaf margins and stems are purple:
● The soil probably has a phosphorus deficiency. Add soft phosphate, bone meal or phosphate rock.

Delayed fruit setting:
● This malady may also be due to a phos-phorus deficiency. Test and amend if needed.

Foliage blue-green, leaves curled and flabby, flowers sparse:
● The soil probably has a copper deficiency. Test and amend if needed by adding more manure to your soil.

Leaves become brittle, curl up and turn yellow:
● The soil may have a magnesium deficiency. Test and amend if needed with limestone or Epsom salts.

Stems turn thick and woody and upper leaves yellow:
● The soil may have a calcium deficiency. Test and amend if needed with limestone, wood ashes, bone meal or oyster shells.

Plants grow slowly and have light green foliage:
● The soil probably has a manganese deficiency. Additional symptoms are few blossoms and no fruit. Test and amend if needed by adding more manure to your soil.

Plants are abnormally bushy and have stunted, blackened and wilted tips:
● The plants may have a boron deficiency—which, in turn, may be because overly acid soil makes boron less available to them. Check soil pH. If it's at or below 6.5, add lime. If that's not the problem, you have a real soil boron deficiency. Mix 1½ teaspoons of common borax into 15 gallons of water and apply to 100 square feet of garden space.

Plants generally growing slowly:
● The problem could be generally poor soil or any of the nutrient deficiencies just mentioned. Test and correct if needed.
● The weather may be too cool. Time your plantings appropriately and/or grow short-season varieties.
● The plants may need water.
● The plants may be in too shady a location. Tomato plants need full sun unless your summers are scorching.

Plants finished bearing too early:
● A heavy crop that is not helped along by lots of compost, side-dressings and/or manure teas will exhaust the plants. Give prolific plants a nutrient boost, or plant a later tomato crop timed to begin maturing when the first ones give out.

Common pests:
● Colorado potato beetle (p. 82).
● Corn earworm (p. 82).

● Cutworm (p. 84).
● European corn borer (p. 84).
● Flea beetle (p. 86).
● Hornworm (p. 88).
● Leafhopper (p. 90).
● Stalk borer. This thin, 1¼″-long caterpillar is creamy white with a dark purple band around its body. Young ones also have several brown or purple stripes down the length of their bodies. It bores into the stem of the plant, wilting the plant. To control, slit the stem above the borer's entrance hole and remove the pest. Then pamper the plant with extra water for a few days.
● Thrips (p. 100).
● Whitefly (p. 100). This pest is mostly a problem on greenhouse tomatoes.

Common diseases:
● Anthracnose (p. 140) attacks quickly when the fruit starts to ripen. At first pea-size, sunken, soft spots appear on the fruits. These enlarge and eventually whole fruits may collapse.
● Bacterial canker (p. 140) has a peculiar trait: It first affects only one side of the leaves on one side of the plant. They wilt, curl up, dry and fall off, yet the little stems that held them to the vine remain attached. The whole plant may be afflicted and its stem core become yellow and mealy.
● Bacterial spot (p. 140) thrives in damp, rainy conditions. It starts with dark, greasy spots on leaves. Then small, watery blisters with white rings appear on green fruits. The spots enlarge and become sunken, dark and dry.
● Bacterial wilt (p. 140) does not create yellowing or spots, but rapidly wilts and kills the entire plant. The inner core of the main trunk stem appears dark and exudes a gray, slimy substance when squeezed.
● Blossom-end rot (above and p. 141) starts as a small, dark, leathery patch on the blossom end of the fruit. It grows until it covers from ⅓ to ½ of the fruit.
● Botrytis fruit rot (or gray mold) afflicts greenhouse tomatoes. It causes watery-looking spots that grow quickly over the fruit. Diseased parts have a gray mold. To control, lower greenhouse humidity and raise temperature.
● Curly top stunts plant growth, producing yellow foliage and purple veins. Leaves may roll up and stiffen. Older plants can often stave off curly top's effects, but young plants

may produce few or no fruits.

● Early blight (p. 141) is a very common leaf disease that produces brown spots with outer yellow circles. It usually starts on lower leaves and then spreads, causing leaves to turn brown and die. It may also affect stems and rot the stem end of fruits.

● Fusarium wilt (p. 141), or yellows, is another very common disease, prevalent when temperatures are high. Leaves and branches turn yellow and wilt. Transport cells show a dark, brown discoloration.

● Late blight (p. 141) is worst in cool, moist areas. It first hits older leaves with green-black, watery patches. These enlarge quickly and become covered with a powdery white fungus. Fruits are infected with large, rough, leathery patches.

● Mosaic (p. 142) mottles, puckers and curls leaves. New growth tips look wrinkled and deformed.

● Septoria leaf spot, or septoris blight, is a very damaging disease that usually starts slowly on the older, lower leaves. They develop water-soaked spots that eventually turn gray in the middle and develop lots of tiny, dark spores. Anywhere from a few leaves to most of the foliage will be lost, leaving fruit open to sunscald. To control, collect and burn infected plant materials, cultivate the garden deeply in fall and spring, keep weeds down, and stay out of the tomatoes when they're wet to avoid spreading disease.

Turnips

Poor production:

● You may not have kept the turnips well watered.

● You may not have kept them well weeded.

● You may not have thinned them properly. Thin them as they grow so that when the leaves have reached a height of about 5″ the plants are all 6″ to 8″ apart.

● The soil may be too hard. Root crops like loose, well-worked soil. Incorporate more organic matter and sand if necessary.

● The soil may be low in phosphorus. Add soft phosphate, bone meal or phosphate rock.

Roots have scars:

● Insect pests (see below) may be scraping the young roots.

● Drought conditions followed by lots of water can cause cracks. Water in dry times to even out soil moisture. Add more humus to help the soil retain moisture.

● The soil may be short on lime. Test and amend if needed.

Roots are long and thin:

● The soil probably is short on potash. Add wood ashes, greensand or crushed granite.

Roots are woody or corky:

● Hot weather ruins turnips. Plant in early spring or (the better choice in most areas) midsummer for a fall crop.

● The soil may have too much nitrogen. Go easy on nitrogen fertilizers and concentrate on phosphorus and potash sources.

Taste is too strong:

● Turnips may have been harvested too late. Harvest when young for best flavor.

● The weather may be too hot and dry. Plant at the right times of year and water as needed.

● Some turnip varieties are more strongly flavored than others. Try growing a milder variety.

Common pests:

● Aphid (p. 78).

● Blister beetle (p. 80).

● Cabbage looper (p. 80).

● Cabbage maggot. These ¹/₃″-long, white grubs chew on young plants just below the soil surface. (You can find them or their white eggs if you pull a little dirt away from the plants.) Control maggots by using tarpaper collars around your plants, practicing clean soil cultivation, covering the plants with a protective row cover to deter the adult flies, or interplanting with mint.

● Cutworm (p. 84).

● Flea beetle (p. 86).

● Imported cabbageworm (p. 88).

● Stinkbug. This ¹/₂″-long, green, brown or black, beetlelike insect has a shield-shaped back and emits an unpleasant odor when crushed. It sucks plant juices, causing blackening, wilting and distorted growth. Control by handpicking; keeping weeds down; planting radishes, nasturtiums or marigolds as repellents; practicing good crop rotation; or (for serious infestations) applying sabadilla.

Common diseases:

● Blackleg (p. 140) starts as light brown or gray spots that turn to dark patches. It may affect leaves or stems.

● Club root (p. 141) makes leaves turn yellow and wilt in hot weather but perk up if it cools off. The roots are enlarged, bumpy and distorted.

● Downy mildew (p. 141) usually affects only seedlings. It starts with small gray or purple downy spots that enlarge and turn yellow.

● Yellows (p. 143), also called fusarium wilt, is common when temperatures are high. Lower leaves first turn yellow, then brown; then they die. Leaf veins may also turn brown.

PART FIVE

References

Useful information from
other people and places to help
your garden flourish

Major Seed Companies

About the only way most ardent back-yard cultivators manage to get through the late winter months—when last year's carefully tended rows or beds are, in most parts of North America, buried in snow or mired in mud—is by curling up with a bunch of seed catalogues and dreaming about the coming spring's gardens.

So, when the pregarden doldrums hit, consult this list of the major seed companies that supply catalogues. Write to any of the firms in the list below (don't forget to add the charge for postage if one is indicated).

Alberta Nurseries & Seeds, Ltd.
Box 20
Bowden, Alta.
Canada T0M 0K0
Catalogue $2 to U.S.A.

Burgess Seed & Plant Company
905 Four Seasons Rd.
Bloomington, IL 61701

Burpee Seed Company
300 Park Ave.
Warminster, PA 18991-0003

D.V. Burrell Seed Company
Box 150
Rocky Ford, CO 81067-0150

Caprilands Herb Farm
534 Silver St.
Coventry, CT 06238

DeGiorgi Company, Inc.
Box 413
Council Bluffs, IA 51502
Send $1 for postage.

Henry Field and Company
407 Sycamore St.
Shenandoah, IA 51602

Gurney Seed & Nursery
Yankton, SD 57079

Harris Seeds
3670 Buffalo Rd.
Moreton Farm
Rochester, NY 14624

H.G. Hastings & Company
Box 4274
Atlanta, GA 30302-4274

Heirloom Gardens
Box 138
Guerneville, CA 95446
Catalogue, mostly herbs,
$2; botanical listing $1.

Jackson & Perkins
1 Rose Ln.
Medford, OR 97501

Johnny's Selected Seeds
305 Foss Hill Rd.
Albion, ME 04910
Please use postcard.

J.W. Jung Seed Company
Randolph, WI 53957

Orol Ledden & Sons, Inc.
P.O. Box 7
Sewell, NJ 08080-0007

Lost Prairie Herb Farm
805 Kienas Rd.
Kalispell, MT 59901
Catalogue $1.

Earl May Seed & Nursery Co.
Shenandoah, IA 51603

Mellinger's
2310 W. South Range Rd.
North Lima, OH 44452-9731

Nichols Garden Nursery
1190 N. Pacific Hwy.
Albany, OR 97321

Geo. W. Park Seed Company, Inc.
Cokesbury Rd.
Greenwood, SC 29647-0001

Pinetree Garden Seeds
New Gloucester, ME 04260

Porter & Sons Seedsmen
Box 104
Stephenville, TX 76401-0104

Sandy Mush Herb Nursery
Rt. 2, Surrett Cove Rd.
Leicester, NC 28748
Catalogue $3.95.

Seedway, Inc.
Box 250
Hall, NY 14463

Semences Laval Inc.
3505, Boul. St. Martin ouest
Laval, Que. Canada H7T 1A2

Stokes Seeds
28 Water St.
Fredonia, NY 14063

Thompson & Morgan
Box 1308
Jackson, NJ 08527

Otis Twilley Seed Company
Box 65
Trevose, PA 19047

Vermont Bean Seed Company
P.O. Box 250
Fair Haven, VT 05743

Vesey's Seeds
York, P.E.I.
Canada C0A 1P0

Well-Sweep Herb Farm
317 Mt. Bethel Rd.
Port Murray, NJ 07865
Catalogue $1.

Wyatt-Quarles Seed Company
Box 739
Garner, NC 27529

Specialty Seed Companies

Morning raspberries shrouded in dew, just-picked greens fairly singing with life, early carrots dug young and sweet, and crunchy, juice-dripping apples are delights that can be savored only when they're homegrown. Such fruits and vegetables are too fragile (or cosmetically "imperfect") to be shipped long distances and sold as supermarket fare. Commercial crops have been bred for toughness (to withstand machine harvesting and long-distance transportation), to thrive on agricultural fertilizer (even if it gives them a sour, "chemical" taste), to mature uniformly ("Company, ripen!") and to have perfect—if skin-deep—beauty.

But while diversity is almost a four-letter word to the big grower, the home gardener doesn't *have* to raise "chain store" varieties. The back-yard grower, thank goodness, can raise tomatoes that practically ooze with flavor, melons perfectly suited to an area's climatological quirks, succulent foods that don't even *exist* in supermarkets and even such exotics as red carrots or blue potatoes. And, surely, half the pleasure provided by such flavor-packed, site-specific and unusual varieties is that of discovering them. The companies listed in "Major Seed Companies" on the opposite page—good as they are—could be said to really represent just the surface of home-gardening possibilities: There's a host of other family-run companies and seed-exchange organizations. Many of these are helping to maintain heritage plant breeds that are in serious danger of extinction. And *all* of them are going against the current grain of horticultural homogenization.

The following is only a representative sampling of lesser-known seed sources. All these outfits offer catalogues or information sheets free of charge unless otherwise mentioned. But please consider sending stamps or donations with any requests, as one small way of showing your support and of thanking these people for helping to give us all gardening freedom of choice.

Seed Exchanges and Nonprofit Groups

Seed Savers Exchange
RR 3, Box 239
Decorah, IA 52101

North American Fruit Explorers
c/o Jill Vorbeck
Route 1, Box 94
Chaplin, IL 62628

CORNS
c/o Carl and Karen Barnes
RR 1, Box 32
Turpin, OK 73950

Native Seeds/SEARCH
3950 W. New York Dr.
Tucson, AZ 85745
Catalogue $1.

Abundant Life Seed Foundation
P.O. Box 772
Port Townsend, WA 98368
Catalogue $1.

KUSA Research Foundation
P.O. Box 761
Ojai, CA 93023
Endangered cereal grasses;
$1 for information.

Northern Nut Growers Assoc.
P.O. Box 247
Chetopa, KS 67336

Home Orchard Society
P.O. Box 776
Clackamas, OR 97015

Vegetables

Midwest Seed Growers
10559 Lackman Rd.
Lenexa, KS 66219
Traditional garden varieties (25 sweet corns alone) sold by weight. Not much description. Good for those who know what they want and appreciate bulk buying.

Natural Food Institute
Box 185, WMB
Dudley, MA 01570
Wonderful $5 catalogue dedicated to permaculture, sustainable agriculture and health in general. Lists nonhybrid vegetables, fruits, nuts, grains, amaranth, millet, pawpaws, wild rice, etc.

Southern Exposure Seed Exchange
P.O. Box 158
North Garden, VA 22959
Open-pollinated and heirloom varieties. Has a seed exchange policy. Catalogue, $3, is practically a gardening minimanual.

Seeds Blüm
Idaho City Stage
Boise, ID 83707
"Heirloom seeds and other garden gems." Also runs a seed exchange and a plant-finder service. Catalogue $2.

Liberty Seed Co.
P.O. Box 806
New Philadelphia, OH 44663
A third-generation family seed company that lists vegetables and flowers and believes we are "borrowing the earth from our children."

Peace Seeds
2385 SE Thompson St.
Corvallis, OR 97333
Vegetables, flowers, herbs and grasses. "A planetary gene-pool service." Catalogue $1.

Oriental Vegetables

Sunrise Enterprises
P.O. Box 10058
Elmwood, CT 06110-0058
A great, diverse selection: Green-in-Snow leaf mustard, goat horn pepper, daikon radishes, baby corn, Oriental greens and cabbages, sprouts and much more.

Tsang & Ma
P.O. Box 294
Belmont, CA 94002
Vegetable seeds from China, the Philippines, India, Vietnam, Malaya and Sri Lanka.

Gourmet and International Varieties

The Cook's Garden
Box 65
Londonderry, VT 05148
"The salad lover's catalogue." These folks are market growers of most of the varieties (from around the world) that they offer. Catalogue $1, refundable with first order.

Le Jardin du Gourmet
West Danville, VT 05873
A very small catalogue packed with seeds from France, Germany, Africa, Holland, Romania, etc. Offers 22¢ sample packets with approximately 20–30 seeds each. Catalogue 50¢.

Horticultural Enterprises
P.O. Box 810082
Dallas, TX 75381-0082
Free price list of hot peppers and other Mexican vegetables. LSASE.

Le Marché Seeds International
P.O. Box 190
Dixon, CA 95620
American heirlooms to European varieties. Catalogue, $2, is laced with growing information and traditional international recipes.

Shepherds Garden Seeds
7389 West Zayante Rd.
Felton, CA 95018
Offers selections chosen for flavor, tenderness and fresh-eating quality. Beautiful catalogue $1.

Wildlife Nurseries
P.O. Box 2724
Oshkosh, WI 54903-2724
Specialists in plants and seeds for the development of natural feeding grounds for wild ducks, fish and other wildlife. Catalogue $1.

Herbs

Catnip Acres Farm
67-E Christian St.
Oxford, CT 06483
Extensive list of plants and seeds. Catalogue $2.

Casa Yerba Gardens
3459 Days Creek Rd.
Days Creek, OR 97429-9604
Rare and unusual herb seeds and plants as well as potpourris, herbal teas and bee pollen. Catalogue $1.

McCrory's Sunny Hill Herb Farm
Star Rt. 3, Box 844
Eustis, FL 32726
Good selection of well-established, affordable plants in 4″ pots. Catalogue 50¢, refundable with order.

Herb Gathering, Inc.
5742 Kenwood Ave.
Kansas City, MO 64110
Average packet $1. Catalogue $1.

Exotic Perennials

Endangered Species
12571 Redhill
Tustin, CA 92680
Bamboo, cycads, exotic foliage, trees, succulents, palms, etc. Catalogue $5 per year for four seasonal copies.

Siskiyou Rare Plant Nursery
2825 Cummings Rd.
Medford, OR 97501

Water Exotics

Lilypons Water Gardens
P.O. Box 10
Lilypons, MD 21717-0010
Artificial ponds, wet-area culture and equipment. Beautiful catalogue $4.

Van Ness Water Gardens
2460 N. Euclid
Upland, CA 91786-1199
Pond-culture plants, frogs, snails, turtles, insects and fish. Large, colorful catalogue $2.

Specialties

Mushroompeople
P.O. Box 159
Inverness, CA 94937
Mushroom spawn and growing supplies. Catalogue $2.

Peaceful Valley Farm Supply
11173 Peaceful Valley Rd.
Nevada City, CA 95959
Seeds for cover crops, hay, pastures and lawns. Catalogue $2.

Kalmia
P.O. Box 3881
Charlottesville, VA 22903
Mostly onions, shallots, garlic and books. Family business uses mostly hand labor to grow seeds.

Steve Ray's Bamboo Gardens
909 79th Pl. South
Birmingham, AL 35206
Bamboo has great usefulness (including edible shoots), and many varieties are hardy to zero degrees.

Wilton's Organic Seed Potatoes
Box 28
Aspen, CO 81612
"The only organic high-altitude certified seed potato in the U.S."

High Altitude And Short Season

Good Seed
Box 702
Tonasket, WA 98855
"Quality-grown, open-pollinated, public-domain seeds for northern gardeners." Specializes in heirlooms. Catalogue $1.

High Country Rosarium
1717 Downing at Park Ave.
Denver, CO 80218

Warm-Weather Crops

The Banana Tree
715 Northampton St.
Easton, PA 18042
Banana tree corms, loquat, rose of Sharon, kangaroo ivy, coffee, true custard apple and more. Catalogue 50¢.

Plants of the Southwest
1812 Second St.
Sante Fe, NM 87501
Drought-tolerant varieties and hard-to-locate Indian crops. Catalogue $1.

Flowers and Wildflowers

The Country Garden
Rt. 2, Box 455A
Crivitz, WI 54114
"The cutting-flower specialist." Catalogue $2. Price list free.

C.A. Cruickshank, Inc.
1015 Mt. Pleasant Rd.
Toronto, Ont.
Canada M4P 2M1

Girard Nurseries
6839 North Ridge East
P.O. Box 428
Geneva, OH 44041
Mostly trees and shrubs.

Moon Mountain Wildflowers
P.O. Box 34
Morro Bay, CA 93442
Annuals, perennials, wildflower mixes and cultivation directions. Sells in bulk or by packet. Beautiful catalogue $1.

Painted Meadows Seed Co.
P.O. Box 1865
Kingston, PA 18704
A collection of 12 eastern-U.S. wildflower seeds. Catalogue $1.

Trees

Frosty Hollow Nursery
P.O. Box 53
Langley, WA 98260
Seeds, plants and design services for a sustainable future. Send SASE for free catalogue.

Lawson's Nursery
Rt. 1, Box 294
Yellow Creek Rd.
Ball Ground, GA 30107
Specializes in old-fashioned and unusual fruit trees.

May Nursery Co.
P.O. Box 1312
Yakima, WA 98907
Since 1909.

Mayo Nurseries
Alton Lyons Rd.
Lyons, NY 14489
Dwarf, semidwarf and standard fruit varieties.

Perennials

Busse Gardens
635 E. 7th St.
Rt. 2, Box 238
Cokato, MN 55321
Wildflowers, rock garden plants, hostas, daylilies, peonies, etc. Catalogue $2, refundable.

Carroll Gardens, Inc.
Box 310
Westminster, MD 21157
Herbs, perennials, bulbs, rock garden plants, roses, shrubs, trees, evergreens. Catalogue $2, refundable with first $10 order.

Fruit and Berries

Southmeadow Fruit Gardens
Lakeside, MI 49116
Good selection of hard-to-find plants. Price list free; excellent, in-depth directory $8.

Makielski Berry Nursery
7130 Platt Rd.
Ypsilanti, MI 48197

Boston Mountain Nurseries
Rt. 2, Box 405-A
Mountainburg, AK 72946
Catalogue 25¢.

Cooley's Strawberry Nursery
Rt. 3, Box 530
Bald Knob, AR 72010

Finch Blueberry Nursery
P.O. Box 699
Bailey, NC 27807

Hartmann's Plantation Inc.
P.O. Box E
310 60th St.
Grand Junction, MI 49056
Blueberry specialists.

Atlantic Blueberry Co.
Galletta Bros. & Sons
Hammonton, NJ 08037

Good Info Sources

The Graham Center Seed and Nursery Directory
Rural Advancement Fund
P.O. Box 1029
Pittsboro, NC 27312
A gardener's and farmer's guide ($2) to sources of traditional, old-timey vegetables, fruits, nuts, herbs and native plants.

Seed Savers Exchange
RR 3, Box 239
Decorah, IA 52101
Membership in Kent Whealy's Seed Savers Exchange is $12 a year ($9 for those on fixed incomes). It includes a 256-page *Winter Yearbook*, the *Fall Harvest Edition*, free listing in the *Yearbook* or with SSE's "Plant Finder Service" and access to the "Growers' Network Collection" of rare garden seeds.

Whealy's new *The Garden Seed Inventory* ($15 softcover postpaid) is a large, computer-compiled inventory of *all* nonhybrid vegetable and garden seeds still sold in the U.S. and Canada.

The Heirloom Gardener
Sierra Club Store
730 Polk St.
San Francisco, CA 94109
Carolyn Jabs' hardbound book ($17.95 plus $3 shipping and handling prepaid) includes such chapters as "A Heritage of Fruits and Vegetables," "Who Is Saving Seeds?," "How to Find and Grow Heirlooms" and "Resources for Heirloom Gardeners."

Guerrilla Gardening
Putnam Publishing Group
200 Madison Ave.
New York, NY 10016
John F. Adams' book (out of print, but should be available in libraries or may still be in stock at bookstores for $14.95) explores the finding and saving of vegetables, fruits, berries and nuts. Includes useful directory and resource lists. His opening line best sums up what this listing stands against: "When the plant breeders at the University of California were requested to design a tomato for mechanical harvesting, they were instructed to think of the tomato not as a fruit but as a projectile."

Plant Yields
What to expect

Did last summer's garden give you plenty of potatoes but only a tiny bit of beans? Have you already eaten all the broccoli you stored in your freezer—while your pantry holds more canned tomatoes than you'll ever consume?

It's not easy to design a vegetable patch so it will supply exactly the amounts of food you want. To that end, this Garden Yield Planner will help you figure out how much produce you should get from 18 garden crops that are commonly preserved (as well as eaten fresh) whether you garden in raised beds or in rows.

The Planner first estimates the yield (in pounds) for 100 square feet of raised-bed garden and 100 linear feet of row. Then it cites how many pounds of each crop it takes to make a canned or frozen quart, and combines that fact with the yield figures to esti-mate the number of square (raised-bed) and linear (row) feet it takes to "grow a quart" of the crop. Standard plant spacings in beds, in rows and between rows come next. Last, the Planner suggests the approximate num-ber of plants you'll need to supply your needs for fresh, in-season produce, (but be sure to *double* that number if you want to preserve the food as well).

Of course, these figures are just estimates. Yields vary, depending on climate, garden-ing skill, pests, soil conditions and that always-fickle factor, the weather. So combine these guideline figures with the wisdom gained from your own growing experiences for a garden that's just right for your needs.

PLANNING THE PLOT

Vegetable	Yield in Pounds		Av. Lb. per Quart	Ft. per Qt.		Inches Apart		Inches Bet. Rows	Approx. Plants per Person
	Per 100 Sq. Ft. Bed	Per 100 Linear Ft. Row		Sq. Ft. Bed	Linear Ft. Row	In Beds	In Rows		
Asparagus	9.5	30	3–4	.38	1.2	12	12	48–60	10
Beans, green	30	60	1.5–2	.6	1.2	4	4	18–30	10
Beans, lima	11.5	25	4–5	.58	1.25	4	8	18–30	30
Beets	55	60	2.5–3	1.7	1.8	3	3	12–18	10–15
Broccoli	26	60	2–3	.78	1.8	18	18	30–36	4–6
Brussels sprouts	71	100	2	1.4	2	18	18	30–36	5
Carrots	100	75	2.5–3	3	2	2	2	12–18	30
Cauliflower	44	120	2	.88	2.4	18	18	30–36	4–6
Corn	17	100	4–5	.85	5	18	12	24–48	20–30
Kale	76	160	2–3	2.3	4.8	18	18	30–36	7
Peas	25	40	4–5	1.25	2	2	3	18–30	30–35
Peppers	36	60	1.5	.54	.9	12	18	18–24	3–5
Potatoes, sweet	82	80	2.5–3	2.46	2.4	10	12	36–48	8–10
Potatoes, white	100	150	2.5–3	3	4.5	10	12	30–36	15
Pumpkin	48	300	3	1.44	9	30	120	84–120	4–6
Spinach	50	50	2–3	1.5	1.5	4	4	12–18	15–20
Squash, winter	50	400	3	1.5	12	30	120	84–120	4–6
Tomatoes	100	380	2.5–3	3	11.4	24	24	36–48	3–5

Soil Nutrients

The basic building blocks for healthy crops

Farmers and gardeners of bygone days would taste a pinch of soil and determine its approximate pH (they meant it when they said a soil was "sweet" or "sour"). And they could judge what nutrients were lacking in the soil from the appearance and growth habits of certain plants.

Since few of us have the knack of such analyses today, but still need to know the nutritional health of our soil, we use soil testing. You can buy an at-home test kit (the best ones use large test tubes and ample testing liquid) or send a soil sample off to an independent testing company or (often the most economical choice) the local agricultural extension service. The results should show you the pH of your soil and its nutrient content.

Don't just go out and dig up a hole to collect your sample. Soil taken from only one location would not give a very complete picture of your garden as a whole. Instead, collect four to eight samples from different locations in your plot. Using a clean trowel, dig holes about 4" or 5" deep and collect about a tablespoon of soil from each. Don't handle the soil with your bare hands. Mix all the scoops together in a clean bowl or cardboard box to create a uniform batch, do (or get) your test, then feed the soil—not the plants.

13 NECESSARY NUTRIENTS FOR OPTIMUM PLANT GROWTH

Major Elements (macronutrients)	Symbols	Symptoms of Deficiency
Nitrogen	N	Yellow or pale leaves; poor growth.
Phosphorus	P	Purplish or reddish leaves; limited cell division.
Potash	K	Little immunity to diseases; thin-skinned, small fruit; weak stalks and puny appearance.
Secondary Elements		
Calcium	Ca	Retarded growth.
Magnesium	Mg	Chlorosis (yellowed or blanched color) of mature leaves; reduced yield.
Sulfur	S	Stunted growth; discolored leaves.
Minor Elements		
Boron	B	Multiple buds; small leaves; heart rot.
Copper	Cu	Multiple buds; gummosis (pockets of gum or exudations of gum).
Iron	Fe	Green veins on yellow leaves.
Manganese	Mn	Chlorosis affecting leaves in spots; growth retardation.
Molybdenum	Mo	Nitrogen not being used to capacity; symptoms vary.
Zinc	Zn	Poor yield; foliage thin and small.
Chlorine	Cl	Less-than-adequate growth.

Planting Times

When to sow where

The planting times on this chart are based on U.S. Department of Agriculture records. These are general estimates to give you a sense of the best approximate planting times for specific crops.

Use them only as starting points. After all, a garden at the very top of any given lettered zone will most likely have a later last spring frost than one located in the very bottom portion of the same zone. And there are innumerable microclimates that could never be portrayed on any map.

One of your jobs as a gardener is to observe—to discover over time, through trial and error, the uniqueness of your own plot of earth. Old-timers used to say such things as "Plant corn and bush beans when apples are in bloom," and "Don't set out tomatoes until the barn swallows are back." These observations are based on the way nature really works in an area and are often better than any "official" textbook chart. But gathering such wisdom takes time and requires watching the world around you as you hoe the potatoes and weed the beets.

You can become your own "old-timer." Make connections and take notes. Eventually, patterns will emerge. You will use general planting charts less and trust your own knowledge of nature more.

PLANTING TIMES FOR VEGETABLES

Vegetables	Areas A	Areas B	Areas C	Areas D
Asparagus	March–April	March–April	March–May	April–June
Beans	April–August	April–June	May–June	May–June
Beets	January–December	February–October	March–July	April–July
Broccoli	July–October	February–March	March–April	March–April*
Brussels sprouts	February–May	February–April	March–April*	March–April*
Cabbage	January–March	January–April	March–May	March–May*
Carrots	January–December	January–March	March–June	April–June
Cauliflower	March–April	March–April	March–April*	April–May*
Celery	March–June	March–May	April–June	March–June
Collards	January–May	February–May	March–June	April–June
Corn	April–June	March–June	May–July	May–July
Cucumbers	April–June	April–June	April–June	May–June
Eggplant	February–March	February–April	March–May*	April–May*
Kale	February–June	February–May	March–May	May–June
Kohlrabi	March–June	March–May	April–May	May–June
Lettuce	January–December	August–May	March–June	April–June
Muskmelons	April–June	April–June	April–June	May–June
Mustard	February–May	February–May	March–June	May–July
Okra	April–June	April–June	April–June	May–June*
Onions	December–March	December–April	February–May	March–June
Parsnips	March–June	February–June	April–June	May–June
Peas	January–May	January–April	February–May	March–June
Peppers	February–March	February–April	March–May*	March–May*
Potatoes	January–December	January–March	March–June	April–June
Pumpkins	April–June	April–June	April–June	May–June
Radishes	January–December	February–October	March–August	April–July
Rhubarb	February–May	February–May	March–May	April–June
Rutabagas	July–September	July–September	July–August	July–August
Soybeans	March–April	March–April	April–May	April–May
Spinach	January–December	February–October	March–September	April–August
Squash	April–June	April–June	April–June	May–June
Sweet potatoes	May–June	May–June	———	———
Swiss chard	January–December	February–September	March–August	April–July
Tomatoes	January–March	February–March	March–May*	March–May*
Turnips	February–March	January–March	February–April	March–May
Watermelons	April–June	April–June	April–June	May–June

Transplants are recommended.

The planting times suggested on the chart above correspond to the map on page 184 and are based on U.S. Department of Agriculture records which give average dates of the final killing frost in the spring. For more specific areas of the country, of course, dates may vary.

Average Spring & Fall Frost Chart

Twice a year, gardeners nearly everywhere get to play a guessing game called "Beat the frost." It's a game of chance, but there are ways to improve the odds. Timing plantings to work with the estimated average frost date for your area is a good starting point if you want to keep cold autumn snaps from killing your crops. Observing how your local conditions differ from the area average is the next logical step. The third is to take steps to alter your particular microclimate.

Choose spots that "swing" the temperature in your favor. Buildings block winds, absorb heat during the day and release it at night. The crest of a hill is the windiest spot on it, while cold air flows downward and collects in frost pockets at the bottom. The side of a hill, then, is a good growing site; the south-facing side is the warmest. Lakes and ponds reflect heat and light (but can also act as unobstructed pathways for winds). Trees and bushes can act as windbreaks.

A few other tricks for your season-lengthening repertoire: Use seed companies that specialize in selling varieties adapted to cold climates. Grow in raised beds—they warm up more quickly in the spring than flat ground. And mulch the ground in the fall to help hold in the soil heat a bit longer.

NOTE: This is obviously a very generalized map. Sharp changes in the dates of frosts can occur within short distances because of differences in altitude, slope of land, type of soil, proximity to bodies of water, etc. Contact your local weather bureau for information.

First Fall Frost

September   October   November   December

Last Spring Frost

February   March   April   May   June

Plant Hardiness

You can't
fool Mother Nature.

You can count on one hand the number of common garden fruits and vegetables that originated here in North America. Tomatoes came from Peru, corn and peppers from Mexico, watermelon and okra from Africa, cantaloupe from Italy, and carrots from the Near East. Crops in these various locations became accustomed over many, many years to the regional seasonal temperature changes and the amount and intensity of daylight hours.

Such imported crops still do best under their age-old optimum growing conditions. Oh, sometimes it's possible to get them started earlier by sowing seeds indoors or covering them with some sort of cold-protection device, and cooler conditions can be created in summer by using shade cloths and mulches.

But you can only go so far with such tactics. Day length, as well as temperature, signals plants when to grow best. So, in the long run, growing crops in the season they were intended for—as indicated by their weather hardiness shown here—makes for the happiest plants. Otherwise, with March pride, you may be the first in your area to get your peas planted, but you could eat June humble pie when your neighbors' later plantings have caught up with yours.

TENDER OR TOUGH?

Very Tender Vegetables
These may be harmed by continued cool weather and should be planted quite late:
Beans, lima bush
Beans, lima pole
Eggplant
Muskmelons
Okra
Peas, Southern
Peppers
Pumpkins
Soybeans
Squash, winter
Sweet potatoes
Watermelon

Tender Vegetables
These are easily injured by frost:
Beans, green bush
Beans, green pole
Corn
Cucumbers
Squash, summer
Tomatoes

Hardy and Semihardy Vegetables
These can tolerate a light frost but not a freeze:
Beets
Broccoli
Brussels sprouts

Cabbage
Chinese cabbage
Carrots
Cauliflower
Celery
Collards
Kale
Kohlrabi
Lettuce, head
Lettuce, leaf
Mustard
Onions
Peas, English
Potatoes, white
Radishes
Rutabagas
Spinach
Swiss chard
Turnips, greens
  and roots

Very Hardy Vegetables
These are not harmed by winter freezing:
Asparagus
Parsnips
Rhubarb

A

Aeration, 14, 19, 21
Agricultural mustard, 28
Alfalfa, as green manure crop, 27, 28
Alliums, 35–36
Alsike clover, 28
Animals
    harmful, 77, 126–31
    helpful, 77, 132–34
Animal traps, 65
Anise, 124
Anthracnose, 140, 148, 149, 158, 160, 162, 163, 166, 167, 174
Anti-feedants, natural, 135
Ants, 75, 79
Aphid lion. *See* Lacewing
Aphids, 57, 75, 78, 79
    peak infestation times, 70, 71
Apple-of-Peru, 124
Araneae, 75, 114, 115
Armyworm, fall, 86, 87
Asochyta blight, 140, 162
Asparagus, 187
    planting times for, 185
    remedies for problems, 148
    yields, 182
Asparagus beetle, 70, 78, 79
Asparagus rust, 140, 148
Assassin bugs, 92, 102, 103
Aster yellows, 91, 154–55, 157, 159

B

Bacillus popilliae (milky spore disease), 88, 91
Bacillus thuringiensis (BT), 67, 80 83, 84, 87, 88
Bacterial blight, 140, 149
Bacterial canker, 140, 174
Bacterial pustule, 140
Bacterial soft rot, 140, 152, 153, 156, 159, 161
Bacterial spot, 140, 163, 174
Bacterial wilt, 140, 157, 158, 160, 164, 167, 174
Banner fava beans, as green manure crop, 28
Barley, as green manure crop, 29
Barriers, 66
Basil
    companion planting, 53
    opal, 124
Bats, 132
Bean aphids. *See also* Aphids
    peak infestation times, 70
Bean jassid. *See* Leafhopper
Beans, 187
    companion planting, 53
    planting times for, 185
    remedies for problems, 149

resistant varieties of, 56
    starting seeds, 36
    yields, 182
Bed preparation, 24-25
Bed protectors, 51-52
Bees, 75
Beet leafhopper, 90, 91
Beetles
    asparagus, 78, 79
    blister, 80, 81, 87
    Colorado potato, 82, 83
    cucumber, spotted, 96, 97
    cucumber, striped, 98, 99
    firefly, 104, 105
    flea, 86, 87
    ground, 87, 106, 107
    Japanese, 90, 91
    ladybugs, 108, 109
    Mexican bean, 92, 93
    rhubarb curculio, 166
    rove, 112, 113
    soldier, 112, 113
    strawberry crown borer, 169
    tiger, 116
Beets, 187
    companion planting, 53
    planting times for, 185
    remedies for problems, 150
    starting seeds, 37
    yields, 182
Berry, Wendell, 19
Biodynamic/French intensive (BFI) gardening, 24
Birdbaths, 132
Birdhouses, 132, 133
Bird netting, 65
Birds, 128, 132
Blackheart, 156
Blackleg, 140–41, 151–53, 164–66, 175
Black light traps, 64–65
Black root, 141, 162, 165, 169
Black rot, 141, 151, 152, 156, 171
Black scurf, 164
Blight, 141, 149, 157, 158, 160
    Asochyta, 140, 162
    bacterial, 140, 149
    early, 142, 163, 164, 175
    late, 142, 164, 175
    leaf, 142, 155, 157, 169
Blister beetles, 80, 81, 87
Blossom-end rot, 141, 163, 167, 174
Borage, 124
    companion planting, 53
Boron deficiency, 150, 154–56, 163, 174, 183
Botanic insecticides, 68
Botrytis rot (neck rot), 161, 174
Braconid wasps, 88, 102, 103
Broccoli, 187
    companion planting, 53
    times for planting, 185
    remedies for problems, 151
    resistant varieties of, 56
    starting seeds, 37
    yields, 182
Brown rot. *See* Bacterial wilt

Brussels sprouts, 187
    companion planting, 53
    planting times for, 185
    remedies for problems, 151–52
    starting seeds, 37
    yields, 182
BT (*Bacillus thuringiensis*), 67, 80, 83, 84, 87, 88
Budworm. *See* Fall armyworm
Bug juice, 67
Bugs
    assassin, 92, 102, 103
    harlequin, 151, 156
    identifying, 75
    minute pirate, 108, 109
    squash, 96, 97
    stinkbugs, 152, 153
    tarnished plant, 98, 99
    wheel, 103
Buildings, weather and, 48
Butterflies, identifying, 74

C

Cabbage, 187
    companion planting, 53
    planting times for, 185
    remedies for problems, 152–53
    resistant varieties of, 56
    starting seeds, 37
Cabbage looper, 56, 80, 81
    peak infestation times, 70
Cabbage maggots, 151–53, 156, 162, 175
Cabbageworm, imported, 56
Calcium deficiency, 183
Canker, bacterial, 140, 174
Cantaloupe. *See also* Melons
    companion planting, 53
    resistant varieties of, 56
    starting seeds, 37
Carbon, 21
Carrot rust fly, 80, 81
Carrots, 187
    companion planting, 53
    planting times for, 185
    remedies for problems, 153–55
    starting seeds, 36
    yields, 182
Carrot worm (celery worm), 154, 157
Castor beans, 129
Caterpillars, 74
    beet or garden webworm, 150
    cabbage loopers, 80, 81
    celery leaf tier, 157
    celery worm (carrot worm), 154, 157
    corn earworm, 57, 70, 82, 83
    cutworm, 84, 85
    European corn borer, 84, 85
    fall armyworm, 57, 86, 87

squash vine borer, 98, 99
    strawberry leaf roller, 169
    wireworm, 58, 64, 100, 101
Cat feces, 20
Cats, 129
Cauliflower, 187
    companion planting, 53
    planting times for, 185
    remedies for problems, 155–56
    resistant varieties of, 56–57
    starting seeds, 37
    yields, 182
Celery, 187
    planting times for, 185
    remedies for problems, 156
    starting seeds, 36–37
Celery leaf tier, 157
Celery mosaic, 141
Celery worm (carrot worm), 154, 157
Centipede, garden (garden symphilid), 148
Chadwick, Alan, 40
Chalcids, 102, 103
Chamomile tea, 30–31, 35
Chickens, 79, 80, 83, 84, 133
Chinese cabbage, 187
Chives, 53
Chlorine deficiency, 183
Cicadas, 75
Citrus peel insecticide, 135
Cloches, 50, 51
Clover, alsike, 28
Club root, 141–42, 151, 152, 156, 175
Coleoptera. *See also* Beetles identifying, 74
Collards, 187
    planting times for, 185
    resistant varieties of, 57
Colorado potato beetle, 57, 82, 83
    peak infestation times, 70
Comfrey, 30
Companion planting, 12, 53–55
Compositae family, 37
Compost(ing), 12, 16, 19–23
    benefits of, 19–20
    containers for, 20–23
    essentials for, 21–22
    green manure, 17
    place for, 20
    for seed-starting soil, 32
    speed of making, 23
    what not to use in, 20–21
Compost tea, 30
Copper deficiency, 183
Coriander, 124
Cork, internal, 171
Corn, 187
    companion planting, 53-54
    planting times for, 185
    remedies for problems, 157
    resistant varieties of, 57
    yields, 182
Corn borer, European, 84, 85
Corn earworm, 57, 82, 83
    peak infestation times, 70
Corn smut, 142, 157
Costmary, 124

Cover cropping, 50
Coverings, 65
Crab spiders, 114, 115
Crickets, 74
Crop rotation, 12, 59
Crown borer, strawberry, 169
Crown rot, 148, 166
Cucumber beetle
  spotted, 96, 97
  striped, 98, 99
Cucumbers, 187
  companion planting, 54
  planting times for, 185
  remedies for problems, 158
  resistant varieties of, 57
  starting seeds, 37
Cultivation, 12, 14–17
Curculio, rhubarb, 166
Curly top (virus), 91, 149, 150, 160, 174–75
Cutworm, 84, 85

D

Dahlia, 124, 125
Damping off, 33, 35, 142
Deer, 128
Dennis, Paul G., Jr., 24
Diatomaceous earth (DE), 68
Dicots, 36–37
Dill, 54
Diptera. See also Flies
  identifying, 74
Dogs, 129
Double-digging, 15, 16
Downy mildew, 142, 149, 151–53, 156, 158, 159, 161, 162, 165, 166, 175
Drainage, 14, 19
Drip irrigation, 44
Ducks, 95, 133
Dusts, irritant, 69

E

Early blight, 142, 163, 164, 175
Ear rot, 157
Earworm, corn, 82, 83
Edovum puttleri wasps, 83
Eelworm. See Nematodes
Eggplant, 187
  companion planting, 54
  planting times for, 185
  starting seeds, 37
Encarsia formosa wasps, 100, 104, 105
Environmental stress, 12
European corn borer, 84, 85

F

Fall armyworm, 57, 86, 87
Fall frost chart, 186
False mildew, 142
Fava beans, as green manure crop, 27, 28
Feeding insect pests to death, 69
Fences, 48, 66
  for deer, 128
  for raccoons, 131
Fertilizers, 12. See also Compost
  organic, 18
  for seedlings, 34
Fertilizing teas, 30–31, 34
Feverfew, 118, 119
Firefly, 104, 105
Flax, 124, 125
Flea beetle, 70, 86, 87
Flies
  carrot rust, 80, 81
  identifying, 74
  leaf miner, 92, 93
  pepper maggots, 163
  robber, 110, 111
  syrphid, 114, 115
  tachinid, 116, 117
Flower fly. See Syrphid fly
Fodder radish, 28
Foot rot, 171
Foul muddammas beans, as green manure crop, 29
Four-o'clock, 118, 119
Fowl, 79, 88, 133. See also Chickens
Frogs, 134
Frost charts, 186
Fruit rot, 142
  strawberry, 169
Fryer, Lee, 18
Fusarium wilt, 142, 157, 158, 160, 162 165–67, 171, 175

G

Garden symphilid (garden centipede), 148
Garlic, 35–36, 118, 119
  companion planting, 54
  remedies for problems, 158–59
Garlic oil, 135
Geese, 133
Geranium, white, 124
Germination problems. See specific plants
Glutathione, 12
Gnats, 74
Goosefoot family, 37
Gophers, 129
Gourd family, 37
Grasshoppers, 74, 86, 87
Gray mold, 174

Green manure, 27–29
Ground beetles, 87, 106, 107
Groundhog, 130
Grubs, 74
  cabbage maggots, 151–53, 156, 162, 175
Guineas, 79

H

Hand-picking insects, 69
Hardiness of plants, 187
Harlequin bugs, 151–53, 156
Heat absorption, compost and, 19
Hedgerows, 48–49
Hemiptera. See also Bugs
  identifying, 74–75
Hoeing for weed control, 46
Homoptera. See also Aphids; Leafhoppers; Whitefly
  identifying, 75
Horsetail teas, 31
Hoses and hose attachments, 44
Hover fly. See Syrphid fly
Humus, 19
Hymenoptera. See also Wasps
  identifying, 75

I

Ichneumon wasps, 106, 107
Information sources, 181
Insecticides. See also Pesticides
  botanic, 68
  limonene, 135
  neem, 135
  pathogenic, 67
Insects, 63. See also specific names
  defining characteristics of, 72
  hand-picking, 69
  harmful, 76, 77, 78–101
  helpful, 76–77, 102–17
  identifying, 74–75
  keys to dealing with, 63
  mail-order sources for, 136–37
  metamorphosis of, 72–73
  netting and coverings for, 65
  peak infestation times, 70–71
  plants resistant to, 56–58
  repellents for, 66–67
  traps for, 64–65
Insidious flower bug. See Minute flower bug
Internal black spot, 142
Internal cork, 171
Iron deficiency, 183
Irrigation, drip, 44
Irritants, 66, 69

J

Japanese beetle, 90, 91
Jar traps, 64
Jeavons, John, 17, 18, 34, 45
Jumping spiders, 114, 115

K

Kale, 187
  companion planting, 54
  planting times for, 185
  resistant varieties of, 57
  yields, 182
Kissing bug. See Assassin bug
Kohlrabi, 187
  companion planting, 54
  planting times for, 185
  starting seeds, 37

L

Lacewings, 75, 106, 107
Ladybird beetle. See Ladybugs
Ladybugs, 79, 108, 109
Larkspur, 124, 125
Late blight, 142, 164, 175
Lavender, 124
Leaf blight, 142, 155, 157, 169
Leaf droop, 44
Leafhoppers, 75, 90, 91
Leaf miner, 92, 93
Leaf roll, 173
Leaf roller, strawberry, 169
Leaf scorch, 169
Leaf spot, 142, 150, 166, 169
Leaf variegation (June or spring yellows), 169
Leak, 164
Leeks, 35
Lepidoptera. See also Caterpillars
  identifying, 74
Lettuce, 187
  bacterial soft rot, 140
  companion planting, 54
  planting times for, 185
  remedies for problems, 159
  starting seeds, 37
Lettuce drop, 142
Light
  hardening off seedlings and, 41
  for starting seeds, 33–34
Lightning bug. See Firefly
Lima beans, 36, 182
Limonene insecticide, 135
Location of garden, 48
Looper, cabbage, 80, 81

M

Maggots, 74
    cabbage, 151–53, 156, 162, 175
    onion, 161
    root, 165
Magnesium deficiency, 183
Mail-order sources, 136–37
Mammal traps, 65
Manganese deficiency, 154, 166,
    183
Mantises, praying, 74, 110, 111
Manure, 16, 18, 21
    green, 27–29
Manure teas, 30
Margined blister beetle, 80, 81
Marigolds, 95, 100, 101, 120, 121
    companion planting, 54
Marjoram, companion planting, 54
Melons. *See also specific types*
    remedies for problems, 160
Metamorphosis, 72–73
Mexican bean beetle, 56–58, 92, 93
    peak infestation times, 71
Mice, 130
Microorganisms, 15–17
    compost and, 22
Mildew
    downy, 142, 149, 151–53,
        156, 158, 159, 161, 162, 165,
        166, 175
    powdery, 142, 149, 160, 162,
        167, 169
Milky spore disease (*Bacillus
    popilliae*), 88, 91
Mint, 120, 121
Minute pirate bugs, 108, 109
Mites, 168–69
Mole plant, 129
Moles, 129
Mollusks (slugs and snails), 64, 75,
    94, 95
Molybdenum deficiency, 156, 183
Monocots, 35–36
Mosaic, 142, 149, 150, 155, 157, 158,
    159, 160, 163, 164, 167, 175
    celery, 141
    tobacco, 143
Mosquitoes, 74
Moths, identifying, 74
Mowat, Farley, 63
Mulch, 12, 24–26
    as insect barrier, 66
    water conservation and, 45
    weatherproofing and, 50
    weeding and, 46
Muskmelons, 57, 185, 187
Mustard, 187
    companion planting, 54
    planting times for, 185
    resistant varieties of, 57
Mustard family, 37

N

Nasturtium, 120, 121
    companion planting, 54
Neck rot (*Botrytis* rot), 161, 174
Neem insecticide, 135
Nematodes, 75, 94, 95, 151, 153
    beneficial, 87
    controls for, 135
Netting, 65
Neuroptera. *See also* Lacewings
    identifying, 75
Nightshade family, 37
Nitrogen, 17, 18, 21
Nitrogen deficiency, 183
    Nosema locustae, 87
NPV (nuclear polyhedrosis virus), 67,
    88
Nutrients, 183
Nutrients (nutrition), 17
    compost and, 19
    in fertilizer, 18
    for seedlings, 40

O

Oats, as green manure crop, 29
Odor repellents, 66
Okra, 185, 187
Onion maggots, 161
Onions, 35, 187
    companion planting, 54
    planting times for, 185
    remedies for problems, 161
Onion thrips, 161
Opal basil, 124
Oregano, companion planting, 54
Organic fertilizers, recipes for,
    18
Organic matter
    green manuring and, 27–29
    in soil, 15–17
Orthoptera. *See also*
    Grasshoppers; Praying mantis
    identifying, 74
Owls, 133

P

Pak choi, 87
Parsley, 36, 54
Parsnips, 187
    companion planting, 54–55
    planting times for, 185
    starting seeds, 36
Pea aphid, peak infestation times of,
    71
Peas, 187
    companion planting, 55
    planting times for, 185
    remedies for problems, 162
    yields, 182

Pea weevil, 162
Pediobius foveolatus wasps, 92
Pepper maggots, 163
Peppers, 187
    companion planting, 55
    planting times for, 185
    remedies for problems, 163
    starting seeds, 37
    yields, 182
Pepper weevil, 163
Pesticides. *See also* Insecticides
    organic, 137
Petunia, 124, 125
pH, 17, 19
Pheromone traps, 64, 91
Phosphorus, 17, 18, 183
Pickleworm, 158, 160, 167
Pink rot, 142, 157, 159, 161
Pirate bugs, minute, 108, 109
Plant allies, 77, 118–25
Plant hardiness, 187
Planting
    companion, 12, 53–55
    in raised-mulch gardens, 25–26
    times for, 184–85
Plant louse. *See* Aphid
Plant yields, 182
Potash deficiency, 183
Potassium (potash), 17, 18
Potato beetle, Colorado, 57, 70, 82, 83
Potato bug. *See* Potato beetle,
    Colorado
Potatoes, 187
    blackleg, 140–41
    companion planting, 55
    planting times for, 185
    remedies for problems, 164
    resistant varieties of, 57
    ring rot, 143
    scurf, 143
    starting seeds, 37
    yields, 182
Potato hopperburn, 91
Potato leafhopper, 57, 90, 91
Powdery mildew, 142, 149, 160, 162,
    167, 169
Praying mantis, 63, 110, 111
Pricking out, 33–35
Psyllid yellows, 142–43
Pumpkins, 187
    planting times for, 185
    remedies for problems, 167
    resistant varieties of, 57
    starting seeds, 37
    yields, 182
Pustule, bacterial, 140
Pyrethrin, 68
Pyrethrum, 122, 123

Q

Quassia, 68

R

Rabbits, 131
Raccoons, 131
Radishes, 87, 99, 187
    companion planting, 55
    fodder, 28
    planting times for, 185
    remedies for problems, 165
    resistant varieties of, 57–58
Rain(fall), 44, 49
    diverting run-off from, 49
Raised beds
    deep-mulch garden with, 24–26
    water conservation and, 44–45
    weatherproofing and, 49–50
Red stele, 169
Resistant plants, 12, 56–58
Rhizoctonia, 142, 151, 152, 153, 156,
    164
Rhubarb, 187
    planting times for, 185
    remedies for problems, 165–66
Ring rot, 142, 164
Robber fly, 110, 111
Root maggots, 165
Root rot, 148
Rosemary, 124, 125
    companion planting, 55
Rot
    black, 141, 151, 152, 156, 171
    blossom-end, 141, 163, 167, 174
    crown, 148, 166
    foot, 171
    fruit, 142, 169
    pink, 142, 157, 159, 161
    ring, 142, 164
    root, 148
    seed, 143
    soft. *See* Soft rot
    stem, 143, 157
Rotenone, 68
Rove beetles, 112, 113
Rue, 122, 123
Rust, 143, 149
    asparagus, 140, 148
Rutabagas, 187
    companion planting, 55
    planting times for, 185
    starting seeds, 37
Ryania, 68
Rye, as green manure crop, 27, 28

S

Sabadilla, 68, 99
Safer's Insecticidal Soap, 67–68
Sage, companion planting, 55
Sandy soil, compost and, 19, 42
Sanitation, 12
Savory, summer, 124
Scab, 143, 158, 160, 164, 167

Scare tactics, 69
Scurf, 143, 171
    black, 164
Seedbeds, 15
Seed companies, 178–81
Seedlings, 38–41
    damping off and, 33, 35
    fertilizing, 34
    hardening off, 35, 38, 40–41
    light for, 33–34
    pricking out, 33–35
    transplanting, 34–35, 38, 41
    watering, 33
Seed rot, 143
Seeds, starting, 32–37
Seed trays, 32
Septoria leaf spot, 175
Serpentine leaf miner, 57, 58
Shelterbelts, 48–49
Shoo-fly plant, 124
Shrubs, shelterbelts and hedgerows
    of, 48–49
Skunks, 131
Slopes, 48
Slugs, 75, 94, 95
    trap for, 64
Smut, 143, 161
    corn, 142, 157
Snail Barr, 66, 95
Snails, 75, 94, 95
Snakes, 134
Soap, insecticidal, 67–68
Soft rot
    bacterial, 140, 152, 153, 156,
      159, 161
    vegetable, 155
    watery, 151–53, 156
Soil. *See also* Nutrients
    organic matter in, 15–17
    preparation of, 14–18
    testing, 17
    texture of, 14–15
Soil mixers
    for seedlings, 34
    seed starting, 32
Soldier beetles, 112, 113
Southern corn rootworm. *See*
    Spotted cucumber beetle
Southern potato wireworm, 58
Soybeans, 187
    bacterial pustule, 140
    companion planting, 55
    planting times for, 185
    starting seeds, 36
Spiders, 75, 114, 115
Spinach, 187
    companion planting, 55
    planting times for, 185
    remedies for problems, 166
    starting seeds, 37
    yields, 182
Spot
    bacterial, 140, 163, 174
    internal black, 142
    leaf, 142, 150, 166, 169
Spotted cucumber beetle, 56–58, 96,
    97
    peak infestation times, 71

Sprays
    homemade, 66–67
    water, 69
Spring frost chart, 186
Sprinklers, 44
Squash, 187
    planting times for, 185
    remedies for problems, 167
    resistant varieties of, 58
    starting seeds, 37
    yields, 182
Squash bugs, 58, 96, 97
    peak infestation times, 71
Squash vine borer, 98, 99
    peak infestation times, 71
Stalk borer, 166, 174
Stem rot, 143, 157
Stickem, 64, 66
Stinging nettle, 30
Stinkbugs, 152, 153, 156, 175
Stout, Ruth, 24
Strawberries, 55, 168–69
Striped blister beetle, 80, 81
Striped cucumber beetle, 57, 58, 98,
    99, 167
    peak infestation times, 71
Striped flea beetle, 56–58
Sulfur deficiency, 183
Summer savory, 124
Sunflowers, 55
    remedies for problems, 170
Sunscald, 163
Suppliers of insects, 136-137
Sweet potatoes, 187
    black rot, 141
    planting times for, 185
    remedies for problems, 170–71
    resistant varieties of, 58
    stem rot, 143
    yields, 182
Sweet potato flea beetle, 58
Sweet potato weevil, 171
Swiss chard, 187
    companion planting, 55
    planting times for, 185
    starting seeds, 37
Syrphid fly, 114, 115

T

Tachinid fly, 116, 117
Tanglefoot, 64, 66
Tansy, 122, 123
Tarnished plant bug, 98, 99
Tarragon, companion planting, 55
Teas, fertilizing, 30–31, 34
Temperature, hardening off
    seedlings and, 40
Terracing, 49
Thrips, 75, 100, 101
    onion, 161
Thyme, companion planting, 55
Thysanoptera, identifying, 75
Tiger beetles, 116, 117
Tip burn, 143, 159
Toads, 134

Tobacco hornworms, 88, 89
Tobacco mosaic, 143
Tomatoes, 187
    bacterial canker, 140
    companion planting, 55
    planting times for, 185
    remedies for problems, 171-75
    resistant varieties of, 58
    starting seeds, 37
    yields, 182
Tomato fruitworm. *See Corn*
    earworm
Tomato hornworms, 88, 89
Tomato yellows, 91
Trace elements, 17, 18
Transplanting seedlings, 34–35, 38,
    41
Traps, 64–65
    groundhog (woodchuck), 130
Trees, shelterbelt of, 48–49
Trichogramma wasps, 88, 116, 117
Tunnel cloches, 51
Turnips, 187
    companion planting, 55
    planting times for, 185
    remedies for problems, 175
    resistant varieties of, 58
    starting seeds, 37
Two-spotted mite, 58

V

Vegetable soft rot, 155
Vegetable weevil, 152, 156
Verticillium wilt, 143, 163, 164, 166,
    169

W

Walls, 48
Wasps
    braconid, 88, 102, 103
    chalcid, 102, 103
    Encarsia formosa, 104, 105
    ichneumon, 106, 107
    identifying, 75
    Pediobius foveolatus, 92
    trichogramma, 88, 116, 117
Water
    compost and, 19, 21
    conserving, 44–45
    importance of, 42
Watering, 42–45
    frequency and amount of, 43–44
    seed flats, 33
    seedlings, 40, 41
    times of day for, 42–43
Watering cans, 33
Watermelons, 187
    planting times for, 185
    resistant varieties of, 58
    starting seeds, 37
Water sprays, 69
Watery soft rot, 151–53, 156

Weatherproofing methods, 48–52
    cover cropping, 50
    diverting run-off, 49
    individual plant protectors,
      50–51
    location, 48
    mulch, 50
    raised beds, 49–50
    shelterbelts and hedgerows,
      48–49
    suppliers, 52
    terracing, 49
    walls and fences, 48
Webworm, beet (garden), 150
Weeding, 46–47
Weevil
    pea, 162
    pepper, 163
    sweet potato, 171
    vegetable, 152
Wheat, hard red spring, as green
    manure crop, 29
Wheel bugs, 103
Whiptail, 156
Whitefly, 100, 101, 174
White geranium, 124
Wilt, 44
    bacterial, 140, 157, 158,
      160, 164, 167, 174
    fusarium, 142, 157, 158, 160,
      162, 165–67, 171, 175
    verticillium, 143, 163, 164,
      166, 169
Wind
    hardening off seedlings and, 40
    protection against, 48–49
Windbreaks, water conservation
    and, 45
Wireworm, 58, 64, 100, 101
Wolf spiders, 114, 115
Woodchuck, 130
Woollypod vetch, 28-29
Worms. *See also* Caterpillars
    carrot, 154, 157
    pickleworm, 158, 160, 167
    tobacco hornworms, 88-89
    tomato hornworms, 88, 89
Wormwood, 124, 125

Y

Yankee bug. *See* Blister beetle
Yellows, 150-53, 156, 165, 166,
    175. *See also* Fusarium
    wilt, 142
    aster, 154-55, 157, 159
    June of spring, 169
    psyllid, 142-43
Yellow sticky traps, 64

Z

Zappers, 65
Zinc deficiency, 183

Credits

Cover: Michael Soluri.
Contents: Richard W. Brown.
Foreword: Joel Popadics.

Part I

p. 13: Richard W. Brown. **pp. 20-21:** Weststar Photographic. **p. 25:** Michelle White. **p. 29:** John Jeavons. **p. 41:** Steven J. Charny. **p. 45:** Kay Holmes Stafford. **pp. 49-51:** Kay Holmes Stafford. **pp. 54-56:** The Bettmann Archive. **p. 59:** Joel Popadics.

Part II

p. 62: Richard E. White. **pp. 64-67:** Kay Holmes Stafford. **pp. 72-73:** *Silk moth life cycle*, The Granger Collection. *Grasshopper*, Culver Pictures. **pp. 74-75:** Anastasia Vasilakis. **p. 76:** Joe DiStefano/Photo Researchers, Inc. **p. 77:** Donald Specker/Animals Animals. **p. 78:** *Aphid*, Holt Studios, Ltd./Animals Animals (3). E.R. Degginger/Bruce Coleman, Inc. Dwight R. Kuhn. Hans Pfletschinger/Peter Arnold, Inc. *Asparagus Beetle*, Grant Heilman/Grant Heilman Photography (2). Alfred Renfro, FPSA/Photo Researchers, Inc. **p. 81:** *Blister Beetle—Margined and Striped*, Harry Rogers/Photo Researchers, Inc. Ken Brate/Photo Researchers, Inc. *Cabbage Looper*, Comstock. Dan Guravich/Photo Researchers, Inc. *Carrot Rust Fly*, Oregon State University Extension Service (2). **p. 82:** *Colorado Potato Beetle*, Donald Specker/Animals Animals (3). *Corn Earworm*, Grant Heilman Photography. Harry Rogers/Photo Researchers, Inc. Jack K. Clark/Bio-Tec Images. John MacGregor/Peter Arnold, Inc. **p. 85:** *Cutworm*, John MacGregor/Peter Arnold, Inc. S.J. Krasemann/Peter Arnold, Inc. *European Corn Borer*, Ray R. Kriner. Runk/Schoenberger/Grant Heilman Photography (2). Ray R. Kriner. **p. 86:** *Fall Armyworm*, Runk/Schoenberger/Grant Heilman Photography. Ray R. Kriner. *Flea Beetle*, Jack K. Clark/Bio-Tec Images. *Grasshopper*, Animals Animals. **p. 89:** *Grub*, Ron West. E.R. Degginger. *Hornworm—Tomato and Tobacco*, Breck P. Kent/Animals Animals. Grant Heilman/Grant Heilman Photography. Ron West. *Imported Cabbageworm*, Runk/Schoenberger/Grant Heilman Photography (2). **p. 90:** *Japanese Beetle*, Runk/Schoenberger/Grant Heilman Photography (2). *Leafhopper*, William E. Ferguson. Jack K. Clark/Bio-Tec Images. **p. 93:** *Leaf Miner*, Ray R. Kriner. Jack K. Clark/Bio-Tec Images. *Mexican Bean Beetle*, E.R. Degginger/Bruce Coleman, Inc. Wallace Kirkland/Photo Researchers, Inc. E.R. Degginger/Bruce Coleman, Inc. **p. 94:** *Nematode*, Runk/Schoenberger/Grant Heilman Photography. Ray R. Kriner. *Slugs and Snails*, Jeff Lepore/Photo Researchers, Inc. Yva Momatiuk/Photo Researchers, Inc. **p. 97:** *Spotted Cucumber Beetle*, Ray R. Kriner. Oregon State University Extension Service. Mike Schick/Animals Animals. *Squash Bug*, Harry Rogers/Photo Researchers, Inc. Bob Gossington/Bruce Coleman, Inc. Harry Rogers/Photo Researchers, Inc. **p. 98:** *Squash Vine Borer*, Dan Fischer/Illinois State Natural History Survey. E.R. Degginger/Animals Animals. *Striped Cucumber Beetle*, Jack K. Clark/Bio-Tec Images. Grant Heilman Photography. *Tarnished Plant Bug*, Grant Heilman Photography. Donald Specker/Animals Animals. **p. 101:** *Thrips*, William E. Ferguson. E.R. Degginger. Bob Gossington/Bruce Coleman, Inc. *Whitefly*, Dwight R. Kuhn. Jack K. Clark/Bio-Tec Images. Animals Animals. *Wireworm*, Ron West. William E. Ferguson. **p. 102:** *Assassin Bug*, L. West/Photo Researchers, Inc. J.H. Robinson/Photo Researchers, Inc. *Braconid Wasp*, Hans Pfletschinger/Peter Arnold, Inc. Patrick Grace/Photo Researchers, Inc. Dwight R. Kuhn. *Chalcid*, L. West/Bruce Coleman, Inc. E.R. Degginger. Dwight R. Kuhn. **p. 105:** *Encarsia formosa*, William E. Ferguson. Max E. Badgley. *Firefly*, L. West/Photo Researchers, Inc. Runk/Schoenberger/Grant Heilman Photography. **p. 106:** *Ground Beetle*, Ron West. E.R. Degginger. Donald Specker/Animals Animals. *Ichneumon Wasp*, Peter C. Aitken/Photo Researchers, Inc. L. West/Photo Researchers, Inc. *Lacewing*, Robert P. Carr/Bruce Coleman, Inc. Dwight R. Kuhn. Joe DiStefano/Photo Researchers, Inc. **p. 109:** *Ladybug*, Robert E. Pelham/Photo Researchers, Inc. E.R. Degginger/Animals Animals. K.G. Preston-Mafham/ Animals Animals. *Minute Pirate Bug*, Oregon State University Extension Service. William E. Ferguson. **p. 110:** *Praying Mantis*, Laura Riley/Bruce Coleman, Inc. Stan Schroeder/Animals Animals. Harold R. Hungerford/Photo Researchers, Inc. *Robber Fly*, John MacGregor/Peter Arnold, Inc. (2). **p. 113:** *Rove Beetle*, Ron West. John MacGregor/Peter Arnold, Inc. *Soldier Beetle*, William E. Ferguson (2). Robert P. Carr/Bruce Coleman, Inc. **p. 114:** *Spider*, J.H. Robinson/Photo Researchers, Inc. Runk/Schoenberger/Grant Heilman. John Shaw/Bruce Coleman, Inc. J. Gerlach/Animals Animals. *Syrphid Fly*, Dwight R. Kuhn/Bruce Coleman, Inc. Robert Carlyle Day/Photo Researchers, Inc. Robert L. Dunne/Bruce Coleman, Inc. **p. 117:** *Tachinid Fly*, C.W. Perkins/Animals Animals. *Tiger Beetle*, Peter Ward/Bruce Coleman, Inc. Kjell Sanved/Bruce Coleman, Inc. L. West/Bruce Coleman, Inc. *Trichogramma Wasp*, Jack K. Clark/Bio-Tec Images. **p. 118:** *Feverfew*, E.R. Degginger. *Four-O'Clock*, Eric L. Heyer/Grant Heilman Photography. Barry L. Runk/Grant Heilman Photography. E.R. Degginger. *Garlic*, Norman Owen Tomalin/Bruce Coleman, Inc. **p. 121:** *Marigold*, Peter B. Kaplan/Photo Researchers, Inc. Park Seed Co., Greenwood, SC. E.R. Degginger. *Mint*, Runk/Schoenberger/Grant Heilman Photography. Grant Heilman Photography (2). *Nasturtium*, S. Rannels/Grant Heilman Photography. Alan Pitcairn/Grant Heilman Photography. **p. 122:** *Pyrethrum*, Park Seed Co., Greenwood, SC. *Rue*, E.R. Degginger. *Tansy*, Pat Lynch/Photo Researchers, Inc. **p. 125:** *Wormwood*, George Whiteley/Photo Researchers, Inc. *Other Flowers*, Helen Marcus/Photo Researchers, Inc. Alford W. Cooper/ Photo Researchers, Inc. Edna Douthat/Photo Researchers, Inc. Robert Lee/Photo Researchers, Inc. George Whiteley/Photo Researchers, Inc. **pp. 126-133:** Kay Holmes Stafford. **pp. 136-137:** Rita Pocock.

Part III

pp. 140-141: *Corn Smut*, Larry Lefever/Grant Heilman Photography. *Leaf Blight*, Grant Heilman/Grant Heilman Photography. *Fruit Rot*, Norm Thomas/Photo Researchers, Inc. *Leaf Spot*, Grant Heilman Photography.

Part IV

pp. 146-147: Philippe-Louis Houzé. **p. 149:** Murray Alcosser. **p. 150:** Murray Alcosser. **p. 151:** George W. Park Seed Co. **p. 153:** Grant Heilman/Grant Heilman Photography. **pp. 154-155:** Philippe-Louis Houzé. **p. 156:** The Bettmann Archive. **p. 157:** Murray Alcosser. **p. 159:** *Garlic*, Murray Alcosser. **p. 162:** Murray Alcosser. **p. 163:** Larry Lefever/Grant Heilman Photography. **p. 165:** Murray Alcosser. **p. 166:** *Rhubarb*, Murray Alcosser. *Spinach*, John Colwell/Grant Heilman Photography. **p. 167:** Judy Pack. **pp. 168-169:** Murray Alcosser. **p. 170:** George W. Park Seed Co. **pp. 172-173:** Philippe-Louis Houzé. **p. 175:** Murray Alcosser.

Part V

p. 187: Joel Popadics. **p. 188:** Janice Fried. **p. 191:** Janice Fried. **p. 192:** Joel Popadics.